SCIENCE FICTION AND SPECULATIVE FICTION

Critical Literacy Teaching Series: Challenging Authors and Genre

Volume 3

Series Editor:

P. L. Thomas, Furman University, Greenville, USA

Editorial Board:

Leila Christenbury, *Virginia Commonwealth University*
Jeanne Gerlach, *University of Texas-Arlington*
Ken Lindblom, *Stony Brook University*
Renita Schmidt, *Furman University*
Karen Stein, *University of Rhode Island*
Shirley Steinberg, *McGill University, Montreal*

This series explores in separate volumes major authors and genres through a critical literacy lens that seeks to offer students opportunities as readers and writers to embrace and act upon their own empowerment. Each volume will challenge authors (along with examining authors that are themselves challenging) and genres as well as challenging norms and assumptions associated with those authors' works and genres themselves. Further, each volume will confront teachers, students, and scholars by exploring all texts as politically charged mediums of communication. The work of critical educators and scholars will guide each volume, including concerns about silenced voices and texts, marginalized people and perspectives, and normalized ways of being and teaching that ultimately dehumanize students and educators.

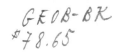
Science Fiction and Speculative Fiction

Challenging Genres

Edited by

P. L. Thomas
Furman University, Greenville, SC, USA

SENSE PUBLISHERS
ROTTERDAM / BOSTON / TAIPEI

A C.I.P. record for this book is available from the Library of Congress.

ISBN 978-94-6209-378-2 (paperback)
ISBN 978-94-6209-379-9 (hardback)
ISBN 978-94-6209-380-5 (e-book)

Published by: Sense Publishers,
P.O. Box 21858, 3001 AW Rotterdam, The Netherlands
https://www.sensepublishers.com/

Cover original artwork "quarternickeldimepenny", by Roymieco A. Carter

Printed on acid-free paper

TABLE OF CONTENTS

Acknowledgements   vii

Introduction: Challenging Science Fiction and Speculative Fiction   1
P. L. Thomas

1. A Case for SF and Speculative Fiction: An Introductory
   Consideration   15
   P. L. Thomas

2. SF and Speculative Novels: Confronting the Science
   and the Fiction   35
   Michael Svec and Mike Winiski

3. SF Novels and Sociological Experimentation: Examining Real
   World Dynamics through Imaginative Displacement   59
   Aaron Passell

4. "Peel[ing] apart Layers of Meaning" in SF Short Fiction:
   Inviting Students to Extrapolate on the Effects of Change   73
   Jennifer Lyn Dorsey

5. Reading Alien Suns: Using SF Film to Teach a Political Literacy
   of Possibility   95
   John Hoben

6. Singularity, Cyborgs, Drones, Replicants and Avatars:
   Coming to Terms with the Digital Self   119
   Leila E. Villaverde and Roymieco A. Carter

7. Troubling Notions of Reality in Caprica: Examining "Paradoxical
   States" of Being   133
   Erin Brownlee Dell

8. "I Try to Remember Who I Am and Who I Am Not":
   The Subjugation of Nature and Women in The Hunger Games   145
   Sean P. Connors

9. "It's a Bird ... It's a Plane ... It's ... a Comic Book in the Classroom?": Truth: Red, White, and Black as Test Case for Teaching Superhero Comics   165
Sean P. Connors

10. The Enduring Power of SF, Speculative and Dystopian Fiction: Final Thoughts   185
P. L. Thomas

Author Biographies   217

ACKNOWLEDGEMENTS

This volume in the Critical Literacy Teaching Series: Challenging Authors and Genres represents yet another shifting journey for me as an author, scholar, and editor. *Science Fiction and Speculative Fiction* began as an authored volume by me, but I soon found myself seeking a collection of assorted voices on a range of genres dear to me as a reader and fan.

My first acknowledgement, then, must be Peter de Liefde, Founder and Owner of Sense Publishers. Peter allowed me to change direction after the volume was planned and has again offered outstanding support for this series and the pursuits of critical literacy and critical pedagogy.

Next, as editor of this volume, I am deeply indebted to the contributing authors in the pages that follow: Mike Svec, Mike Winiski, and Aaron Passell, colleagues of mine at Furman University; Jennifer Lyn Dorsey; John Hoben; Leila E. Villaverde; Roymieco A. Carter, who also provided the artwork for the cover; Erin Brownlee Dell; and Sean Connors, who served double-duty addressing young adult and comic books/graphic novels within the science fiction and speculative fiction genres. The range of expertise and fandom offered among this group has produced a volume that I believe is both unique to the field of SF scholarship and powerful in its confrontation of experiencing and teaching genre, medium, and form.

As I have acknowledged before and as I do in this volume, I am deeply indebted to my parents and my childhood, where I came to know the world of SF through the black and white movies on TV that my mother loved. I had the great fortune of being raised in a home that fed my voracious appetite for words, and although my parents never intended the outcome, their love, support, and trust in my intellect all led to my life as a critical academic and scholar—and to the reality that I still read and watch SF with the joy of child.

It would be remiss, then, not to thank Arthur C. Clarke and innumerable authors of my childhood and youth, and then Kurt Vonnegut and Margaret Atwood for maintaining my fascination by challenging my understanding of literature, fiction, SF, and scholarship. To all creators of SF in every medium and form possible, then, I offer my most sincere appreciation.

Finally, I must acknowledge Furman University for the outstanding professional environment that allows me to pursue a wide range of scholarly pursuits in a way that I determine. The conditions of my university commitments are truly yet another great fortune in my life.

P. L. THOMAS

INTRODUCTION

Challenging Science Fiction and Speculative Fiction

My childhood and adolescence can accurately be characterized as a menagerie of genre and media: From *Go, Dog, Go!* and *Green Eggs and Ham* to E.B. White's *Charlotte's Web* and *Stuart Little* to Saturday afternoons watching *The Fly* and *The Day the Earth Stood Still* as well as an assortment of classic horror films on *Shock Theater* to the 7,000 Marvel comics I read and collected throughout the 1970s and then to the novels of Arthur C. Clarke, Larry Niven and Jerry Pournelle, and Ray Bradbury.

My mother's fascination for books of all sorts and science fiction (SF) cannot be discounted in how this came to be. From her, I acquired my own naïve but budding love for a wide range of genres in an assortment of media. My life as a high school teacher of English (for 18 years in the rural town where I was born and raised) and then as a university professor and scholar in teacher education has pushed me to examine more closely the inherent allure of genre and medium as well as the complexity of the paradigms and drawing clear distinctions among either those genres or media (Thomas, 2010). With the clarity of hindsight, I see the inevitable transition from —in my life as a teen drawn to "other worlds" (Atwood, 2011, p. 1)—Arthur C. Clarke's *Childhood's End* and *Rendezvous with Rama* to— in my budding academic years as an undergraduate and early career teacher— William Faulkner's Yoknapatawpha County stretching over several novels that spoke to my shared Southern roots.

Eventually my literary life brought me to Kurt Vonnegut, an on-again, off-again fascination that finally clicked in adulthood and led to my writing a volume about Vonnegut's work and teaching his canon (Thomas, 2006) as well as becoming a sometimes Vonnegut scholar (Thomas, 2009). Well before he attained his cult-fame after the publication of *Slaughterhouse-Five*, Vonnegut (1965) confronted his initial and lasting association with science fiction:

> Years ago I was working in Schenectady for General Electric, completely surrounded by machines and ideas for machines, so I wrote a novel about people and machines, and machines frequently got the best of it, as machines will. (It was called *Player Piano* ....) And I learned from the reviewers that I was a science-fiction writer.
>
> I didn't know that. I supposed that I was writing a novel about life, about things I could not avoid seeing and hearing in Schenectady, a very real town, awkwardly set in the gruesome now. I have been a sore-headed occupant of a

P. Thomas (ed.), Science Fiction and Speculative Fiction, 1–13.

file-drawer labeled "'science-fiction" ever since, and I would like out, particularly since so many serious critics regularly mistake the drawer for a tall white fixture in a comfort station.

Vonnegut's "sore-headed" response to the SF labeling highlights the hierarchy (fair or unfair) that exists for genres and media, but that distinction was absent in my childhood until I ran against it in my tenth-grade English class, taught by Lynn Harrill (who would become after my father the second most important man in my life as well as a mentor and friend [Thomas, 2003]).

After tolerating my SF obsession for much of the school year, Lynn imposed a wrong-headed mandate on me in my sophomore year when he banned my reading any more Clarke and SF, insisting that I turn my time to literary fiction (F. Scott Fitzgerald, Ernest Hemingway, Thomas Wolfe). In the years since, Lynn has admitted he was mostly misguided, but this moment in my experiences as a student and reader has paid inadvertent dividends to my life as a writer and scholar since it introduced me to a corrosive snobbery in society and education that I acknowledge and reject, what Kohn (2009) calls "negative learning."

Vonnegut's antagonistic and paradoxical relationship with SF lasted throughout his career. In *Man without a Country*, Vonnegut (2005) continues to wrestle with the inherent nature of technology in contemporary life and the responsibility of writers to address that reality: "I think that novels that leave out technology misrepresent life as badly as Victorians misrepresented life by leaving out sex" (p. 17). But by sticking to this simple truism, Vonnegut believed he was unduly labeled a SF writer, just for acknowledging technology, and then marginalized.

I also discovered a similar but more nuanced tension within a writer venturing into works labeled (or mislabeled, she contends) "science fiction"—Margaret Atwood (Thomas, 2007)—who has confronted SF and her works being labeled SF in essays (Atwood, 2005) and then a book on the genre (Atwood, 2011). While Vonnegut wrestled with his commitment to the conventions of SF and the realities of being labeled SF bringing dedicated fandom but scorn from literary critics, Atwood lends to the discussion a central thread I plan to weave through this volume on SF and speculative fiction.

Atwood's being associated with SF began with *The Handmaid's Tale* that, like Vonneguts' *Player Piano*, received the SF label and led to her own argument against the classification: "So I think of *The Handmaid's Tale* not as science fiction but as speculative fiction; and, more particularly, as that negative form of Utopian fiction that has come to be known as the Dystopia" (Atwood, 2005, p. 93). Also like Vonnegut, Atwood acknowledges the role of satire as well as literature intended as "dire warnings" (p. 94). With "Writing Utopia," Atwood begins to wrestle with a complex interplay of genre considerations—SF, speculative fiction, Utopian fiction, Dystopian fiction—as well as writer intent—satire, "dire warnings."

"Like *The Handmaid's Tale*, *Oryx and Crake* is a speculative fiction, not a science fiction proper," Atwood (2005) continues to argue when she returned to the genre, adding, "It contains no intergalactic space travel, no teleportation, no Martians" (p. 285). Atwood's nuanced consideration of genre speaks to my own evolving recognition that all sorts of texts (print, graphic, digital, film) work within genre conventions, against genre conventions, and by blending genre conventions in ways that remind me of the "other worlds" of my childhood books and even films such as Vincent Price's *The Fly*, a powerful mix of horror and SF conventions (echoed masterfully in Ridley Scott's 1979 *Alien*, starring Sigourney Weaver). In her discussion of *Oryx and Crake*, Atwood offers a framework for distinguishing genre, for her the blurred line between SF and speculative fiction:

> As with *The Handmaid's Tale*, [*Oryx and Crake*] invents nothing we haven't already invented or started to invent. Every novel begins with a *what if* and then sets forth its axioms. The *what if* of *Oryx and Crake* is simply, *What if we continue down the road we're already on? How slippery is the slope? What are our saving graces? Who's got the will to stop us?* (pp. 285-286, emphasis in original)

The lineage leading to Atwood's four novels (as of 2013) that contribute to some of her work being labeled SF and then her subsequent denial (and the controversy that creates) is examined by Atwood (2005) herself in "George Orwell: Some Personal Connections." Reminding me of my own early reading of Clarke, Atwood read *1984* as an adolescent:

> At the same time, I absorbed its two companions, Arthur Koestler's *Darkness at Noon* and Aldous Huxley's *Brave New World*. I was keen on all three of them, but I understood *Darkness at Noon* to be a tragedy about events that had already happened, and *Brave New World* to be a satirical comedy, with events that were unlikely to unfold in exactly that way....But *1984* struck me as more realistic, probably because Winston Smith was more like me...and who was silently at odds with the ideas and the manner of life proposed for him. (pp. 288-289)

This on-going and developing consideration of genre by Atwood, both in her fiction and her nonfiction, reveals her life as a young reader and her own journey with literature.

In the summer of 2011, I dove into novels written by Neil Gaiman, a writer whose work I had come to know and appreciate through his comic books and graphic novels (notably his *Sandman* series) as well as his blog and Twitter account. One thing I noticed was that his novel *American Gods* was identified by the publisher as SF. Once I read that work and then *Anansi Boys*, I was struck by my own struggle with classifying Gaiman's work, a struggle I find compelling in Atwood (2011), who discusses how others tend to classify *The Handmaid's Tale*, *Oryx and Crake*, and *The Year of the Flood* as SF:

> Though sometimes I am not asked, but told: I am a silly nit or a snob or a genre traitor for dodging the term.... I didn't really grasp what the term *science fiction* meant anymore. Is this term a corral with real fences that separate what is clearly "science fiction" from what is not, or is it merely a shelving aid, there to help workers in bookstores place the book in a semi-

accurate or at least lucrative way?...These seemed to me to be open questions. (p. 2)

And it is here—genre and medium as "open questions"—that I want to focus this volume, as I did when considering comics and graphic novels (Thomas, 2010). Instead of defining and classifying a variety of texts (print, print and graphics, film, digital) as SF or speculative fiction (I still feel compelled to classify *American Gods* and *Anansi Boys* as fantasy or create some new terminology such as "contemporary mythology"), a variety of authors dive into genre and medium throughout this volume as a vibrant but never-ending quest to confront, challenge, and embrace the shifting conventions of SF and speculative fiction, here as readers, fans, and scholars but also in parallel ways to Vonnegut and Atwood as artists. This, then, will be a journey filled with tension, contradictions, false starts, and possibly more questions raised than answered.

* * *

The lens for this discussion of SF and speculative fiction, as offered in my volume on comics and graphic novels (Thomas, 2010), is critical pedagogy (Kincheloe, 2005a, 2005b) and critical literacy. SF and speculative fiction are ideal genres for confronting the nature of text, genre, medium, and reading, providing students and teachers rich and complex avenues for reading and rereading the world, writing and rewriting the world as well as creating classrooms that honor teacher/student and student/teacher dynamics (Freire, 1993, 1998, 2005).

In discussions of teaching, and particularly in discussions of what is often deemed *basic* education (such as literacy), we tend to focus on the *what*'s: What texts or what teaching strategies or what content? But in this volume, we are asking that readers step back further than the *what*'s and consider the *why*'s: Why are we engaging with texts? Why are some texts allowed in formal education settings and others excluded? Why do we perpetuate a narrow view of "text," "medium," "reading," and "genre"? Of course, there are many more *why*'s, but in this introduction, I want to pull us back so that throughout the coming chapters we remain focused on those *why*'s as we do examine the *what*'s.

As I noted in my comics/graphic novels volume:

> "Doctrinaire or explicitly revolutionary literature is not needed when literary works of art have the capacity to move readers to imagine alternative ways of being alive," Greene (1995) notes, shifting our criteria for selecting text from some imagined qualities within the text to the impact that text has on the reader. Like Rosenblatt (1995), Greene is expanding our views of the reader-writer-text dynamic. (Thomas, 2010, p. xii)

Similar to comics/graphic novels, SF and speculative fiction are genres that "move readers to imagine alternative ways of being alive"—notably in that they have thrived in a wide range of media from traditional text-only works to TV and movies to comics/graphic novels.

The canon of works endorsed and even allowed in the English classrooms— recall my own experiences with Mr. Harrill during my sophomore year of high school as well as Vonnegut's feelings of being marginalized—is a powerful and corrosive dynamic:

> As Greene (1995) continues, she clarifies that authoritarian views of genre, text, and literature impose onto students implicit messages *that their own worldviews do not matter, at best, or are wrong, at worst* [emphasis added]. Part of Greene's own "begin[ning] again" involved that realization: "I have not easily come to terms with the ways in which education, too often following the lines of class, gender, and race, permits and forbids the expression of different people's experiences" (p. 110) …. [W]hen I had committed myself fully to the world of reading, drawing from, and collecting comics, I never saw that rich literacy experience as something that mattered in school. This chasm between the literacy lives of our students and the normalized literacy of school is a profound failure of schooling. (Thomas, 2010, p. xiii)

To recognize, embrace, and explore the SF and speculative texts that flourish in our culture and in the lives of students is to open up the possibilities of text and to honor the possibilities of other ways of knowing, most notably the other ways of knowing that our students bring to their learning:

> Many of the alienated or marginalized are made to feel distrustful of their own voices, their own ways of making sense, yet they are not provided alternatives that allow them to tell their stories or shape their narratives or ground new learning in what they already know. The favored ones, in contrast, seldom question the language of dominance or efficiency or efficacy in which they are reared, although they may seek out discourses more appropriate for a shared young culture or for moments of rebellion or adolescent discontent. (Greene, p. 111)

The life and career of Vonnegut (Shields, 2011; Sumner, 2011) reveal the power of being marginalized on an influential and popular writer; as teachers, we must consider how our choices and biases instill that same distrust in our own students, effectively silencing them.

This volume's consideration of SF and speculative fiction, then, is not intended to suggest that SF and speculative fiction are somehow superior to other genres, but to advocate for expanding what texts we consider, how we examine texts, and what conclusions we reach (tentatively) *with our students* by viewing texts as a way to knowing, not a fixed goal to be achieved. As well, this volume seeks to infuse further into the classroom both critical pedagogy and critical literacy as necessary for education as empowerment, individual autonomy, community, and social responsibility.

SF, SPECULATIVE FICTION, AND HONORING LITERACY

As I noted above, I can clearly trace my literary and scholarly life back to SF roots, a vibrant life that was nurtured by a blend of genres and media that allowed a

Southern young man from a working-class family excel throughout formal schooling. My literary experiences as a boy and young man were primarily steeped in the SF world, notably moments such as watching *The Andromeda Strain* (1971) run on TV after its theatrical life, and I am convinced that SF/speculative fiction are powerful genres for building critical literacy, *but I also believe that a person's being deeply engaged with a genre or series is ultimately what builds the foundation for empowering literacy.*

In other words, this volume is in many ways about how and why readers (or viewers) fall in love with particular genres or series (whether that be novels, as with the *Hunger Games* or *Twilight* series for young adults, or TV and movies series, as with *Star Wars* or *Star Trek*, or cable phenomena such as *True Blood* and *Game of Thrones*). My serial fascination manifested itself in *Shock Theater*, collecting and reading Marvel comics, and devouring SF novels from Clarke, Bradbury, and Niven/Pournelle. While I believe SF has a powerful, although not unique, quality (or set of qualities) that help trigger and feed the serial loyalty found in many children, young adults, and adults who are highly literate, I recognize that other genres (fantasy, romance, horror, detective) have a parallel power and thus am arguing that we reconsider the value of genre fiction, which, as Vonnegut lamented, often is unduly and routinely marginalized.

SF, like fantasy, often builds and develops entire and seemingly new worlds (sometimes as thin disguises for our own world and often genuinely speculative or uniquely alternative existences) with characters that exist in extended narratives that readers and viewers can come to know and love (or hate). I can now see that my serial fascination embedded in watching TV's *Star Trek* or collecting Spider-Man comics blurred into my love for J. D. Salinger's Glass family spanning the few works Salinger offered this world. The fictional "other worlds"—whether SF, speculative, or literary—always have spoken to me as *real* and *True.*

And it is here that I connect SF and speculative fiction with my educational foundations of critical pedagogy and critical literacy. Critical pedagogy views the content of education as a mechanism for unmasking the world, not as a goal of teaching. In other words, I see SF novels, for example, as an ideal format for seeking the value in the novel for the novel's sake as well as a window into students reading/re-reading the world and writing/re-writing the world. As we sit in a classroom with texts of all kinds, the teacher seeks to be the teacher-student while the student is a student-teacher.

SF and speculative fiction, then, are not here being suggested as something teachers assign, but possibilities that teachers allow students to explore and even encourage students to explore. Critical literacy is both a goal of bringing text into the classroom and a commitment to honoring a students' autonomy and the dignity of engaging with a wide variety of texts for a wide variety of purposes (including that a person simply loves the experience).

The concept of *reading* becomes a problem here. Some (if not many) people conflate *pronunciation* with *reading.* Some do argue to move beyond mere decoding, though, and stress that reading is comprehension. Both of these positions ultimately fail text and students, however. If readers merely decode (the ability to pronounce all the words), but have no sense of what the meaning of those sounds are, then of course, the *reading* has little empowering qualities (in fact, that some children can decode often masks that they are not truly engaging fully with text and the *appearance of reading* can then work against their autonomy). To then push a student to mere comprehension (the ability to paraphrase accurately what the text presents) is not enough since that does not address how text positions a reader, what credibility lies within that text, and a whole range of contexts and assumptions that must be exposed and confronted for readers to be autonomous and empowered.

The chapters in this volume seek to offering SF and speculative fiction in a wide variety of media as challenging texts as well as challenging the genres and media in order to honor critical literacy and human agency. The role and purposes of texts are combined with re-thinking the role and purposes of teachers and students.

SF AND SPECULATIVE FICTION: "A HARD AND FAST DEFINITION?"

Atwood (2011) found herself in the middle of a debate over not just what qualifies a text or medium as SF, or some other genre similar to SF, but by addressing those defining qualities, the broader debate over the quality inherent in genres. For the *New Scientist*, Atwood explained her own process as it stands against people with "a hard and fast definition of 'science fiction,'" adding:

Here I myself would include such items as Body Snatchers—if of extraterrestrial rather than folklore provenance—and Pod People, and heads growing out of your armpits, though I'd exclude common and garden-variety devils, and demonic possession, and also vampires and werewolves, which have literary ancestries and categories all their own. (p. 3)

Part of understanding and even defining SF includes the details that any audience associates with that genre, and why. Atwood admits that SF can be identified by how the medium is presented, such as a book cover, as anything else: "Thus: looks like science fiction, has the tastes of science fiction—it IS science fiction!" (p. 3).

Eventually, Atwood's struggle to define SF and her own works' relation to the genre built to a peak that included Ursula K. Le Guin's reviews of Atwood's *Oryx and Crake* and *The Year of the Flood*. Le Guin, a major writer of SF and fantasy, believes Atwood's works are SF because they blend an imaginative look at worlds that might be as well as satirizing the world that has been and is, and Le Guin also bristles as Atwood's arguments against the SF label: "This arbitrarily restrictive definition seems designed to protect her novels from being relegated to a genre still shunned by hidebound readers, reviewers and prize-awarders. She doesn't want the literary bigots to shove her into the literary ghetto" (Atwood, 2011, pp. 5-6).

Le Guin's argument pushed Atwood (2011) to examine the nuances of SF, speculative fiction, and fantasy as well as Bruce Sterling's term "slipstream":

In short, what Le Guin means by "science fiction" is what I mean by "speculative fiction," and what she means by "fantasy" would include some of what I mean by "science fiction." So that clears all up, more or less. When it comes to genres, the borders are increasingly undefined, and things slip back and forth across them with insouciance. (p. 7)

Atwood is not only confronting the complexity of defining any genre, but also recognizing that the term "genre" itself is perplexing, noting Sterling's consideration of "genre" and "category" (much like the debates and confusions surround the status of comic books as medium or genre [Thomas, 2010]).

Ultimately, Atwood (2011) returns to the source of the title of her book, "other worlds": "in another time, in another dimension, through a doorway into the spirit world, or on the other side of the threshold that divides the known form the unknown" (p. 8). SF and speculative fiction, or at least works that appear to fall within one genre/category or the other, allow students and teachers to apply what they know about text, genre, medium, and reading while also challenging that awareness. It is the same tension that I felt over Gaiman's *American Gods* or my recent fascination with the HBO series *True Blood* (I've never been a real horror or vampire fan, but the serialization and dark humor clearly overlap the essence of my love for SF).

* * *

Sterling (2011) returned in 1999 to his category, "slipstream," coined in the 1980s, just before Atwood published *The Handmaid's Tale* and well before Atwood and Le Guin entered into a literary argument over SF. While Sterling notes that his term appears never to have gained a hold, especially in marketing and publishing (recall the publisher's labeling *American Gods* as SF), he also recognizes some of the complexity with coherence within genres:

> There would be a certain amount of solidarity within the genre; they would have a generic sensibility. But they clearly don't. Trying to get slipstream writers together is like herding cats. I don't think they have a temperament with which they can unite.

So is coherence, or some sort of official organization necessary for a genre to be defined and even valued? Maybe or maybe not, but Sterling does equate genre with the organic needs of a contemporary time:

> But the reason I think it's ["slipstream" as a possible category/genre] still interesting, and is still compelling public attention years later, is that I think our society *has room* [emphasis in original] for a new genre. A genre arises out of some deeper social need; a genre is not some independent floating construct. Genres gratify people, they gratify a particular mindset. They gratify a cultural sensibility, and there is a cultural sensibility that is present today that would like to have a literature of its own and just can't quite get it together to create one. This would be a nonrealistic genre of a postmodern sensibility. But since it doesn't exist, I think slipstream is probably best defined by talking about things that it isn't.

Regardless of the tension between and among genres felt by authors, readers, teachers, students, and critics, Sterling (2011) identifies the power of classification or at least the power of debating these distinctions and the hegemony embedded in such debates. And with the organic nature of genre in mind, we have organized the following chapters around broad categories that support and inform a consideration and confrontation of SF and speculative fiction within a variety of media and forms.

In Chapter One, "A Case for SF and Speculative Fiction: An Introductory Consideration," Thomas details and rejects the traditional and lingering reality that SF as a genre has often been marginalized, with a few works and writers allowed into the official canon, almost begrudgingly—Aldous Huxley, George Orwell, Kurt Vonnegut, Margaret Atwood. But those SF works tend to be embraced when the writers are also considered literary, leaving works and writers dedicated exclusively to SF to a second-class status. This chapter examines what constitutes SF as a genre and discusses the complex debate surrounding that classification, building on Atwood's (2011) arguments about SF, speculative fiction, and dystopian fiction. This chapter also introduces a consideration of SF/speculative fiction across several medium forms—novels, short stories, film, and graphic novels. The chapter includes an annotated listed of resources that consider SF and speculative fiction in a variety of contexts including introductions to the genres; framing the genres against feminism, race, sexuality, and politics; placing the genres against other genres and media (young adult literature and comics/graphic novels); and highlighting key authors in the genres (Philip K. Dick, Ursula K. Le Guin).

Next, "SF and Speculative Novels: Confronting the Science and the Fiction," Chapter Two, authored by science educators Michael Svec and Mike Winiski, discuss how they confronted the tensions between SF and science during a first-year seminar for college students focusing on Mars. Their argument is described in the chapter as follows:

As we move toward a pedagogical definition of SF, we are guided by the goals of providing students with the opportunity to develop both their sense of informed skepticism and wonder. Selecting SF only for its realistic portrayal limits the opportunity for students to explore the social, political, and ethical implications of the science that are so powerfully revealed through story. A focus on realism can also squelch the "what if?" questions which foster openness to new ideas and curiosity. On the other hand, stories that play too loose with the science diminish opportunities to teach its content and process. Our evolving scientific understanding over time complicates the mix.

Chapter Three, "SF Novels and Sociological Experimentation: Examining Real World Dynamics through Imaginative Displacement," by sociologist Aaron Passell, argues that SF novels "pose sociological questions." This chapter explores the dialogical relationship between SF and sociological speculation "because we cannot perform on real people the experiments that we can imagine." Speculative topics include sex and gender, race and ethnicity, human evolution, and other themes and topics common within the field of sociology. The chapter ends by offering a number of powerful pairings of specific SF novels and sociological considerations.

In Chapter Four, "'Peel[ing] apart Layers of Meaning' in SF Short Fiction: Inviting Students to Extrapolate on the Effects of Change," doctoral student Jennifer Lyn Dorsey confesses that punk rock and SF helped shaped her during adolescence, and then she argues how the two "offered something the rest of my life and education lacked. They asked questions." Using the context of critical literacy and critical thinking, Dorsey explores SF short fiction, focusing first on a brief history of that intersection. She then deals with the ethical issues connected with technology as viewed through the lens of SF. Next, she examines questions around power and then SF's powerful look at defining humanity—all through a variety of SF short fiction works.

Despite the best efforts of many scholars to trivialize SF film, in Chapter Five, "Reading Alien Suns: Using SF Film to Teach a Political Literacy of Possibility," John Hoben argues that "SF film offers a model of public life as a web of unexplored possibility, and an anticipatory *space*, positioned between the human and the virtual." Through a number of key SF films, Hoben deals with the connection between SF's interest in self, time, and place as a parallel process to critical thinking, particularly as a goal of critical classrooms. This is followed by a discussion of traditional, behavioral education complicated by Stanley Kubric's *Clockwork Orange*: "What would we do, Kubrick seems to be asking us, if we knew the future was a camp being prepared for us, and the momentum of the present pushed us along like some dark infernal train?"

Chapter Six, "Singularity, Cyborgs, Drones, Replicants and Avatars: Coming to Terms with the Digital Self," by cultural scholar Leila E. Villaverde and artist-scholar Roymieco A. Carter, offers a direct challenge that "technology is the new opiate of the masses." To make their case, Villaverde and Carter use several SF films—*The Island, Logan's Run, Minority Report, Ghost in the Shell*, and *In Time*—as contemporary examples of key themes and topics related to cloning, reality, class, the body, work, time, and wealth as they intersect scarcity and fate. The discussion seeks critical literacy as a mechanism for rethinking the nature of curriculum and learning.

Erin Brownlee Dell in Chapter Seven, "Troubling Notions of Reality in *Caprica*: Examining 'Paradoxical States' of Being," considers how simulation allows for multiple representations of reality so that any distinction is ultimately blurred and any one *true* reality questioned, building on philosopher Jean Baudrillard's "paradoxical state." This postmodern stance complicates perceptions of what is real, welcoming the chaos of uncertainty. Her chapter concentrates on SF in television since a "paradoxical state" of being frames much of the *Battlestar Galactica* series prequel *Caprica*. This prequel helps highlight that identity, technology, and reality exist in a state of flux, calling on viewers to reconsider what constitutes reality, the self, and human existence.

In Chapter Eight, "'I Try to Remember Who I Am and Who I Am Not': The Subjugation of Nature and Women Represented in *The Hunger Games*," English education professor Sean Connors wades into the popularity and complexities surrounding SF adolescent literature, Suzanne Collins's *The Hunger Games*, as a novel trilogy crossing over into mainstream adult pop culture and as a statement on empowered young women. Connors "advocate[s] reading [Katniss's] character as a metaphor for the damage that patriarchal institutions inflict on young females by inundating them with a steady stream of messages that function to actively limit the subject positions they recognize as available to them." Sections in the chapter consider young adult dystopian fiction as social criticism and ecofeminism literary criticism, building to an extended discussion of *The Hunger Games* as an argument for the power of both SF and young adult literature.

Connors, next in Chapter Nine, "'It's a Bird … It's a Plane … It's … a Comic Book in the Classroom?': *Truth: Red, White, and Black* as Test Case for Teaching Superhero Comics," opens by acknowledging the powerful connection between SF, speculative fiction, and comic books. The pop culture icon, Superman, stands as a central image for the mix of genre and medium found in superhero comic books and narratives, including crime, horror, fantasy and—perhaps most famously—SF. This chapter situates speculative superhero comics and graphic novels as texts rich in possibilities for confronting how those text mirror and challenge cultural norms. Connors provides a brief overview of the history of comics and then focuses on the graphic novel *Truth* that began as a seven-issue comic book anchored by an African American super soldier within the Captain America narrative.

Thomas's Chapter Ten, "The Enduring Power of SF, Speculative and Dystopian Fiction: Final Thoughts," anchors this volume by outlining a series of public commentaries linking SF works with key social, political, and educational issues. This final section helps contextualize why and how SF remains a powerful and insightful genre that is enduring, a central characteristic often associated with literary texts held in greater esteem than SF.

* * *

In her father's cellar, Atwood (2011) read H. Rider Haggard's *She*: "I was a teenager, it was the 1950s, and *She* was just one of the many books in the cellar" (p. 106). While Haggard's novel from the 1890s fits well into the blur of genre that Atwood confronts, it is also important to recognize the context of her first reading:

> I had no socio-cultural context for these books then—the British Empire was the pink part of the map, "imperialism and colonialism" had not yet acquired their special negative charge, and the accusation "sexist" was far in the future. Nor did I make any distinctions between great literature and any other kind. *I just liked reading.* (p. 106, emphasis added)

As a teen reader who loved to read, Atwood (2011) associated She of the novel with her reading Wonder Woman comics, and "[t]hen I graduated from high school and discovered good taste, and forgot for a while about *She*" (p. 109). And this is where I want to frame what the authors seek in the chapters to come—a balance between the naïve but passionate love of texts and the informed and critical challenging of text.

If awareness and problematizing "genre," "medium," "text," and "reading" destroy the naïve but passionate reader, then the acts of being a scholar and student have the exact opposite effect that learning and scholarship should achieve. So it is cautiously that we move forward with a detailed consideration and confronting of science fiction and speculative fiction because the authors here, like Atwood (2011), found have found ourselves in love with the genres and media before we really understood what we had given our literary and scholarly hearts to.

CAVEATS, MOTIFS, AND ASSORTED THREADS

Let me pause here, before moving into the volume proper, to offer a clear set of statements that can help any readers of this volume understand for whom, why, and how we are proceeding in a volume purporting to examine and *challenge* a genre. In each chapter, these caveats, motifs, and assorted threads should hold the volume together as a tentative but cohesive whole:

– As an editor and chapter author, I am not a SF writer, scholar, or expert. I am a critical pedagogue (Kincheloe, 2005a, 2005b), a life-long SF and comic book fan as well as collector, and a part-time or tangential literary scholar (Kurt Vonnegut and Margaret Atwood, along with Barbara Kingsolver, Ralph Ellison, and the interplay of genre and medium in comic books and graphic novels) who has spent nearly three decades as a serious teacher of writing and literature at the high school, undergraduate, and graduate levels. As such, I remain more a *seeker* and a fan (Roberts, 2005) than authoritarian scholar on SF. If I make too many references to and spend too much time on Steven Soderbergh's *Solaris* (2002), that may well rub some readers and scholars the wrong way, but it is no claim to the quality of the work as much as how that work has informed me in my journey with SF.

– Readers may wonder, ironically, what type of work this is as well as who the audience is, and therein lies a key aspect of this work. This volume is eclectic in its own genre and purpose(s) as it is part literary scholarship, part *fanfare* (as a bit of a pun), part pedagogical and methodological musing for teachers, and part advocacy for the appreciation of and value in SF and speculative fiction for readers/fans, teachers, scholars, and students. And the discourse as well as mode of discussion and argument blends a variety of styles that integrate the conventions of scholarship and academic writing with personal narrative.

– Scholarship on SF tends to offer stances on definitions, authoritative lists of authors and works, and nuanced commitments to terminology ("genre," "medium"), but this volume is much more enamored with the arguments, the evolution, the journey with SF, speculative fiction, and the whole host of terms and concepts that accompany that journey—genre, medium, reading, text, Truth/truth. Thus, we are allowing ourselves to experiment and makes errors, recycle and confront again and again some of the issues that many scholars would declare "finished," partly as naïve and evolving fans/scholars/teachers, and then partly to maintain the freshness of the questions for readers, students, and teachers all along the spectrum of expertise with SF and speculative fiction.

REFERENCES

Agamben, G. (1998). *Homo sacer: Sovereign power and bare life*. Stanford, CA: Stanford University Press.

Agamben, G. (2005). *State of exception*. Chicago: University of Chicago Press.

Atwood, M. (2011). *In other worlds: SF and the human imagination*. New York: Nan A. Talese/ Doubleday.

Atwood, M. (2005). *Writing with intent: Essays, reviews, personal prose: 1983-2005*. New York: Carroll and Graf Publishers.

Freire, P. (1993). *Pedagogy of the oppressed*. New York: Continuum.

Freire, P. (1998). *Pedagogy of freedom: Ethics, democracy, and civic courage*. P. Clarke (Trans.). Lanham, MD: Rowman and Littlefield.

Freire, P. (2005). *Teachers as cultural workers: Letters to those who dare to teach*. D. Macedo, D., Koike, & A., Oliveira (Trans.). Boulder, CO: Westview Press.

Greene, M. (1995). *Releasing the imagination: Essays on education, the arts, and social change*. San Francisco: Jossey-Bass.

Kincheloe, J. L. (2005a). *Critical constructivism primer*. New York: Peter Lang.

Kincheloe, J. L. (2005b). *Critical pedagogy primer*. New York: Peter Lang.

Kohn, A. (2009, September 16). The value of negative learning: How traditional education can produce nontraditional educators. *Education Week*. Retrieved from http://www.alfiekohn.org/teaching/edweek/negativelearning.htm

Roberts, A. (2005). *The history of science fiction*. New York, NY: Palgrave Macmillan.

Shields, C. J. (2011). *And so it goes: Kurt Vonnegut: A life*. New York: Henry Holt and Company.

Sterling, B. (2011, March). Slipstream 2. *Science Fiction Studies #113, 38*(1). Retrieved from http://www.depauw.edu/sfs/abstracts/a113.htm#sterling

Sumner, G. D. (2011). *Unstuck in time: A journey through Kurt Vonnegut's life and novels*. New York: Seven Stories.

Thomas, P. L. (2003, November). A call to action. *English Journal, 93*(2), 67-69.

Thomas, P. L. (2006). *Reading, learning, teaching Kurt Vonnegut*. New York: Peter Lang USA.

Thomas, P. L. (2007). *Reading, learning, teaching Margaret Atwood*. New York: Peter Lang USA.

Thomas, P. L. (2009). "No damn cat, and no damn cradle": The fundamental flaws in fundamentalism according to Vonnegut. In D. Simmons (Ed.), *New critical essays on Kurt Vonnegut* (pp. 27-45). New York: Palgrave.

Thomas, P. L. (2010). *Challenging genres: Comic books and graphic novels*. Netherlands: Sense Publishers.

Vonnegut, K. (1965). On science fiction. *The New York Times*. Retrieved from http://www.vonnegutweb.com/archives/arc_scifi.html0301502.html

Vonnegut, K. (2005). *A man without a country*. New York, NY: Seven Stories Press.

P. L. THOMAS

1. A CASE FOR SF AND SPECULATIVE FICTION

An Introductory Consideration

Naming things is innately human, our apparently unique verbal nature, and central to academia and scholarship. In the 2011 film of the Marvel Comics superhero team, *X-Men: First Class*, Charles Xavier as a young man assembles a group of mutants, most of whom have lived in secret and unaware of other mutants. One scene shows those young mutants sharing their mutations, super powers, and then they do something interesting: they assume *new* names—Mystique, Banshee, Darwin, Angel, Havok. What is the purpose of the renaming? Is the name a badge of self-awareness, of a sort of *coming out* for these mutants who have been marginalized? Does a name liberate or restrict?

The Science Fiction Handbook, in fact, begins by confronting the tension surrounding the need to define, to name:

> Most readers of SF spend little time or energy worrying about a definition of the genre or attempting to determine whether any given text is science fiction or not. They tend to know what sorts of stories and books they regard as science fiction and little trouble locating works in the category to read. Scholars and critics tend, however, to be more cautious (and finicky) about categorization, so that many studies of science fiction as a genre begin with lengthy meditations on the definition of science fiction, often in order to distinguish it from other forms of "speculative" fiction, such as fantasy and horror. (Booker & Thomas, 2009, p. 3)

I would add to readers and scholars/critics, writers themselves. Thus, we see Le Guin and Atwood wrestle with SF, fantasy, speculative fiction, and dystopian/ utopian fiction as distinguishing labels:

> To my mind, *The Handmaid's Tale, Oryx and Crake* and now *The Year of the Flood* all exemplify one of the things science fiction does, which is to extrapolate imaginatively from current trends and events to a near-future that's half prediction, half satire. But Margaret Atwood doesn't want any of her books to be called science fiction. In her recent, brilliant essay collection, *Moving Targets*, she says that everything that happens in her novels is possible and may even have already happened, so they can't be science fiction, which is "fiction in which things happen that are not possible today." (Le Guin, 2009)

P. Thomas (ed.), Science Fiction and Speculative Fiction, 15–33.

While Vonnegut (1965) both practiced and shunned the conventions of SF, Sterling (2011) grappled with both the evolution of genre and naming that evolution, "slipstream."

Here in Chapter One, I want to examine the genre of SF as well as the many competing arguments about how to define and characterize the genre, including the various relating and distinguishable genres (notably speculative fiction and dystopian fiction), sub-genres, and multi-genres. But in this introductory consideration, I am proceeding with both the dangers and value inherent in naming things—as an act of classification that can render moribund something vibrant and as a celebration of what names any *thing* what it is. This grounding of the opening chapter and the chapters to follow attempts to honor the broad spectrum of reader, fan, student, teacher, academic, scholar, and artist—recognizing the perspectives of all without marginalizing the voice of any.

I take, then, a somewhat ambivalent stance about, for example, the powerful but esoteric view of SF argued by Suvin (1978):

> SF is distinguished by the narrative dominance of a fictional novelty (novum, innovation) validated both by being continuous with a body of already existing cognitions and by being a "mental experiment" based on cognitive logic [emphasis in original]. This is not only nor even primarily a matter of scientific facts or hypotheses, and critics who protest against such narrow conceptions of SF as the Verne-to-Gernsback orthodoxy are quite right to do so. But such critics are not right when they throw out the baby with the bath by denying that what differentiates SF from the "supernatural" genres or fictional fantasy in the wider sense (including mythical tales, fairy tales, etc., as well as horror and/or heroic fantasy in the narrower sense) is the presence of scientific cognition as the sign or correlative of a method (way, approach, atmosphere, world-view, sensibility) identical to that of a modern philosophy of science.

My ambivalence lies in recognizing the weight and value in Suvin's expertise and careful teasing out of what is and what is not SF, although my scholarly respect is deeply tempered by Booker and Thomas (2009) honoring the "know it when you read it" mentality of many readers and fans of SF who want to enjoy the works themselves and not be sidetracked by the rumblings around and about the classification of the works.

Next, I put the texts and reader upfront before offering a more scholarly and academic consideration that positions SF and speculative fiction within the teaching and learning dynamic. To start, then, I want to look briefly at Michael Crichton's *The Andromeda Strain* as an exemplary text (both novel and film) for characterizing SF and complicating the act of naming.

THE ANDROMEDA STRAIN: KNOWING SF WHEN YOU SEE IT

Most people who have developed some serious or distinct interest in text (whether that be print, film, graphic, or otherwise) has had that fascination and fandom spurred by a seminal work. And of course this event is more or less chance, as well as unique to each of us and universal in its happening. As I have noted in the Introduction, my SF fascination began with films that my mother enjoyed, specifically *The Day the Earth Stood Still* (1951)—she treasures the memorable "Klaatu barada nikto!"—and Vincent Price in *The Fly* (1958).

But my own self-awareness as a SF fan came in the form of *The Andromeda Strain* (1971) running on television. This film experience drove me to the novel, which was Michael Crichton's first novel under his name and published in 1969. Crichton eventually moved to the center of the dinosaur and cloning elements of the SF world with the serialized *Jurassic Park*, but *The Andromeda Strain* offered readers a glimpse into the *other world* where some sort of alien life exists—although Crichton's take isn't the Blob or little green men (at least not "men").

I want to consider what makes *The Andromeda Strain* SF, and I want to explore how other genre elements work in the novel (and film). I also pursue another multi-genre and multi-media question: What do *The Andromeda Strain*, Kurt Vonnegut's *Cat's Cradle* (1963) and *Galapagos* (1985), and Marvel Comics' The Hulk and Iron Man have in common? And why does that matter to this discussion? First, let's focus on *The Andromeda Strain*, the novel.

The initial aspect of the novel worth highlighting here is that its SF elements are reinforced by or parallel to the narrative being a thriller, one genre informing another. The central action of the novel involves the mysterious death of an entire town, Piedmont, Arizona, population 48 people, except for two survivors—the sickly, Peter Jackson, addicted to Sterno, and a crying infant. The science elements in the story are couched in mysteries involving the government and military carrying out clandestine operations, the mass deaths of the citizens of Piedmont, a police officer, and two men sent initially to investigate the event, the nature of the alien virus named The Andromeda Strain, and the precarious contingency plans surrounding the Wildfire facility and ground zero of the virus.

A reasonable argument can be made that the novel is a thriller with SF elements—just as much as classifying the work as SF with thriller elements. What, then, constitutes its SF grounding.

The novel begins with Lieutenant Roger Shawn, and as the story develops, the military becomes central to both the science and the mystery in the work. The connection between SF and the military is one powerful characteristic. *The Andromeda Strain* positions the military as willing to experiment with human life in order to secure an alien virus to use for biological warfare. Science in the hands of the military is also central to Vonnegut's *Cat's Cradle* (possibly a SF novel, but a complex mix of genres in itself, with its *ice-nine* sharing with the alien virus the possible ability to destroy the world) and the comic book superheroes The Hulk and Iron Man in the Marvel Universe.

Tensions exist in many SF works surrounding the potential of science, but many works of SF appear to suggest that less danger exists in science than in who pursues that science and why. The Hulk, for example, was created in 1962 (in the same decade as *Cat's Cradle* and *The Andromeda Strain*) and like many SF works in the context of the threat of nuclear holocaust or disaster. The Hulk as a character

17

can be read as the personification of a modern Frankenstein's monster, but created by the human failure to seek science while ignoring ethical concerns. The Andromeda Strain virus is brought upon humans by the military in much the same way as The Hulk is spawned from a test explosion of a gamma bomb (much of the Marvel Universe grew from science experiments gone wrong, such as Spider-Man, unlike the alien Superman or the self-made hero, Batman from DC Comics).

Thus, one common element of SF may be expressed as an examination of the pursuit of science by highlighting the dangers inherent in *who* is governing that science and *why*. Embedded in this characteristic is also the tendency for SF to warn. It appears to be the place of SF works, novels or films or comic books, to draw readers and viewers to that other world that is close enough to the real world that the audience can see reality, not distorted, as it is in the work, but more clearly. The Hulk helps us see the monster in all of us just as *The Andromeda Stain* forces us to re-examine our faith in the military, the government, scientists, and even medical doctors.

The Andromeda Stain confronts, in fact, the "other world" quality raised by Atwood (2011). While Crichton's novel does examine alien life form, it doesn't transport the reader to an alien planet or onto a human vessel to explore life beyond Earth. In fact, *The Andromeda Stain* sits squarely in the now of its publishing, a slightly askew but significantly realistic 1960s United States. The novel itself is posed through the narration and even typeface as an official document (a technique also employed by Crichton in *Next*), framed masterfully in the Acknowledgements signed "M. C., Cambridge, Massachusetts, January 1969" (p. xv).

While Vonnegut's *Cat's Cradle* shifts readers to San Lorenzo and immerses them in an entirely new religion, Bokononism, and culture—to intensify the drama of the SF elements of the novel (*ice-nine*)—and the Hulk and Iron Man have otherworldliness highlighted by its graphic format as comic books, Crichton masks the other world with realism and accomplishes other worldliness with the Mojave Desert and the five-story underground facility used by Wildfire (the facility, in fact, has many characteristics parallel to spaceships). Wildfire serves as a quasi-inverted outer space, both possible as an act of human engineering and mythically a human-made and leveled hell.

The desert setting and underground, multi-layered facility both suggest hell, in fact—like the hellish nightmare experienced by Bruce Banner as the Hulk. The existential nature of SF is central to *The Andromeda Stain* as a commentary on hell-on-earth as a product of human choices and behaviors. The essential and pervasive affect of the novel is also fear, nested as it is within the very human science of the nuclear bomb. In the novel, a nuclear explosion is not at the core of creating the Hulk or Spider-Man, but the fail-safe device designed to stop the spread of infection brought upon humans by the military.

And the great irony of *The Andromeda Stain* is that the characters, almost too late, discover that the nuclear fail-safe would not cleanse the world of the virus, but provide it energy for massive reproduction. SF exposes, in Crichton, the folly of nuclear weapons regardless of the intent of the weapon.

The other world of *The Andromeda Stain* is both our contemporary world and the otherworldliness of a desert or a hellish subterranean fortress that serve to protect and possibly destroy humanity. This blending of realism, factual or near-factual speculation about science and the military, actual and imagined dangers, and intensified tension reflect the characteristics often found in SF, although not exclusive to SF. Examining *The Andromeda Stain* helps present a simultaneous clarification and muddling of just why we know SF when we see it. Crichton's novel raises questions of ethics (Is it ethical to kill people to save people? And is it in the purview of the government to make such decisions for people?), questions of the nature of life as well as alien life, questions of the role of nuclear power in human existence, and questions of the transparency and cloaked nature of government among a free people. But many genres can and do raise these questions as well.

Now, let me come back to a question I posed above: What do *The Andromeda Strain*, Kurt Vonnegut's *Cat's Cradle* (1963) and *Galapagos* (1985), and Marvel Comics' The Hulk and Iron Man have in common? And why does that matter to this discussion?

I noticed among these works, a mix of media—novels, film, comic books—with threads running through all of them that would reinforce the "we know it when we see it" characterization of SF—both as evidence that we can classify SF and evidence that it is a shifting set of criteria that we use even when we make such pronouncements. And, thus, let me pose our consideration of *The Andromeda Strain* within these other works and our discussion of SF as a few problems before moving on:

- Is the use of the military (in some form) a central thread running through SF? And if so, why does this genre blend science and the military so often?
- How powerful is the role of credible science against speculative science in the mainstream understanding of SF? Consider Atwood (2011) and Le Guin (2009) struggling with how to identify SF, speculative fiction, and fantasy.
- What are the ethical imperatives and dilemmas running through SF? Is SF uniquely concerned with ethical imperatives and dilemmas compared to other genres?
- How is science central to patterns of examining the nature of life on earth and the possibility of life beyond earth in SF?
- Is SF distinctly suitable as a genre to present the simultaneous tensions between the promise and threat of science for humanity? Is that tension between good and evil restricted to science, or is it also an allegory for the dual qualities of human nature, i.e. the Hulk?

One last consideration connected to *The Andromeda Strain* is worth a brief discussion; then I'll turn to a brief history of the genre and further discussions of just what constitutes SF as a genre among other genres and among a variety of media.

The Andromeda virus eventually mutates, adapts, posing a new danger for the main characters and all of humanity. Here is yet another central issue in SF—the use of science to self-reference. Science is both the motivation for SF and the content of SF, in some way. Like the Hulk, the X-Men are a Marvel Comics exploration of mutation, but unlike the Hulk, the mutants of the X-Men appear to be both natural (not primarily created by some human mis-step or creation, like gamma rays or experiments gone wrong) and unnatural (in that these mutants don't belong among those who appear to be *normal*).

At the intersection of musing about mutation, a central element of evolution, *The Andromeda Strain* poses a discussion of the human mind that is eerily similar to the entire premise of Kurt Vonnegut's *Galapagos* (1985):

> No one ever thought to consider whether the human brain, the most complex structure in the known universe, making fantastic demands on the human body in terms of nourishment and blood, was not analogous. Perhaps the human brain had become a kind of dinosaur for man and perhaps, in the end, would prove his downfall. (Crichton, 1969, p. 260)

And in *Galapagos*, Vonnegut speculates in the shadow of Charles Darwin, the personification of science, that the future of humanity involves the evolution of the brain to being smaller, not larger, for the exact reasons speculated upon in Crichton's *The Andromeda Strain*.

And with our too-big brains, we as humans are well suited to wrestle with abstractions such as naming SF, or not, as well as arguing that all this naming gets in the way of simply enjoying the genre that we know when we see it.

SF AMONG THE GENRES: A BRIEF HISTORY

This chapter, along with this section and the entire volume, is a situated work, a critical work. Necessarily, a brief and introductory history of SF and the many sub-genre, genre, and medium overlaps will be an extension of my own perspective as a reader/viewer, a scholar, and a teacher (the following chapters also occasionally integrate some versions of SF and related genre/medium histories as well). I am not suggesting my version is definitive, or even exemplary, but I am offering a critical entry into the broader concerns about genre, medium, text, and reading, and I am acknowledging here that this discussion is skewed to a Western perspective and an English-language bias.

When possible (in that my scholarly range is more narrow than the topic and field itself), I will acknowledge and consider the valuable contributions to SF beyond Western and English-language with the understanding throughout that no single work is enough on a field that remains vibrant and evolving. This, then, is *one critical* way into the SF discussion, and I hope it is a powerful invitation and a provocative consideration as reconsideration.

Here, I am discussing the history of Western culture, English language SF in order to lead to a tentative and incomplete consideration of exemplary works throughout the volume—again, potential touchstones for argument, more so than a claim that citing works (which is strongly influenced by other scholars attempting the same goal) endorses those works as *definitive*. The end of the chapter also includes an annotated bibliography of possible scholarly resources that examine the

SF genre and the many broad themes and concepts the genre returns to again and again. Now, what has come before to lead to what many now view as SF?

For the history of American literature, the works of Edgar Allan Poe and Nathaniel Hawthorne represent seminal moments for the evolution of a wide range of genres, a distinct set of media, and characteristic elements of craft that distinguish American literature from, most directly, British literature. SF has never been solely the domain of American literature or even English-language literature, but, for example, Hawthorne's "Rappaccini's Daughter" serves as a distinct opening example of the brief SF history below.

"Rappaccini's Daughter" is both an early model of essential aspects of SF—the dangers of science and experimentation, the blending of SF qualities with other genre elements (such as mystery, horror, fantasy)—and a work just as easily classified in some other genre than SF (which is likely how the work is traditionally viewed since Poe has been honored as a literary writer despite his genre roots and efforts to attain popular readerships). As well, Hawthorne is never confused for a SF writer, placing a consideration of "Rappaccini's Daughter" as SF within the context framed by Vonnegut and Atwood: Why and how are authors apt to work both within and against genre conventions such as SF, and why does this crossing into genre impact the literary credibility of writers?

Since Hawthorne and Poe worked at the inception of American literature, their self-consciousness was different than Vonnegut's or Atwood's—more a matter of the long and dark shadow of British literature than the literary bias inherent in genres. But the *situatedness* of, for example, Hawthorne's "Rappaccini's Daughter" both in that seminal American literature period and along the entire spectrum of history stretching to the present allows a consideration of the history of SF to raise essential questions and establish tentative essential characteristics to support a consideration of genre broadly and SF narrowly in a scholarly or classroom setting.

Now, I want to outline some of the key historical moments, including a range of media, that help create a framework for understanding the history of SF across those media and as that history interacts with and informs other genres. Many of the sources annotated at the end of this chapter (Booker & Thomas, 2009; Bould & Mieville, 2009; Gunn & Candelaria, 2005; Roberts, 2005) offer fuller discussions of the history of SF and the debates surrounding that history, but I will focus on Booker and Thomas and Roberts while augmenting their historical thread with my own experiences and fleshing out their primary focus on text-based media. If we begin here: "[S]cience fiction might be defined as fiction set in an imagined world that is different from our own in ways that are rationally explicable (often because of scientific advances) and that tend to produce cognitive estrangement in the reader" (Booker & Thomas, p. 4), then an outline of SF includes, but isn't restricted to, the following broad but key developments, essentially within identifiable centuries and decades.

Roberts (2005) argues that making historical claims are framed within both a time and genre distinction, the SF distinction being:

[A] delination of the continuum by which SF can be meaningfully separated out as that form of the Fantastic that embodies a technical (materialist) "enframing," as opposed to the religious (supernatural) approach we would today call "Fantasy." (p. 21)

Form, specifically the novel, also contributes to Roberts's perception of SF history since "the novel [was] … the mode central to SF for much of its life as a genre" (p. 21).

Ancient Roots

The rise of SF shares the rise of the novel in many respects. The Greek novel (Roberts, 2005) and works such as Jonathan Swift's *Gulliver's Travels* (1726) are essential seeds of what comes to be viewed as SF (Booker & Thomas, 2009). Roberts recognizes the "trope of odyssey" (p. 22) as one ancient source of conventions central to SF, space travel for example. Lucian Samosata, Roberts notes, is often invoked as the first SF writer because of his work dealing with a moon voyage; however, earlier works offered similar characteristics.

SF has rich ancient roots, but Roberts (2005) notes that little occurred in its history from about AD 400 until the seventeenth century. This dark period included a shift to religious texts and the rise of poetry over prose.

SF in the 1600s

The rise of science cannot be separated from the rebirth of SF (as Svec and Winiski explore in Chapter Two). Roberts (2005) recognizes Copernicus and Bruno as foundational scientific thinkers upon which SF regained its footing. For example, scientist Johann Kepler (1571-1630), Roberts explains, produced science as well as a prose romance, or early SF. Seventeenth century SF also represents an enduring conflict in terms of classifying genres, presenting an early tension between SF and fantasy: "Stuart Clark has demonstrated at length that, instead of being opposed discourses, 'magic' and 'science' were viewed by most thinker sin the period as complementary and even aspects of the same truth" (Roberts, p. 45).

Broadly, Roberts (2005) identifies SF patterns in the 1600s that endure into the twenty-first century—space travel (see Cyrano de Bergerac), "other" worlds, utopias (as related to Sir Thomas Moore [1477-1535]), narratives set in the future, and stories of scientific development as well as speculation: "The more science itself became an empirical, experimental discourse, and therefore the less place speculative impulse had in the practice of science, the more important science fiction became" (p. 60).

SF in the 1700s

The Enlightenment also provided a fertile period for SF. Roberts (2005) identifies science and poetry: "The same SF dialectic between reason and magic filters through into much of the Newtonian poetry of the time" (p. 67). Prose SF, notably the works of Jonathan Swift (*Gulliver's Travels*) and Voltaire, from this era redefined "the rules of imaginative speculation" (Roberts, p. 68). Key conventions of SF are represented also in the eighteenth century—satire, utopias, aliens, fantastic voyages (notably flight), examining otherness, subterranean narratives, Moon exploration.

The development of SF included the influence of intersecting genres, as Roberts (2005) explains, "most historians of SF link the birth of the genre with Gothic writing. Brian Aldiss ... goes so far as to define SF as an offshoot of Gothic" (p. 82). SF as "future fictions" also flourished in the French Revolution era, fueling the challenging nature of SF into the next century.

SF in the 1800s

Referencing the work of Suvin, Roberts (2005) identifies the work of Mary Shelley and Edgar Allan Poe as key during the nineteenth century shifts in SF:

> an increased interest in the mystical and theological component of interplanetary or interstellar Romances; reflections in imaginative literary form of nineteenth century advances in science, technology and industry; in some cases a direct mapping of Imperialist or political concerns into SF or utopian fantasy; and above all a much greater emphasis on the *future* as the area of science-fictional storytelling. (p. 88)

SF in the 1800s turned to the future, including considerations of the last human in existence. Washington Irving also introduced the green alien, but *Frankenstein: Or, the Modern Prometheus*, by Shelley (1818), is "often identified as the first genuine work of science fiction" because it combines a "[concern] with science overstepping its bounds" with "the various incarnations of the Faust story" (Booker & Thomas, p. 5). Here, SF's roots are established: science and the threat of science, satire, and the quasi-mythological nature of the *new* mythologies embedded in SF characters and narratives.

Poe, Roberts (2005) adds, also "has his enthusiasts as the originator of" SF (p. 99). Roberts add that Poe's focus on imagination as central to science stands as an important moment in SF's history. By the later decades of the 1800s, SF assumed a dual or antithetical quality, between decay and evolution or utopia versus dystopia (Roberts). Other key topics and characteristics during this era include anti-gravity, mystical elements such as telepathy, futuristic war, robots, and the power of the human will (which Roberts links to the force in *Star Wars*, *The Matrix*, and Superman's flying). A powerful if not crucial transition from Jules Verne to H.G. Wells bridges nineteenth century and twentieth-century SF.

SF in the Early- to Mid-1900s

SF parallels, then, the shifting evolution of the novel form by overlapping with other sub-genres, such as historical fiction. SF can often be described as having a historical situatedness, whether in some reshaped past or imagined future: "Science fiction, in short, inherits the mantle once worn by the historical novel as the utopian literary genre par excellence and as the genre most capable of capturing the energies of the historical process" (Booker & Thomas, 2009, p. 6).

Thus, SF blooms out of the "'scientific romances' of H. G. Wells at the end of the nineteenth century" (Booker & Thomas, 2009, p. 6). Booker and Thomas note that the earliest SF is not entirely unique when compared to other forms by Edward Bellamy, William Morris, H. Rider Haggard, or Rudyard Kipling. "Verne's fiction," Roberts (2005) argues, "spools out and reels in the imaginative possibilities of radical change and radical departure" (p. 142). However, Roberts adds, "Wells did not invent science fiction; but he did revivify its core dialectic with promiscuous energy, and with lasting impact" (p. 154).

Like comics and graphic novels (Thomas, 2010), SF is linked strongly to the market: "Science fiction as a selfconscious publishing category is generally considered to have begun in 1926, when editor Hugo Gernsback published the first issue of *Amazing Stories*, the first magazine devoted exclusively to science fiction" (Booker & Thomas, 2009, p. 7). SF short stories are a key element in the development of the genre, as an important connection between genre and medium as well as a powerful element in the double-edged sword of popularity for the genre. By becoming popular, SF essentially created a wedge between the genre and the critics (again, something that is paralleled in the comic book industry). Booker and Thomas explain that *Amazing Stories* established a key arena for the next editor, John W. Campbell, and writers—Isaac Asimov, Lester Del Ray, Robert Heinlein, Theodore Sturgeon, A. E. Von Vogt.

Renamed *Astounding Science-Fiction* in 1938, the magazine reinforced through the work of Campbell what Booker and Thomas (2009) designate as the Golden Age of Science Fiction from the late 1930s through the late 1950s. This era included more magazines—*The Magazine of Fantasy and Science Fiction, Galaxy Science Fiction*—and "the short story continued to be a vital form for the exploration of new sf ideas" (Booker & Thomas, p. 7). Medium is central here as Asimov's success as a SF short story writer translated in this period into novels as well. The pulps also introduced the visual connection between SF and its many media: "Almost as important as the stories was the visual look of the Pulp magazines" (Roberts, 2005, p. 184). SF silent films, serialized films, and the iconic Orson Welles's *War of the Worlds* radio broadcast represent the genre/medium develops of SF also.

The significance of the visual also continued to develop throughout mid-twentieth century. Magazine and SF novel covers became distinctive and created popular SF artists. SF also fed and was itself reinforced by the growing comic book market, again making the graphic central to the impact of the SF genre and the various media. In comics, Roberts (2005) identifies the "human-to-superhuman transforming characters," such as Sub-Mariner, Captain America, The Flash, and Green Lantern (p. 224).

SF distinguished itself as a genre and as a contrast to literary fiction throughout this Golden Age, notably by focusing on "social and political issues" instead of the strong characterization emphasis in literary fiction (Booker & Thomas, 2009, p. 8). Booker and Thomas also identify the importance of SF building a "fan culture that has helped sf readers to establish communities of a kind unknown among devotees of 'high' literature, including an array of popular sf conventions[1] in which fans can meet each other as well as well-known authors" (Booker & Thomas, p. 8). Next, then, comes the rise of SF films in the 1950s—*The Day the Earth Stood Still* (1951) and *The Invasion of the Body Snatchers* (1956), the first of which is my mother's favorite movie and the seed of my childhood fascination with SF and the second is crucial to understanding the allegorical power of SF as it paralleled literary works such as *The Crucible*, by Author Miller, which used the same metaphorical frame to address a social issue under the mask of genre (*Body Snatchers* using SF to mask Cold War fears and *The Crucible* using history to mask a confrontation of the McCarthy Era). Booker and Thomas highlight the power of SF to "avoid censorship": Frederik Pohl, Ben Barzman, Pohl and C. M. Kormbluth (p. 8).

New Wave SF of the 1960s, 1970s

Booker and Thomas (2009) see the 1960s as a turn from Gold Age, "hard" SF to New Age, "soft" SF, "more character driven and more concerned with the social and political ramifications of technological developments than with the technologies themselves" (p. 9): typified in the pages of Michael Moorcock's *New Worlds* magazine and Judith Merril's *England Swings* anthology. Roberts (2005) identifies the influence of the Soviet Union launching Spitnik as well, spurring New Wave SF that "reacted against the conventions of traditional SF to produce avant-garde, radical or fractured science fiction" (pp. 230-231).

New Wave SF appeared determined to address also that the genre had been marginalized; regardless of SF's critical status, however, this era includes foundational works across media and established some of the leading artists in the SF genre: Frank Herbert (*Dune*), Philip K. Dick, J.R.R. Tolkien (blurring the SF and fantasy fan-base), Stanley Kubrick's *2001: A Space Odyssey*, Ursula Le Guin, Anthony Burgess (*A Clockwork Orange*), Joanna Russ, Marge Piercy, Alice Sheldon (James Tiptree Jr.).

The New Wave era should not be underestimated in its impact on the rise of SF in visual media, TV and film, as print-only SF often fed the now-classic TV series and films often most directly associated with SF—such as Dick's *Do Androids Dream of Electric Sheep?* spurring Ridley Scott's *Blade Runner* (1982) and a graphic novel series begun in 2009.

Late Twentieth Century SF Film and TV

While claims that "young people today" have abandoned reading print-texts for the immediate gratification of TV, film, and the Internet are disputed by evidence that traditional reading endures, pop cultures, especially in the U.S., has certainly been grounded in TV and film. SF has been instrumental in that phenomenon, and for many people, the first associations they have with SF is a visual medium. To show how this looks historically, consider this list of TV and film works from the mid- to late-twentieth century: *Fahrenheit 451, 2001: A Space Odyssey, Star Trek, Dr. Who, Star Trek: The Next Generation, Planet of the Apes* (and the sequels), *Star Wars, Batman* (TV series), *Alien* (and sequels), *Blade Runner, The Matrix* (trilogy), *E.T. the Extra-Terrestrial, Terminator* (and sequels), *Mad Max* (and sequels), *RoboCop, Jurassic Park* (and sequels).

Although still incomplete, that listing represents not just the impact of SF on late twentieth century pop culture, but also the enduring qualities associated with SF: androids, post-apocalyptic worlds, space and aliens, time travel, computers and technology. A credible argument can be made that SF during the late twentieth century, on the heels of New Wave SF, gained both the popular and critical respect it deserved. But another transition also came as a consequence

Recent SF and Beyond

Roberts (2005) recognizes that SF ascended to new heights during the decades of the 1960s-2000 with the huge success of SF TV and films, but "during this period the novel stopped being the prime mode of SF. As visual SF (particularly cinema and TV) increasingly came to dominate the mainstream, prose SF became increasingly sidelined" (p. 295). Roberts notes the shift did not mean a drop in quality of print SF or that the print fan base disappeared, but that SF as a popular and respected form appeared to move to visual media (Atwood's *The Handmaid's Tale*, for example, sparked both high praise and the debates about SF noted earlier).

A notable development in SF also included the rise of adaptation: SF superhero comics to films (X-Men, Spider-Man, Batman, Superman, *Watchmen*) as well as SF video games to film. But the adaptation trend also includes prose fiction to comics and graphic novels, and a seemingly endless overlap of comics/graphic novels, prose fiction, TV/cable series, video games, and films. SF continues in these adaptations to cross-pollinate with other genres and a wide array of media.

Critical Response and Scholarship of SF

A final consideration of the history of SF concerns the rise of critical response and scholarship. As SF became more mainstream, including its inclusion in the canon of K-12 and university classrooms, the critical and scholarly response also grew. Briefly here, that scholarship is noted to suggest that it helps clarify and capture the evolution of SF.

Most SF scholarship includes a retelling of its history, either in chapter or sections (Booker & Thomas, 2009; Bould et al., 2009) or entire volumes dedicated to that history (Roberts, 2005). Critical responses to SF also often address controversies and complications associated with teaching SF (Hellekson et al., 2010). As well, SF scholarship tends to highlight the key themes and topics that SF confronts as a genre—post-colonialism (Hoagland & Sarwal, 2010), women and gender (Hellekson, et al., 2010; Reid, 2009), sexuality (Betz, 2011), race (Jackson & Moody-Freeman, 2011; Nama, 2008; Lavender, 2011), communism/Marxism (Bould & Mieville, 2009), and key authors/works (Booker & Thomas), for example. (See the selected annotated bibliography at the end of this chapter.)

* * *

My journey as a SF fan, teacher, and writer has evolved as SF has, a move toward my own changing view of what counts as SF as well as a scholarly and educational focus on exploring adaptation as a quest to understand, and not define, genre, medium, mode, and form. My problem with coming to know and admire the writing of Neil Gaiman has been replicated in a more recent fascination with Japanese writer Haruki Murakami, whose *1Q84* drew me to it in part because that novel was labeled, like *American Gods*, as SF.

Once again, I faced a conflict, echoed by Roberts (2005):

> The gifted Japanese novelist Haruki Murkami (b. 1949) has written science fiction, but his SF novels owe more to the traditions of the ghost story and supernatural fable than to the particularly cultural dynamic that shaped the western genre …. [His novels] might similarly be described as "magical realism," except that Murakami's characters are too passive, in a sense too machinic, and his world too thoroughly immersed in the idiom of contemporary technology. (p. 323)

In short, Murakami's work is both SF and not SF, although it often *feels* SF (maybe passing the *know it when I read it* test).

Yet, the exploration of SF as a problem remains with me the most enduring, just as we read SF as a confrontation of the world and all the unanswered and unanswerable questions that come with human existence. So this volume is both a consideration of SF as confrontation and our collective confrontation of the genre itself.

After the selected annotated bibliography below, Chapter Two turns to SF and speculative fiction novels as they helped professors Svec and Winiski confront science in a first year seminar.

SELECTED ANNOTATED RESOURCE LIST

Atwood, M. (2011). *In other worlds: SF and the human imagination.* New York: Nan A. Talese/ Doubleday.

> Atwood dedicates her examination of SF to Ursular K. Le Guin, with whom Atwood had a public argument over the nature of SF—the apparent genesis of this volume. Atwood notes the book "is an exploration of my own lifelong relationship with a literary form, or forms, or subforms, both as reader and as writer" (p. 1). The book has four broad sections: "In Other Worlds: SF and the Human Imagination" (Atwood's examination of SF as a fan, writer, and scholar), "Other Deliberations" (a collection of Atwood's short pieces on SF), "Five Tributes" (five SF short forms by Atwood), and "Appendices" (an

open letter about the banning of The Handmaid's Tale and a brief essay about the connection between Atwood's *The Blind Assassin* and *Weird Tales*).

Betz, P. M. (2011). *The lesbian fantastic: A critical study of science fiction, fantasy, paranormal and gothic writing*. Jefferson, NC: McFarland and Company, Inc., Publishers.

In her preface to this volume exploring the "otherness" of being lesbian in the context of genre fiction, Betz explains:

The paradox of fantasy literature lies in its balance of attraction and revulsion, its creation of alternative worlds and realities based on the already experienced, its acceptance of difference while attempting to annihilate it. Within these contradictions lesbian authors and their readers have the ability to play out the meanings of Otherness and reconcile the fear that accompanies it. (p. 4)

Chapter Four focuses directly on lesbian science fiction, which she classifies as a subgenre of fantasy.

Booker, M. K., & Thomas, A. (2009). *The science fiction handbook*. Malden, MA: Wiley-Blackwell.

Booker and Thomas assemble an excellent introductory text about SF in western cultures. After a solid introduction, the volume includes a brief survey of SF subgenres (including time-travel narratives, dystopian and utopian SF, and other major types of SF), overviews of nineteen influential SF authors, and a concluding section on twenty major SF works. An outstanding work for scholars, teachers, and students.

Bould, M., Butler, A. M., Roberts, A., & Vint, S., eds. (2010). *The Routledge companion to science fiction*. New York: Routledge.

This edited volume collects a wide range of SF scholars presented in four parts—history, theory, issues and challenges, and subgenres. The individual essays cover all types of SF media and serve as excellent introductions to the complex genre in its many forms: "Sf has always been as much concerned with the past as with the future, and this volume stands at the moment in time, telling what has already passed in some of its richness, richness, detail, and diversity, and looking forward into possible futures," notes the editors (p. xxi).

Bould, M., & Mieville, C., eds. (2009). *Red planets: Marxism and science fiction*. Middleton, CT: Wesleyan University Press.

This edited volume confronts the marginalizing characterizations of SF across media, notably the quality of many SF works and the impact of SF in pop culture. The collected essays address the many and varied aspects of most SF scholarship and weave through those examinations a focus on how

Marxism informs SF and SF informs Marxism: "However one responds to it, Suvin's definition (and its elaboration) itself arrived like a novum, reordering SF theory and criticism around it, idiosyncratically and contingently wedding SF to Marxism" (p. 19). The works are organized in "Things to Come," "When Worlds Collide," and "Back to the Future."

Clarke, A. M. (2010). *Ursula K. Le Guin's journey to post-feminism*. Jefferson, NC: McFarland and Company, Inc., Publishers.

Le Guin is one of the major voices in SF, as well as a powerful advocate for the genre. Clarke's examination of her work frames Le Guin with J.R.R. Tolkien and C.S. Lewis "for the quality and mythic status of her Earthsea series" (p. 1). This volume presents Le Guin's SF and fantasy catalog in the context of her feminism: "I reinforce my position that Le Guin, now a post-feminist, follows the natural trajectory of the feminist evolution and so fully exemplifies the impact of feminism on the work of a significant writer," and we may add on SF as well (p. 4).

Cornea, C. (2007). *Science fiction cinema: Between fantasy and reality*. New Brunswick, NJ: Rutgers University Press.

SF in pop culture may be defined more by film as by any other medium, even print-text. Cornea presents a chronological examination of SF films, but also highlights key and defining topics and elements of SF throughout that chronology. This format allows readers to grasp the evolution of SF as a genre as well as how SF film evolved within the broader classification. Each chapter also present key interviews for even greater insight in SF films, including writers, directors, actors, and one special effects technician.

Gunn, J., & Candelaria, M. (2005). *Speculations on speculation: Theories of science fiction*. Lanham, MD: The Scarecrow Press, Inc.

This often cited edited volume is divided into six sections—identification, location, derivations, excavation, infatuation, and anticipation—in order to present a complex effort to define SF. The essays reflect the attitude of the volume: "Uncertainty is a way of life" (p. xi)—especially in a scholarly work that speculates about the act of speculation (SF). James Gunn's "Toward a Definition of Science Fiction" stands a key work in the field of SF scholarship.

Hellekson, K., Jacobsen, C. B., Sharp, P. B., & Yaszek, L., eds. (2010). *Practicing science fiction: Critical essays on writing, reading and teaching the genre*. Jefferson, NC: McFarland and Company, Inc., Publishers.

This edited volume is rich with diversity and approaches the exploring SF. The SF genre is examined here through the broad categories of teaching, reading and writing, media, and women. As Hellekson notes, the volume is unique in its "address[ing] the intersection among these three topic"—reading, writing, and teaching (p. 1).

Hoagland, E., & Sarwal, R., eds. (2010). *Science fiction, imperialism and the third world: Essays on postcolonial literature and film.* Jefferson, NC: McFarland and Company, Inc., Publishers.

This edited volume acknowledges the essential Western grounding of SF, but also notes the tension between defining SF against the genre both being and becoming: "This introduction," Hooagland and Sarwal explain, "then, seeks to establish a middle ground through which to articulate some thoughts regarding the emerging genre of postcolonial science fiction, a hybrid genre that reflects intriguing affinities between two genres whose own parameters continue to vigorously contested" (p. 5). The essays are collected in four sections: re-inventing/alternate history, forms of protest, fresh representations, and Utopia/dystopia. Moving beyond the Western groundings of SF, the essays examine post-colonialism in and through SF.

Jackson, S., & Moody-Freeman, J. E., eds. (2011). *The black imagination: Science fiction, futurism and the speculative.* New York: Peter Lang.

The editors of this volume argue that SF connected with Black writers, directors, and characters "has begun to come into its own. It is no longer an anomaly" (p. 1). This edited volume also builds on the assertion that Black SF has older and deeper roots than many acknowledge. Eleven chapters explore the intersections of race with SF in a wide variety of forms as well as how Black SF addresses gender, sexuality, and power. This is an important volume both for its complication of defining and understanding SF and how the issues raised in SF reveal the essential critical nature of the genre.

Lavender, III, I. (2011). *Race in American science fiction.* Bloomington: Indiana University Press.

Lavendar includes quotes from Octavia E. Butler and Ralph Ellison to preface this volume—from *Invisible Man*: "Who knows but that, on the lower frequencies, I speak for you?" Ellison's invisible narrator, it is worth noting, distinguishes himself from the popular SF novel; thus, this opening quote serves well to set the tone for Lavender's work. In the introduction, Lavender recounts visiting Little Rock Central and confronting segregation in the U.S., concluding, "My surreal experience is the stuff of science fiction (sf). This rumination cause me to think 'what if...'" (p. 2). This is an ambitious work, in which Lavender "attempt[s] to harness the signature language of modernity—science fiction—to explore and better understand the American heritage of race and racism related to black experiences with displacement, dispossession, and alienation filtered through more familiar racist structures such as slavery, Jim Crow, or offensive language" (p. 20).

Link, E. C. (2010). *Understanding Philip K. Dick*. Columbia, SC: The University of South Carolina Press.

The Understanding Contemporary American Literature series presents writer's works in accessible and thorough volumes, and this volume on Dick is no exception. Link identifies Dick as "a cultural phenomenon and one of the most celebrated writers of science fiction in the twentieth century" (p. xi). Link notes that this examination of Dick is a broad overview and introductory, focusing on themes and addressing the novice reader of Dick's works.

Nama, A. (2008). *Black space: Imagining race in science fiction film*. Austin, TX: University of Texas Press.

"[B]lackness and race are often present in SF films as narrative subtext or implicit allegorical subject," Nama explains in the Introduction to this volume on race in SF films (p. 2). Name focuses on "black racial representation" in SF movies in order to examine broader issues of race in the U.S. (p. 6). This is an excellent work to focus on SF in the film medium.

Reid, R. A., ed. (2009). *Women in science fiction and fantasy*, vols. 1-2. Westport, CT: Greenwood Press.

"This project is the first general reference work focusing on women's contributions to science fiction and fantasy" across form and media, explains Reid (p. vii). Volume one includes 29 essays that span virtually every time frame, text form and media, and related topic imaginable bringing women/gender and SF/fantasy together. Volume two provides 230 encyclopedia-type entries and a wealth of scholarly references. This two-volume set is important as a look at women and SF, but also as a powerful reference for examining SF broadly.

Roberts, A. (2005). *The history of science fiction*. New York, NY: Palgrave Macmillan.

A SF novelist and scholar, Roberts presents a broad but thorough examination of the history of SF, starting with the problem of defining SF and working through the ancient roots of the genre and up to the still evolving twenty-first incarnations of SF. Roberts is knowledgeable and witty in his discussion, offering both neophytes and seasoned readers and scholars valuable insight into SF as well as the controversies surrounding the genre. While Roberts has clear and assertive stances on SF, this volume is effective at raising questions and problems that maintain a sense of SF history as a living, breathing thing.

Rossi, U. (2011). *The twisted worlds of Philip K. Dick: A reading of twenty ontologically uncertain novels*. Jefferson, NC: McFarland and Company, Inc., Publishers.

Rossi explains that "we have not come to terms with Dick yet," arguing that scholarship about Dick has "fallen short of the author" (p. 2). Examining twenty of Dick's novels, Rossi attempts to rectify some of the failures of scholarship on the SF author by connection Dick's works with each other and wit a wide variety of other texts and media. This volume, then, is valuable to anyone interested specifically in Dick, but also as a powerful examination of SF and the many problems with the genre.

Sullivan, III, C. W., ed. (1999). *Young adult science fiction*. Westport, CT: Greenwood Press.

Just as the *Twilight* series promoted a stream of young adult fiction featuring vampires, *The Hunger Games* trilogy revitalized the SF young adult fiction market. While this volume is becoming dated, the edited work's twelve chapters help establish the rich SF young adult fiction history, including SF young adult works internationally. As well, the volume helps examine both SF and young adult fiction as distinct and overlapping genres.

Suvin, D. (1979). *Metamorphoses of science fiction: On the poetics and history of a literary genre*. New Haven, CT: Yale University Press, 1979.

Suvin's now essential scholarship on SF was groundbreaking and confrontational when it was published. The tone and content explores the rich and strained history of SF and the scholarship about SF. As a review of the book notes, "It is almost, then, as if Suvin, instead of defining his genre, avoids defining it out of fear that the "subversive" form might turn out simply another handmaiden of bourgeois ideology" (Slusser, 1980. p. 75).

NOTES

[i] See the 2011 film, *Paul*, which opens with and works against the convention element of SF as part of the film's larger satire and homage to SF fandom and films.

REFERENCES

Atwood, M. (2011). *In other worlds: SF and the human imagination*. New York: Nan A. Talese/ Doubleday.

Betz, P. M. (2011). *The lesbian fantastic: A critical study of science fiction, fantasy, paranormal and gothic writing*. Jefferson, NC: McFarland and Company, Inc., Publishers.

Booker, M. K., & Thomas, A. (2009). *The science fiction handbook*. Malden, MA: Wiley-Blackwell.

Bould, M., & Mieville, C. (Eds.). (2009). *Red planets: Marxism and science fiction*. Middleton, CT: Wesleyan University Press.

Bould, M., Butler, A. M., Roberts, A., & Vint, S. (Eds.). (2010). *The Routledge companion to science fiction*. New York: Routledge.

Clarke, A. M. (2010). *Ursula K. Le Guin's journey to post-feminism*. Jefferson, NC: McFarland and Company, Inc., Publishers.

Cornea, C. (2007). *Science fiction cinema: Between fantasy and reality*. New Brunswick, NJ: Rutgers University Press.

Crichton, M. (1969). *The Andromeda strain*. New York: Harper.

Gunn, J., & Candelaria, M. (2005). *Speculations on speculation: Theories of science fiction*. Lanham, MD: The Scarecrow Press, Inc.

Hellekson, K., Jacobsen, C. B., Sharp, P. B., & Yaszek, L., eds. (2010). *Practicing science fiction: Critical essays on writing, reading and teaching the genre.* Jefferson, NC: McFarland and Company, Inc., Publishers.

Hoagland, E., & Sarwal, R., eds. (2010). *Science fiction, imperialism and the third world: Essays on postcolonial literature and film.* Jefferson, NC: McFarland and Company, Inc., Publishers.

Jackson, S., & Moody-Freeman, J. E., eds. (2011). *The black imagination: Science fiction, futurism and the speculative.* New York: Peter Lang.

Johns, A. M. (2008). Genre awareness for the novice academic student: An ongoing quest. *Language Teaching, 41*(2), 237-252.

Lavender, III, I. (2011). *Race in American science fiction.* Bloomington: Indiana University Press.

Le Guin, U. K. (2009, August 28). *The year of the flood* by Margaret Atwood. *The Guardian.* Retrieved from http://www.guardian.co.uk/books/2009/aug/29/margaret-atwood-year-of-flood

Link, E. C. (2010). *Understanding Philip K. Dick.* Columbia, SC: The University of South Carolina Press.

Nama, A. (2008). *Black space: Imagining race in science fiction film.* Austin, TX: University of Texas Press.

Reid, R. A. (Ed.). (2009). *Women in science fiction and fantasy,* vols. 1-2. Westport, CT: Greenwood Press.

Roberts, A. (2005). *The history of science fiction.* New York, NY: Palgrave Macmillan.

Rossi, U. (2011). *The twisted worlds of Philip K. Dick: A reading of twenty ontologically uncertain novels.* Jefferson, NC: McFarland and Company, Inc., Publishers.

Sterling, B. (2011, March). Slipstream 2. *Science Fiction Studies #113, 38*(1). Retrieved from http://www.depauw.edu/sfs/abstracts/a113.htm#sterling

Sullivan, III, C. W., ed. (1999). *Young adult science fiction.* Westport, CT: Greenwood Press.

Suvin, D. (1978, March). On what is and is not an SF narration; with a list of 101 Victorian books that should be excluded from SF bibliographies. *Science Fiction Studies #14, 5*(1). Retrieved from http://www.depauw.edu/sfs/backissues/14/suvin14art.htm

Thomas, P. L. (2010). *Challenging genres: Comic books and graphic novels.* Netherlands: Sense Publishers.

Vonnegut, K. (1963). *Cat's cradle.* New York, NY: Delta.

Vonnegut, K. (1965). On science fiction. *The New York Times.* Retrieved from http://www.vonnegutweb.com/archives/arc_scifi.html

Vonnegut, K. (1985). *Galapagos.* New York, NY: Delta.

MICHAEL SVEC AND MIKE WINISKI

2. SF AND SPECULATIVE NOVELS

Confronting the Science and the Fiction

Today there is a nuclear-powered, laser-firing robot exploring Mars. This isn't fiction. Martian rocks are being zapped, not in defense of the planet Earth, but for the sake of knowledge. The rover is aptly named Curiosity, and she represents not only our advancing technical understanding but also our intense desire to explore, imagine, and create. Many scientists trace their inspiration to science fiction (SF), but as Carl Sagan (1996) notes, the relationship between science and SF is cyclical and mutually reinforcing.

> Science and science fiction have done a kind of dance over the last century, particularly with respect to Mars. The scientists make a finding. It inspires science fiction writers to write about it, and a host of young people read the science fiction and are excited, and inspired to become scientists to find out more about Mars, which they do, which then feeds again into another generation of science fiction and science; and that sequence has played major role in our present ability to get to Mars.

In this chapter we describe how we leveraged this interplay between SF and science in a first year undergraduate seminar about Mars to create an environment in which students learned not only the facts about the red planet but also the habits of mind necessary to understand the scientific process and imagine its implications within the context of story.

Becoming and being a scientist or engineer no doubt requires deep content knowledge; however, a laser-like focus on "just the facts" comes with a cost. In the American Association for the Advancement of Science's seminal book *Science for all Americans* (1990) the authors describe the current science curriculum as "overstuffed and undernourished" (p. xvi) to the detriment of students' conceptual understanding and their ability to foresee and solve messy problems. According to the report, the development of values that undergird scientific habits of mind is of equal (if not greater) importance than content. Science-minded students are characterized by informed skepticism, curiosity, and openness to new ideas. Productive skeptics are more than just fact checkers, however. They understand where we've been and how we got where we are. This perspective reminds them not to hold too tightly to an idea and that the unraveling of a current theory may just be the next step towards a great discovery. When these values are cultivated, students begin to ask, "What if?," and science and SF can offer productive environments in which to explore.

P. Thomas (ed.), Science Fiction and Speculative Fiction, 35–57.

Taking informed skepticism to an extreme ruined SF for author Mike Winiski—for a while anyway. As a high school physics teacher, he used clips of Keanu Reeves and Sandra Bullock jumping fifty-foot gaps in the highway in a bus to teach projectile motion and illustrate the implausibility of such a venture. This practice extended to SF. In the movie *Mission to Mars* (2000), the dismemberment of a crewmember as he was pulled into a spinning vortex provided a wonderful opportunity to teach rotational physics. For a time, this instructor was the assassin of suspended disbelief, but the teaching moments were just too ripe for him to feel much regret.

Debunking bad science is important; the realistic portrayal and detail in contemporary movies may corrode the general public's understanding. A cartoon coyote violating the laws of gravity is easily recognized as implausible, but advanced special effects can trick moviegoers into thinking that flames in the vacuum of space are perfectly reasonable. With this in mind, The National Academies of Sciences has started a program, The Science & Entertainment Exchange (2013), which connects filmmakers with scientists to enhance the accuracy of the science portrayed on the big screen. Teachers use movies in classes to increase the students' scientific literacy and their ability to critique and analyze scientific images and arguments in film and television. Skepticism is a scientific value after all. While use of SF in the classroom has been found to help foster positive student attitudes (Freudenrich, 2000; Kilby-Goodwin, 2010; Firooznia, 2006; Barnett & Kafka, 2007), focusing solely on debunking can cause students to doubt even the solid science represented in the story (Czerneda, 2006) and certainly the extended possibilities. We are going to argue for another use, feeding the imagination and creative side of the future scientist.

For author Michael Svec, his love of astronomy was born one summer night at a Boy Scout camp during a star hike. It was the first time he had seen the moonless night sky away from city lights. No planetarium show had prepared him for what he saw that evening. When Svec returned to the yellow night sky of Chicago, it was Carl Sagan's *Cosmos* that fueled his new passion for astronomy. Sagan was a master at taking science, mixing in a human story, and asking speculative questions. Sagan's story telling was able to engage Svec such that he was angered by the burning of the Alexandria library, fascinated by the relationship of Johannes Kepler and Tycho Brahe, and intrigued by the possibility of large floating life forms in the atmospheres of Jupiter-like planets. Later as an undergraduate science major he had the opportunity to use the historic telescope at the university observatory and could not help but recall the episode "Blues for a Red Planet" as he drew his own pictures of Mars resembling those of Percival Lowell's (see Figure 1).

While not SF, Sagan's *Cosmos* engaged in speculation based on current science and provoked inspiration, curiosity, and imagination. SF likewise asks the "what if?" questions. The *Cosmos* episode of "Encyclopaedia Galactica" caught Svec's interest the most because of the concept of catalogues of hundreds of planets and civilizations. Sagan's foreshadowing of an encyclopedia of planets is current reality with well over 800 planets beyond our solar system known and more being discovered. Good SF can possess many of the same characteristics of *Cosmos* and in that way feed the curious mind of the science-minded student and build on the central role of questioning in science.

As we move toward a pedagogical definition of SF, we are guided by the goals of providing students with the opportunity to develop both their sense of informed skepticism and wonder. Selecting SF only for its realistic portrayal limits the opportunity for students to explore the social, political, and ethical implications of the science that are so powerfully revealed through story. A focus on realism can also squelch the "what if?" questions which foster openness to new ideas and curiosity. On the other hand, stories that play too loose with the science diminish opportunities to teach its content and process. Our evolving scientific understanding over time complicates the mix. The plausible and the possible are a moving and interwoven target. But we can't think of a better learning environment for students to experience the "rough and tumble enterprise" (Furman University, 2005, p. 9) of deep learning.

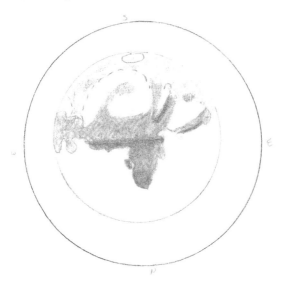

Figure 1. Mars on September 25, 1988 by Michael Svec at the University of Illinois Observatory.

DEFINING SCIENCE FICTION

What is SF? Classifying rocks and minerals or plants and animals is probably easier than classifying literature. Darko Suvin (1979) suggests that SF is a literary genre "whose necessary and sufficient conditions are the presence and interaction of estrangement and cognition, and whose main formal device is an imaginative framework alternative to the author's empirical environment" (pp. 7-8). The empirical environment is literally the real world and the imaginative framework is the introduction of something new. The novum, the intrusion of something new into a world not unlike our own and validated by cognitive logic, is a defining characteristic of SF (Suvin, 1979, p. 63). The novum could be an alien, a discovery, or a new technology, but it must be possible, an extrapolation of our current understanding of science.

Margaret Atwood (2011) saw SF as descending from H.G. Well's *War of the Worlds* with speculative fiction tracing its origins to Jules Verne. Speculative fiction is about things, technologies that *could* happen but just haven't when the book was written, such as submarines and balloons. She did not see Martians arriving on Earth in metal cylinders, as portrayed in *War of the Worlds,* as possible. For Atwood, aliens are SF, not speculation. Atwood contrasted her meaning with Ursula Le Guin's belief that SF represented what could really happen. To Atwood's point, the idea of intelligent tentacle, blood-sucking Martians does seem more like fantasy based upon our current understanding of Mars, although Le Guin would counter that at the time *War of the Worlds* was written, it did represent commonly accepted thoughts about intelligent life on Mars and was thus speculative but grounded in the science of the time.

Paul Kincaid (2010) argued there is no such thing as a pure genre and "[e]verything is capable of being read in different ways. So the way we read a work, sometimes the way we *choose* to read a work, is crucial in determining how we identify it" (para. 35). Using Kincaid's logic, the authors are going to provide guidelines for selecting and reading SF and effectively integrating it into a course that also focuses on science content. From a pedagogical perspective we have assumed an understanding of speculative SF more consistent with Ursulua Le Guin's broader conception of the genre (Atwood, 2011), which provides some leeway based on perspective. The inclusion of historical perspective (the scientific understanding of the time which formed the basis of the speculation) has immense pedagogical value because it illustrates the cycle of science feeding speculation and vice-versa, which Sagan so beautifully captures.

We have identified four overlapping and interwoven elements necessary for our pedagogical use of the speculative SF genre;

1. Deep description of the science content or technologies that were plausible or accurate to the time period.
2. The novum: A plausible innovation as a key element in the speculation.
3. Big Picture: Exploration of the impact on society and humanity.
4. Nature of Science: Science and technology as human endeavors

These elements guided our selection of SF for the course as well as the science content.

Plausible Science and Technologies

For use in our classes, the science needed to shape the story and play an integral role. The plausibility of the science being portrayed was important as it served as a launching point for connecting to current science—a major portion of the course. For the students with a science background, inaccurate science within a novel can often become a distraction resulting in disconnect from the fictional story. In an interview, Sam, an Earth and Environmental science major, shared that realistic science pulled him into SF. He traced his SF roots to Jules Verne and found the author's inclusion of projectile motion calculations in *From the Earth to the Moon* made him more willing to engage with the story.

Some readers require less hard science to draw them in. John, a physics major we interviewed, did not draw a distinct line between SF and fantasy. He sought out both because he read to have his imagination engaged and stretched. He was willing to adapt his expectations accordingly; however, some readers find it difficult to be so fluid with their approach.

A famous cartoon by Sidney Harris (1977) illustrates our desire for a reasonable scientific explanation. The illustration shows two scientists standing in front of a chalkboard covered in complex formulas. One scientist says to the other, "I think you should be more explicit here in step two" while pointing to a spot on the board that reads, "Then a miracle occurs." Some moments in fiction play that way, like the scene in *A Princess of Mars* in which John Carter is magically transported to Mars from a cave on Earth. For some readers this deux ex machina (god from the machine) moment is too grand a leap and moves the story into the realm of the impossible or fantasy. But through story, SF can allow us to imagine in the fuzzy scientific space. While we may not be comfortable with a miracle, we may be willing to set aside the debunker in us and imagine "what if?" scenarios, as long as the story starts with the plausible and leads us to imagine the possible.

The Novum

Readers of any piece of fiction must find a touchstone, a place, person, or emotion, where they can connect and engage in the story. SF then introduces a novum as a means to create cognitive dissonance. In social psychology, cognitive dissonance is the discomfort people experience when there is a clash between their expectations and reality (Festinger, 1962). Within the context of the SF story, the novum becomes the mechanism to challenge our preconceived notions. It must be a scientifically or technologically plausible device such as a new technology, scarcity scenario, distant location, or future time that provides the catalyst sparking examination of our beliefs and expectations. The planet orbiting multiple suns in Asimov and Silverburg's *Nightfall* presents a society with many connections to our own familiar context, but when an unexpected eclipse reveals a night sky filled with stars, that society collapses into chaos. The reader may well have their beliefs in the stability of their society's foundational assumptions challenged. In our daily lives we try to reduce cognitive dissonance, sometimes by altering or modifying our beliefs or by ignoring the dissonance. Fiction becomes a safer place for exploration and helps us resolve dissonance.

The novum, within the context of our class, is the source of speculation, which connects to both curiosity and openness to new ideas. Scientists thrive on curiosity.

Science education should foster and then channel that curiosity into productive investigations. In addition, the scientific value of openness to new ideas can be demonstrated with the novum. The growth of scientific knowledge and technology comes from generating new ideas, and the novum can serve as the means to generate those innovations (Strauss, 2012). As *Science for all Americans* points out:

> The purpose of science education is not exclusively to produce scientists, it should help all students understand the great importance of carefully considering ideas that at first may seem disquieting to them or at odds with what they generally believe. The competition among ideas is a major source of tensions within science, between science and society, and within society. (AAAS, 1990, p. 185)

Big Picture: Impact on Society and Humans

Important issues in our communities and society never involve questions of science and technology alone. Science is a human endeavor and part of a larger human ecosystem that includes other goals and institutions. SF can explore the impacts of science and technology at a variety of scales, from the individual to all of humanity.

The products of technology and discoveries of science impact society. Robots are frequently explored beginning with the robot rebellion in Karel Čapek's play *R.U.R.* (*Rosumovi Umělí Roboti*) to Marge Piercy's *Body of Glass*, a SF/cyber punk novel that examines gender roles, human identity, and artificial intelligence. Our student Sam enjoyed the way SF can play with the ethical dilemmas in ways that other societal institutions tend not to. For example, the life extending treatments in *Red Mars* are only made available to insiders, posing ethical and moral dilemmas that closely mirror current controversies related to access to health care based on income.

Science itself is a complex social activity with its own set of cultural values that can be examined in SF. Beyond the common mad scientists or independent gentlemen scientist hero stereotypes, there are examples that provide insight into the culture of scientists. Radio astronomer Ellie Arroway as the main protagonist in Carl Sagan's *Contact* (1985) provides one illustrative example. *Contact* also explores the influence of society on science. Society's concerns and needs often dictate research priorities through funding and public opinion, as Ellie learns as she struggles to secure financial backing for her research. Corporate funding and economic goals drove the cloning of dinosaurs in *Jurassic Park*, for example.

Nature of Science

Science is built on curiosity. *A framework for K-12 science education* (2012) includes as one of its guiding principles the importance of connecting science to student interests and experiences. Science education should both capture the students' wonder and spark their desire to continue to learn about science. SF may well have a place among university science programs as a means to help sustain student interest as they progress through the science majors. For some science students, SF provides the larger picture and engages them in the speculative questions that might have served as their initial motivation for pursing a science major. When Alex, a chemistry graduate, was asked if science majors should read SF, he responded: "Should pigs roll in the mud?"

SF can be read for enjoyment but also for the way in which it explores scientific concepts. As Czerneda (2006) noted:

> Most science fiction authors ask, "What if?" and speculate about what could happen if a certain aspect of science or technology existed – or did not exist. By bringing science into the realm of individual lives as well as entire cultures, these stories are thought experiments about anything we can imagine, from global warming to evolution. (p. 39)

Good SF, from a pedagogical position, does not violate scientific principles but relies on them to spark the discussion of not only "what if?" but also "so what?" SF often engages in both science and technology.

> Any education that focuses predominantly on the detailed products of scientific labor – the facts of science – without developing an understanding of how these facts were established or that ignores the many important applications of science in the world misrepresents science and marginalizes the importance of engineering. (NGSSF, p. 43)

Science for all Americans lists recommendations on what constitutes essential scientific literacy for all citizens including: science cannot provide complete answers to *all* questions, science is a blend of logic and imagination, science is a complex social activity, science is conducted based on generally accepted ethical principles, and scientists participate in public affairs as both specialists and citizens. SF can serve as a powerful means to explore these elements of science, for both majors and non-majors.

Being a science major often immerses students in a very narrow and deep exploration of one discipline. As science majors, the authors often felt that the larger issues were lost and the connection of the content to the larger world was difficult to see. Many science majors seek to find that relevance. SF is one means for science majors to explore the larger issues about the content's implication. Emma, one of our students now majoring in chemistry, reflected one year after the seminar: "[O]f course, it [SF] reminds you why you started to like science in the first place."

IN THE CLASSROOM

The first year seminar "Mars: On the Shoulders of Giants" was designed to be consistent with the university's curricular goal for the seminars: to ignite students' intellectual curiosity and to develop their ability to analyze and craft arguments.

Small class sizes of 15 encourage intellectual risk taking and foster community. The course was developed and taught by the two authors and David Moffett, the university's professor of astronomy. First offered in 2009, it has been taught four times with revisions along the way. This course focuses on how scientific knowledge is developed through the lens of our changing view of Mars throughout history. Analyses of current studies of Mars are juxtaposed against historical understanding and perceptions of the planet found in scientific and popular literature of the day, as well as the movies. Kim Stanley Robinson's *Red Mars* (1993) provides a unifying story throughout the course complemented by Fredrick Taylor's *The Scientific Exploration of Mars* (2010), Mary Roach's *Packing for Mars* (2010), and William Hartmann's *A Traveler's Guide to Mars* (2003).

A detailed analysis of the progression of our understanding of Mars throughout history was beyond the scope of the course. Instead, we focused on creating assignments that helped students develop habits of mind to better understand historical worldviews. Once students honed those habits, they could apply those experiences to the exploration of the interplay between historical mindset and speculative fiction. Deep dives trumped broad surveys, and we chose to focus on the following periods, which were oftentimes characterized by accelerated change and controversy:

- Tycho Brahe and Johannes Kepler and the role of Mars in shaping our understanding of a heliocentric solar system;
- The Canal Controversy— Percival Lowell, Alfred Russel Wallace, H.G. Wells, Edgar Rice Burroughs;
- The intervening period between Lowell and Mariner 4;
- The modern era and Kim Stanley Robinson's *Red Mars*.

Brahe and Kepler

During this period in history, Mars was just a reddish dot in the night sky; however, the red planet's path through the sky played a pivotal role in shaping our understanding of our place in the universe. Building on the work of his predecessors and analyzing copious observational data, Tycho Brahe nudged Earth's place in the universe slightly off center. His model still posited the earth at the center, and the sun still revolved around the earth. But Brahe claimed the planets revolved around the sun, rather than the earth. Jupiter and Saturn sent Kepler in a different direction. To Kepler, a diagram of the planets' conjunctions suggested divine order, and the astronomer devoted his efforts towards supporting his theory that nested platonic solids predicted planetary distances (Ferguson, 2002).

It's easy to dismiss these and other historical theories as quaint, anthropocentric, overly complicated, and obviously wrong. Brahe and Kepler's conclusions fly in the face of what we *now* know to be true; however, to summarily dismiss their tangents is shortsighted. We can learn a great deal about iterative nature of science and perspective by attempting to understand this moment in history more deeply. The tricky part is shedding our current understanding and putting ourselves in

Brahe's and Kepler's shoes. Envisioning the world through the fragmented and pre-telescope 16th century cannon is difficult. But even attempting to do so sheds light on Kepler's persistence and dedication to the *process* of science. His willingness to follow the data, coupled with the idiosyncratic nature of Mars' orbit (still a red dot at this point), more than just nudged our worldview. Kepler's *New Astronomy* knocked Earth squarely off its pedestal.

In addition to providing a compelling story that helped students develop habits of mind, which included understanding scientific exploration within historical context, Kepler also provided an example of the relation between science and speculation. While we decided to address more modern speculative fiction in lieu of tackling Kepler's *Somnium* in class, we used a description of his work (which provides a fascinating mix of science, personal experience, and fantasy) as a segue to 19th and 20th century works. Could a mind driven by curiosity and reason be predisposed to more creative speculation? Johannes Kepler seemed to be suggesting so.

The Canal Controversy

We summed up (admittedly too briefly) our progress in understanding Mars from the early 17th to the late 19th and early 20th century by showing sketches drawn by Christiaan Huygens, Giovanni Cassini, and others. We also acknowledged the buzz surrounding the possibility of extra-terrestrial life that coincided with publication of many of the Mars sketches (Fontenelle, 1686; Huygens, 1698). Students reviewed Schiaparelli's drawings, which included "canali" and descriptions of Earth analogs including named seas. In lieu of a detailed analysis of Schiaparelli's stance, the instructors summed up the astronomer's conclusions about the implications for intelligent life as non-committal. Flammarion's initial response to the implications of the canali sufficed to illustrate the tentative and cautious tone of many in the scientific community at the time: "… the Known is a tiny island in the midst of the ocean of the Unknown. Moreover, our senses are very limited; our power of perception is still lacking; our science remains, and will always remain, fatally incomplete" (Flammarion, 1981, p. 901; as cited in Markley, 2005, p. 59).

Percival Lowell was not so cautious. Based on meticulous observation, Lowell ignited controversy by suggesting that Mars, with its canals and oases, might harbor intelligent life. Once again, with the benefit of hindsight, it's tempting to dismiss Lowell as a hack, at least when it comes to interpreting observational data. But as with Brahe and Kepler, the reality is more nuanced and steeped in historical context. As instructors, we found ourselves navigating a tricky balance. How do we provide first year undergraduates with a sense of the broad strokes of the controversy, and hence the iterative nature of scientific understanding, and not overwhelm them with details? Rather than provide a comprehensive overview of the controversy, such as the excellent and detailed analysis provided by Markley (2005), we chose to focus on just a few aspects. Helping the students: 1) Understand what Mars actually looked like through an earth-based telescope in the early 20th century; 2) Elucidate the impact of Lowell's vision in the

MICHAEL SVEC & MIKE WINISKI

mainstream; 3) Focus on the particulars of the response to Lowell's conclusions through the writings of Alfred Russell Wallace; 4) Articulate the perspective of individuals on both sides of the canal controversy (and those lost in the middle) through the lens of speculative fiction.

The preceding list suggests a linear progression; however, historical and speculative fiction readings and films were interspersed. Resources that predated the Mariner 4 flyby (and subsequent period of rapid change in our understanding of the red planet) were presented in roughly chronological order and included:

– *War of the Worlds*—H.G. Wells book (1898), recordings of Orson Welles radio broadcast (1938), and RadioLab's podcast (Abumrad &Krulwich, 2008) which chronicles the original and subsequent hoaxes.
– Excerpts from Edgar Rice Burroughs' *A Princess of Mars* (1917)
– The "Green Morning" from Ray Bradbury's *The Martian Chronicles* (1950)
– *Flight to Mars* film (1951)
– "Mars and Beyond" (1957), an episode from the *Disneyland* series
– *Robinson Crusoe on Mars* film (1964)

Telescopic observations of Mars or Jupiter (depending on what was visible during the particular semester) helped students begin to grasp the limits of Lowell's observations. Students read a modern day explanation for the canals (Hartmann, 2003) suggesting that wind streaks, coupled with atmospheric interference, could account for the appearance of Lowell's canals; however, one comment by an exasperated student illustrates just how hard it is to step into a historical perspective:

> One thing I don't understand, is how he [Lowell] drew so much detail into the maps of Mars and how he saw all those lines. Because when I see the original sketches of Mars and what they were looking at, I don't see many of those lines, and I don't connect all the dots to form that map of Mars, with all the lines that he figured were canals and agriculture.

While this statement could be interpreted as proof of the elusive nature of historical perspective, we found it exciting that the student seems to be in the same liminal space as the early observer.

The tendency of the media to give Lowell the lion's share of the spotlight in the controversy and the impact of his speculation on the collective imagination is well-chronicled (Markley, 2005); however personal stories provided an even richer window into Lowell's influence and helped students (and the instructors) form a deeper understanding of historical perspective and Mars' impact on the speculative psyche. Facsimiles of several letters from Alexander Graham Bell to his wife, Mabel, proved to be a goldmine. Bell's admiration for Lowell in the uneven, typewritten letters is unmistakable. In 1901 he tells Mabel, "I wish I had your opportunity of crossing the Atlantic with Percival Lowell. I wonder whether you talked with him about Mars" (Bell, 1901, p. 2).

In a letter written from his houseboat (Bell, 1909), he reflects on man's insignificant size in relation to the planet. He clearly respects and agrees with Lowell's scientific conclusions. For Bell, Lowell's induction that Venus' rotation rate makes the planet inhospitable to life is both convincing and disappointing. "No signs of life, however, have so far been observed; and now Professor Lowell comes forward with a statement concerning rotation that almost deprives us of hope" (p. 2). Bolstered by a 3-page recap of Lowell's observations and inferences regarding Mars, Bell returns his gaze to Venus, unwilling to write off the possibility of life there:

> Surely there must be a narrow belt around the planet, between the frozen and heated sides constituting a temperate zone where life may possibly exist: A region where …, without either setting to freeze, or rising to roast, the living things that might take refuge there. (p. 8)

While discussing these letters in class, one student commented, "It sounds like Bell is working up a science fiction story here." Clearly, hope, science, and speculation could collide to inspire great stories, especially in a time of rapidly changing understanding of the red planet.

A seemingly odd end to Bell's 1901 letter helped us better understand how our present day understanding can obscure historical perspective. After a brief reflection comparing correspondence via telegraph and letter (speed vs. depth) and questions about Queen Victoria's funeral, Bell's letter to Mabel ends abruptly:

> INTERRUPTED. Dear Mrs. Bell:—Mr. Bell was called down the Census Office, and so I will have to send of this fragment of a letter. He was just getting down to write you a nice long letter, it is a shame. (p. 3)

The class was perplexed. Why couldn't Bell just finish the letter the next day? Why send out the fragment? Why was his secretary taking over his letter? It was difficult for us to even articulate why the abrupt finish seemed so strange, until students began describing the assumptions they brought to the reading. We realized that every single one of us (instructor included) pictured Bell hammering away at the typewriter himself, when it's much more likely that he was dictating the letter which was to be typed later. In the age of the keyboard, we had to take a minute and unlearn our ingrained habits of mind surrounding correspondence. Many assumed daily postal pick up and delivery and that waiting a day would not significantly impact delivery. Understanding that we couldn't *fully* inhabit an early 20th perspective paved the way to a more thoughtful approach to speculative fiction of the time and freed us up to imagine alongside our early 20th century friends. From years of teaching science, the instructors knew that scientific misconceptions could be tenacious; we could now add inhabiting historical perspective to the list of challenging concepts. Forgetting what we know doesn't come easily, but we were making strides.

Lowell's 1895 *Atlantic Monthly* article "Mars III: Canals" and Alfred Russel Wallace's critical response in *Is Mars Habitable?* provided the students with the opportunity to wrestle with some of the details of the controversy firsthand. While the readings are dense and difficult, we worked with the students to distill and summarize the arguments from both sides. Students were guided to approach the readings with an eye towards high-level arguments, rather than getting bogged down in the details. Lowell argues that the patterns of canals, visible from Earth only due to the surrounding vegetation, are simply too regular and seasonal to be of similar origin as cracks radiating from craters on the moon (Lowell, 1906). Wallace counters that Mars is too cold and the atmosphere too thin to support liquid water (Wallace, 1907). The arguments are obviously more complex, but having students experience the tenor of the debate and Lowell's leaps from observation to inference were as important as how the authors used conflicting observations to support their claims.

Lowell's focus in future writings on the dying nature of the planet and implications for our own future set the stage for the speculative and environmental focus of *Red Mars* used later in the course. Markley (2005) beautifully summarizes the impact of Lowell's writing on our earthly perspective:

> The analogy between Earth and Mars has been subtly inverted; rather than imposing terrestrial conditions onto the red planet, Lowell reimagines humankind's present and future in terms of a dying world on which "we are able to glimpse, in some sort, our future." (Lowell, 1906, p. 384; as cited in Markley, p. 94)

In a culminating assignment to articulate historical perspective, students were asked to craft a film or book review of their choice from the aforementioned list from both Lowell's and Wallace's perspective. By giving the option to review pieces from Lowell and Wallace's future, we violated our plausibility assumption, exploring together the blurry line between plausibility and possibility.

Our *War of the Worlds* (WoW) discussion was deep and centered around the live RadioLab broadcast (Abumrad & Krulwich, 2008) that posed the question, "Could It Happen Again? (And Again?)." By this time, the students had listened to recordings of Mercury Theatre's 1938 broadcast and read Chapter One ("The Eve of War") of H. G. Wells' novel. Reviewing the broadcast from the perspective of Lowell and Wallace, most students felt the former would find the speculation credible while the latter would roll his eyes at the flimsy science on which the broadcast was based.

The podcast provided additional historical context and explored our penchant for being pulled into a good story. The hosts described Mercury Theater's meticulous attention to the broadcast realities of the day to heighten plausibility. The "we interrupt this broadcast" style of the production was patterned after Edward R. Murrow's reports from war-torn Europe, and one radio actor went so far as to mimic Herb Morrison's (1937) coverage of the Hindenburg disaster to heighten the realistic feel of the broadcast. Plausibility was entrenched in the reality of the day, with Percival Lowell helping to set the stage. Subsequent interviews with radio listeners revealed that many interpreted reports of war machines and poisonous gas as a German invasion. According to interviewees, reports of Martians were just indicative of reporters getting the details wrong, but the perceived threat was just as scary. Other listeners described initial skepticism being allayed by the inclusion of "expert scientific testimony" during the broadcast. The power of suggestion was so trenchant, that many even reported seeing smoke and Martian war machines on the horizon (Abumrad & Krulwich, 2008).

If the modern day observer is tempted to ascribe ignorance of the day to the 1938 panic, the podcast's description of the 1949 Quito incident is enough to provide serious pause. Radio Quito's re-enactment of the WoW production, replacing original locations with local places, wreaked havoc. Reports of strange objects in the sky and radio interference in the days leading up to the main broadcast set the hook. The reaction to the broadcast was so visceral that interviewed residents reported scenes of individuals confessing their sins on the spot and mobilized military heading out to fight the invasion. Once the hoax was revealed, angry citizens stormed the radio station, pelting it with rocks and eventually burning the building to the ground. Six people were killed in the ensuing riot. The perpetrator of the hoax fled to Venezuela, never to return (Abumrad & Krulwich, 2008).

The description of the reaction to a 1968 Halloween adaption of WoW by WKBW radio in Buffalo, NY confirms our predisposition for speculation. Over 4,000 listeners called the radio station to get more details and devise evacuation plans (Abumrad & Krulwich, 2008). We can get fooled again. Perhaps the fact that we are built for story, coupled with our poor understanding of science and anxieties of the day, could suck us in. Plausibility is a nuanced beast, and our relationship with story complicates the picture.

The intervening period between Lowell and Mariner 4

Disney, a master storyteller, sucked us in deeper. The students and instructors were enthralled with "Mars and Beyond," an episode from the *Disneyland* series (Kimbell, 1957). The beautiful images creatively illustrating the impact of Mars on our imagination, including animations inspired by Edgar Rice Burroughs, seemed to break through the stranglehold that science had imposed on our creativity and our willingness to imagine. Speculation about the nature of life on Mars runs wild in the episode, but we set aside our disbelief and current understanding to simply enjoy the art and story. At that moment, speculative fiction wasn't just a place for us to imagine current science extended (or witness historical understanding in snapshot), but it was fodder for wilder, unrestrained speculation.

The second half of the production brought us somewhat back to reality, as Dr. E. C. Slipher described our 1957 understanding of Mars. Blurry traces of Martian canals still cover the Martian globe Slipher uses for his scientific discussion of Martian seasons, tilt, atmosphere, and temperature and the potential the planet holds for life. Based on spectrographic data, Slipher incorrectly concludes that Mars' atmosphere "probably consists mostly of nitrogen and a small amount of carbon dioxide" (Kimbell, 1957), illustrating that our knowledge of Mars in the pre-Mariner days was still quite sketchy. The Sliphers tie to the Lowell observatory also provided an appropriate historical link to our earlier studies of Lowell. But more than provide another historical lens, Disney, like it so often does, reinvigorated our relationship with story.

The students' analysis of *A Princess of Mars* (1917) at first seemed fairly straightforward. Taken to the extreme, Lowell's interpretation of the surface of Mars could serve as a foundation for a rollicking, over-the-top story, given that the reader was willing to play along (and thanks in part to Disney, we were). Students thought Wallace would have hated the premise on which the story was built—bad science, extrapolating too much from naturally formed cracks and more fantasy than speculation. Unable to shed our modern-day experience, we were more apt to agree and classify the tale as fantasy, suggesting that genre may be time-bound.

Despite classification challenges, the students felt that a story of conflict over limited resources on a dying planet could inform our own present and future predicament on planet Earth. At this point, the question of how humans might deal with scarcity (a novum) and its implications was ill-formed but began to persist a bit like Neo's notion of the Matrix. Morpheus tells Neo, "You've felt it your entire life, that there's something wrong with the world. You don't know what it is, but it's there, like a splinter in your mind, driving you mad" (Silver, 1999.) Implanted through the notion of scarcity, the splinter in this case came in the form of loosely articulated questions that we would revisit and shape throughout the latter half of the course:

– What will Earth be like when resources become even more scarce?
– What if another planet could serve as our lifeboat? Do we have a right to stake a claim to that lifeboat and its potential inhabitants?
– Do we have moral obligations to preserve our own or even another planet?
– Do our needs trump natural order or sacredness of place?
– Just because we can, should we?

This discussion marked a subtle shift from analyzing speculative fiction from the perspective of history to asking what the genre could tell us about our potential future and the role science could play—and the sticky questions on the horizon. *Princess of Mars* served as an unintended inflection point.

Ray Bradbury's *The Martian Chronicles* (1950) pushed these blurry questions forward. This compilation of loosely knit short stories launches from a future Earth in peril. In the story "The Green Morning," Benjamin Driscoll speculates and struggles with scarcity—the dearth of breathable air. He looks beyond current mining exploits and envisions a more earth-like Mars, covered in trees that provide oxygen for the new explorers. He plants vigorously to push his vision towards reality. Driscoll awakens to find thousands of trees have grown overnight, transforming Mars into a more habitable home. Unlike his *Red Mars* counterparts, who we visit later in the course, he doesn't hesitate a second to ponder, "Should I?" At this point in the course, the story felt more like a strange aside, but the notion of terraforming had been planted (pardon the pun), and the awareness of our desire for a home that resembled our own had been heightened, albeit in a weirdly wonderful way.

Scarcity is a continued theme in the movie *Flight to Mars (1951)*, as the inhabitants of the red planet struggle with the depletion of their primary energy source, Corium. The class viewing resembled an episode of *Mystery Science Theater*, as students had fun pointing out the low production quality, the fact that the inhabitants (rather than the visitors) wore space suits, the sexist portrayal of the female scientist's excitement over the accouterments of the Martian kitchen, and the Star Trek-like thrashing of the crew as the spaceship hit turbulence. The film seemed more a cheesy diversion than representative of historical plausibility, but the fact that scarcity drove some of the Martian inhabitants to deceit and visions of Earth conquest was now clearly a common organizing story principle.

Robinson Crusoe on Mars portrays a warmer and wetter planet, although the thin atmosphere requires the administration of "air pills" for the earth visitor, Kit Draper. The liner notes to the DVD contain current (circa 1960) facts about Mars and suggest there may be sufficient oxygen closer to the planet's surface. A quote from Dr. Wernher von Braun is included stating that, "A man can stay alive longer on Mars than a native of the tropics could exist in the Arctic." These "Mars facts" highlight our evolving understanding of the planet. In addition to providing a somewhat historical snapshot (or at least a snapshot of historical Hollywood plausibility), the movie hints at the issue of scarcity. Friday, Draper's companion and friend for the remainder of the film, is a Martian native and escaped slave from the Martian mines. In this scenario, scarcity had driven a fictional civilization to subjugate others in the name of survival, subtly posing the question, "What would you do?"

This period of the course, like our understanding of Mars at the time, was one of transition. Our focus shifted from seeing speculative fiction only as a window into scientific understanding, and hence plausibility, to larger themes and ethical questions. At this point, we started looking forward more than back.

The Modern Era and Kim Stanley Robinson's Red Mars

A wide variety of resources guided us into the modern era, during which our understanding of the planet's surface changed drastically. Non-fiction such as *A Traveler's Guide to Mars* (Hartmann, 2003) and *The Scientific Exploration of Mars* (Taylor, 2010) provided much of the foundation to support our goal. We wanted students to get a sense of the gestalt of Mars as we now know it—the relatively young and flat northern plains, the heavily cratered southern highlands, and the canyons and volcanoes of the Tharsis region. Specifics were subservient to process, however, as we asked students to focus on theories of formation and evidence to support those theories.

To foster a process-oriented approach, we asked each student to become an expert on a specific chapter in *Traveler's Guide* which either focused on a particular region (Marte Valles, Olympus Mons, Aram Chaos) or phenomenon (dust devils, dunes, and crater types). While the chapters were well organized, we worried that the sheer density of information could steer students towards presentations that were more information-dump than coherent story. Enter PechaKucha (Japanese for chit-chat), a presentation format devised by architects in Tokyo to slay droning and over-bulleted PowerPoint presentations. In this model, the presenters are constrained to 20 (generally image-based) slides to tell their story, and the slides advance automatically every 20 seconds (Klein Dytham

Architecture, n.d.). With under 7 minutes to tell a story, we hoped that students would be more likely to spend their time selecting and evaluating the importance of a particular concept within the big picture, rather than bombarding the audience with disconnected details. Students also accessed the most recent images from the current spacecraft exploring Mars.

To emphasize patterns of recent discovery, every third student PechaKucha presentation was followed by a comparison discussion, during which the students worked to identify connections. After an especially compelling presentation describing how ice depth can be inferred from crater patterns, we asked the student where she found the crescent-shaped image that succinctly showed the general trend of shallower ice as one progressed from the equator to the Martian poles. She replied, "I made it. I couldn't find an image that summed up the general trend." Score a victory for analysis and synthesis. While far from a panacea, the presentation constraints seemed to help shift the student focus towards process and patterns.

We didn't expect all the details or even general trends to stick, but perhaps revisiting the Martian landscapes in the context of story could help students further develop their geological understanding. In *Red Mars,* which is set in the future (2026), Robinson situates the story within beautiful and accurate descriptions of the Martian surface, at least based on our understanding at the time (1993). The link between story and landscape seemed strong, perhaps because familiarity with Martian geology helped students be more attuned to the setting. During class discussions, several students wondered if Robinson chose different locations on Mars with the intent of aligning landscape with the tone of events that were described in the novel. For example, Olympus Mons (a high spot on Mars) is the scene of a hopeful reunion of characters, while a murder attempt takes place at Senzeni Na, a fictional location in the Thaumasia region of Mars. Thaumasia appears to have been volcanically active and is characterized by faults which spread across the landscape. Was this fracturing symbolic of the political and environmental factions potentially behind the murder attempt or just background for the action?

Place certainly mattered at the planetary scale, but we decided to dig deeper into the relationship between the geologic vibe of specific locations on Mars and events portrayed in the story. Each student chose several passages from the novel that they found revealing, pivotal, or complex, then authored reflections about these different events. The reflections were anchored to the location where the events occurred in Google Mars™. Conveniently, Google Mars provides a layer that corresponds to selected excerpts from *Traveler's Guide*, so that after compiling the student text, we were presented with a virtual planet that was a mix of story, analysis, satellite maps, and technical descriptions of the landscape. Fictional locations like Underhill, Burroughs, Senzeni Na, and Bradbury point were interspersed amongst real Martian features such as Vastitas Borealis, Lunae Planum, and Valles Marineris, blending the known and speculative.

Beyond landscape, we wanted to move further down the speculative scale and explore plausible future scenarios, challenges, and implications. Interweaving fiction and non-fiction helped to push this goal forward. While technically classified as non-fiction, *A Case for Mars* (Zubrin, 1996), hinges on speculation, based on current science. In the first chapter, Zubrin describes a scene from the future:

> At the end of a year and a half on the Martian surface, the astronauts clamber aboard the ERV [Earth Return Vehicle] and blast off to receive a heroes' welcome on Earth some six months later. They leave behind Mars Base 1, with the *Beagle* hab, a rover, a greenhouse, power, and chemical plants, a stockpile of methane/oxygen fuel, and nearly all of their scientific instruments. (p. 12)

More details follow. In fact, only a few aspects seem to distinguish Zubrin's speculation from Robinson's account in *Red Mars*:

– Robinson's speculation is wrapped in story. Add murder, a red-bearded anarchist, high explosives, and a beautiful Russian cosmonaut to Zubrin's vision, and the two accounts begin to converge. But *Red Mars* provides a narrative in which students have more freedom to explore the *implications* of scientific progress than within Zubrin's fairly technical account.

– As our student intimated, the reader brings a different set of expectations to each account. We expect the non-fiction version to include ample backing to support the author's vision, and Zubrin complies. Because Robinson crafts his vision within a story, we seem willing to cut him some scientific slack. It's up to the reader to decide if space elevators, nuclear power, terraforming, and bases on Phobos are plausible, or at least within the realm of possibilities. The onus is on the reader.

While Zubrin touches on the human element, Mary Roach (2010) dives headlong into all the messy and smelly details of space travel in *Packing for Mars*. According to Roach,

> To the rocket scientist, you are a problem. You are the most irritating piece of machinery he or she will ever have to deal with. You and your fluctuating metabolism, your puny memory, your frame that comes in a million different configurations. You are unpredictable. You're inconstant. You take weeks to fix. (p. 15)

Through her humorous and graphic account of experiments in weightless sex, turds floating through space capsules, and the psychological impact of sharing small spaces with other humans, we get it—clearly. But experiencing these issues through the characters in *Red Mars* allowed the students and instructors to go deeper. John, one of the students in the class, pointed out that while the science in the story was compelling, the depiction of the fictional crew in *Red Mars* solidified the political and social implications of the science. As a student in one of the classes noted, "Red Mars helped me realize that humans in space are still humans." In this case fiction and non-fiction paired beautifully.

To explore the broader issues raised through the story, clicker statements such as those below, with the only option to anonymously agree or disagree, were presented to the class to frame and complicate the discussion. Interestingly, students proposed slight modifications to several statements, and re-voting revealed nuance and additional discussion points. Example statements included:

- The first person to land on Mars should own it (Pisaturo, 2002).
- "In other words, it is the explorer, not the homesteader, who may be the creator of the initial value of the body of land. And the creator of the initial value is the rightful owner" (Pisaturo, 2002, p. 214).
- "If no private organization wants to explore Mars in the absence of government financing, then - unless there is a valid military need - Mars should not be explored" (Pisaturo, 2002, p. 215).
- We have far too many problems on this planet to consider exploration of another.
- Humans will land on Mars in my lifetime.
- Despite the risk and length of the trip, if I were selected to be an astronaut on a Mars mission, I'd do it.

The last statement above was posited to one particular class at the beginning and end of the semester. Interestingly, while the majority of the students at the beginning of the term said they would embark on the trip, only one agreed by the last day.

Additional statements regarding terraforming, another novum, were also provided:

- I think the idea of terraforming Mars is heretical - tantamount to humans playing God (adapted from Zubrin, 1996, p. 266).
- "I would say that failure to terraform Mars constitutes a failure to live up to our human nature and a betrayal of our responsibility as members of the community of life itself" (Zubrin, 1996, p. 267).

Like Driscoll in the *Martian Chronicles*, characters in *Red Mars* link the alien landscape to home. Arkady Bogdanov, a Russian with a penchant for anarchy and desire to see the red planet serve as a chance for a more equitable society, names the nuclear plant on the surface "Chernobyl." The first habitats are referred to collectively as "the trailer park," rather than providing them with a more original Martian moniker. Russian engineer, Nadia Chernyshevski, breaks through this earth-bound perspective when she makes an extended journey to the northern plains of Mars. Inspired by the expansive views, Nadia's perspective shifts:

> Beauty could make you shiver! It was a shock to feel such a physical response to beauty, a thrill like some kind of sex. And this beauty was so strange, so *alien*. Nadia had never seen it properly before, or never really felt it, she realized that now; she had been enjoying her life as if it were a Siberia made right, so that really she had been living in a huge analogy, understanding everything in terms of her past. (Robinson, 1993, pp. 141-142)

The settlers' view of the Martian landscape and their place within it doesn't simply influence naming conventions and inspire appreciation. This worldview drives many to call for action. Almost immediately, stifled by their inability to spend significant amounts of time on the surface due to radiation concerns, some of the

Martian colonists advocate for immediate terraforming efforts—despite the fact that it's not their call. Decisions about terraforming ultimately fall to the corruptible United Nations Organization Mars Authority (UNOMA). Two factions quickly form on the red planet and on Earth. The Greens, typified by physicist Sax Russell, want to begin the long process of creating and releasing greenhouses to make Mars more earth-like. Unlike Bradbury's Driscoll, many Greens do ask the question, "Should we?" They conclude, however, that the ends (sustaining the human race in an environment of limited resources, or in Arkady's case, the opportunity for independence), justifies the means (irreversible terraformation).

The Reds, whose position in extreme is represented by geologist Ann Clayborne, want to see Mars left in as much of a pristine state as possible. Ann even regrets the tire tracks they leave as the team explores the northern regions with Nadia. She laments,

> We'll all go on and make the place safe. Roads, cities. New sky, new soil. Until it's all some kind of Siberia or Northwest Territories, and Mars will be gone and we'll be here, and we'll wonder why we feel so empty. Why when we look at the land we can never see anything but our own faces. (Robinson, 1993, p. 158)

Discovery undergirds the Reds' conviction, and they fear that man-made changes will forever render the question about native life on the planet unknowable. The Reds worst fear is realized as UNOMA approves the distribution of windmill heaters, and terraformer enthusiasts secretly, and illegally, seed the heaters with genetically engineered microorganisms (GEMs), polluting the possibility of ever knowing if Mars harbors life. Arkady notes that he and Nadia have become unwitting "Johnny Appleseeds" (Robinson, 1993, p. 191), inextricably linking them to Bradbury's Benjamin Driscoll and home.

Empathizing with the Reds didn't come naturally for many students. At least it appeared that way on the surface. Many that did see merit in the Reds' position, or agreed with it, were willing to let hypothetical terraforming activities commence if cursory searches for life yielded negative or rudimentary results. If there was support for Ann's view that we "value consciousness too high, and rock too little" (Robinson, 1993, p. 179), it was overshadowed by a sentiment more sympathetic to the Greens, once the possibility of life was deemed improbable or lowly-evolved.

The class dug into the details of terraforming via lectures based on *The Case for Mars*, and readings proposing less conventional means like *Terraforming Mars with Four War-Surplus Bombs* (Mole, 2002). When the tenor of the class suggested more of a focus on the *could we* aspects of the reading than the *should we*, we decided to challenge the students to explore the Reds' position more deeply by adding readings from environmentalist Edward Abbey (1968, 1975). Abbey's description of a similar earthly landscape, the American desert, seemed an appropriate way to ponder more about the value of wild places in a more familiar setting. His story of eco-terrorist tactics (1975) foreshadowed the sabotage in *Red Mars*. Like Abbey's protagonists George Hayduke, Seldom Seen Smith, Bonnie Abbzug, and Doc Sarvis, Martian settlers were willing to take drastic and destructive action based on their convictions. Lastly, Arkady and Abbey seemed to be kindred spirits when it came to their views on government and big corporations. The following passage from Abbey (1989) would have flowed just as naturally from either man: "Anarchism is founded on the observation that since few men are wise enough to rule themselves, even fewer are wise enough to rule others" (p. 23). Although they would have disagreed vehemently about terraforming, an introduction and comparison seemed in order.

The final exam in the course took the form of a debate between the Reds and the Greens and provided the students with an opportunity to revisit and fortify their stance. To even up the teams (the Green sentiment seemed prevalent, or at least the most vocal), students were randomly assigned to each side. Several students told us later that they appreciated being forced to argue a side that conflicted with their own belief. Students designed the debate format and ground rules and developed the evaluation criteria. A spirited but respectful debate ensued. A significant portion of the dialogue focused on terraforming details and unknowns (*could we?*), but the latter half shifted to the *should we?* question.

The Greens cited scarcity and the necessary resources Mars could provide. The instructors found themselves secretly rooting for a counter punch in the form of an Abbey quote. While students enjoyed Abbey, several shared in course evaluations that they struggled to connect his ideas to the ethical questions raised by the prospect of terraforming, and Abbey never surfaced during the debate; however, the student Reds had found something more impactful and direct—*The Value of Wilderness* by William Godfrey-Smith (2008). The Reds pointed out that all the arguments ascribing value to Mars by the Greens did so from a human-centered perspective, a worldview we had seen humans wrestle with throughout the course. Using a mix of quotes and summary of ideas from the paper, the Reds ended the debate with hanging questions. Is it possible that Mars has intrinsic value, which is obscured by our anthropocentric view? Could our experiences both enable and interfere with deeper understanding? It was an appropriate way to end the course.

CONCLUSION

We have defined four elements in our pedagogical definition of SF and illustrated those elements using experiences from a first year seminar that mixed SF and science content. The four elements created a classroom that encouraged speculation and fostered the very habits of mind consistent with being a scientist. The science portrayed in *Red Mars* and other SF used in the class was plausible yet one step beyond current capabilities—satisfying the skeptics at the same time encouraging them to open their minds to new perspectives.

The course went beyond using a single work of SF to incorporate several selections spanning over a century of time. This historical progression of SF, matched to the historical development of our understanding of Mars, illustrated the nature of science. In the process, the very values necessary to become a scientist such as curiosity, imagination, and creativity, were exalted and the connections between science, technology, and society were richly explored based upon the SF selected. As our student Alex stated, "Science fiction glorifies the men and women of the future—they invent, innovate, develop and think of new solutions. [Science] Research is about new discoveries, and about expanding frontiers—the unknown." At the same time SF also highlights the potential downsides of unrestrained scientific "progress."

The novums often created cognitive dissonance and presented an opportunity to examine how scientists and engineers resolve that dissonance. The stories also highlighted the fact that some of the dissonance generated by scientific speculation, such as the "should we?" questions raised during the terraforming debate, can't be resolved by science alone. Ironically, SF simultaneously pushes our scientific boundaries and reminds us that science has its limits.

Speculative SF as a genre has at least a supporting role to play in the preparation of the undergraduate interested in the sciences. We believe this model could be extended to other science disciplines and speculative novels. Michael Crichton's *Jurassic Park* or *The Andromeda Strain* would be examples that fit the four elements. SF, biographies, and other genres that include science as a theme can engage, enrich and extend the scientific knowledge learned within the science classroom and textbooks. "A love of reading produces a person who is literate. A love of reading science fiction produces a literate person open to new ideas, critically aware of the consequences of change, and ready for the future" (Czerneda, 2006, p. 42). For many students interested in science and engineering, SF is another source of nourishment that helps develop, sustain and motivate them in their pursuit.

REFERENCES

Abbey, E. P. (1968). *Desert solitaire.* New York, NY: McGraw-Hill.

Abbey, E. P. (1975). *The monkey wrench gang.* Philadelphia, PA: Lippincott Williams & Wilkins.

Abbey, E. P. (1989). *A voice crying in the wilderness.* New York, NY: St. Martin's Press.

Abumrad, J., & Krulwich, R. (Hosts). (2008, March 24). *War of the worlds.* RadioLab. Podcast retrieved from http://www.radiolab.org/2008/mar/24/

American Association for the Advancement of Science. (1990). *Science for all Americans.* New York: Oxford Press.

Atwood, M. (2011). *In other worlds: SF and the human imagination.* New York: Nan A. Talese/ Doubleday.

Austin, B., Menasco, J., & Vannette, T. (2008). The nature of science in popular nonfiction. *The Science Teacher, 75*(5), 27-32.

Barnett, M., & Kafka, A. (2007). Using science fiction movie scenes to support critical analysis of science. *Journal of College Science Teaching, 36*(4) 31-35.

Bell, A. G. (1901, February 11). [Letter to Mabel Bell]. The Alexander Graham Bell Papers at the Library of Congress. Retrieved from
http://memory.loc.gov/cgi-bin/query/P?magbell:11:./temp/~ammem_j7u7::

Bell, A. G. (1909, November 29). [Letter to Mabel Bell]. The Alexander Graham Bell Papers at the Library of Congress. Retrieved from http://memory.loc.gov/cgi- bin/query/P?magbell:2:./ temp/~ammem_j7u7::

Bould, M., Butler, A. M., Roberts, A., & Vint, S. (Eds.). (2010). *The Routledge companion to science fiction.* New York: Routledge.

Bould, M., & Mieville, C. (Eds.). (2009). *Red planets: Marxism and science fiction.* Middleton, CT: Wesleyan University Press.

Bradbury, R. D. (1950). *The Martian chronicles.* New York, NY: Doubleday.

Burroughs, E. R. (1917). *A princess of Mars.* Chicago, IL: A.C McClurg.

Czerneda, J. E. (2006). Science fiction and scientific literacy. *The Science Teacher, 73*(2), 38-42.

Ferguson, K. (2002). *Tycho & Kepler: The unlikely partnership that forever changed our understanding of the heavens.* New York, NY: Walker & Company.

Firooznia, F. (2006 March/April). Giant ants and walking plants. *Journal of College Science Teaching, 35*(5) 26-31.

Festinger, L. (1962). *A theory of cognitive dissonance* (Vol. 2). Stanford University Press.

Fontenelle, B. (2008). *Conversations on the plurality of worlds.* (E. Gunning, Trans.). London: Tiger of the Stripe. (Original work published 1686).

Freudenrich, C. (2000, November). Sci-fi science. *The Science Teacher, 67*(9), 42-45.

Furman University. (2005). *Invigorating intellectual life: A proposal for Furman University's Academic Program and Calendar.*

Godfrey-Smith, W. (2008). The value of wilderness. *Environmental Ethics, 1*(4), 309-319.

Harris, S. (1977). *What's so funny about science?* Los Altos, CA: William Kaufmann, Inc.

Hartmann, W. K. (2003). *A traveler's guide to Mars.* New York, NY: Workman Publishing.

Huygens, C. (2010). *Cosmotheoros: The celestial worlds discovered – New conjectures concerning the planetary worlds, their inhabitants, and productions.* Farmington Hills, MI: Gale ECCO. (Original work published 1698.)

Jacobson, T. (Producer), & De Palma, B. (Director). (2000). *Mission to Mars* [Motion picture]. United States: Touchstone Pictures.

Kilby-Goodwin, K. (2010). Putting the 'science' in 'science fiction.' *The Science Teacher, 77*(5) 60-63.

Kimbell, W. (Director). (1957, December 4). Mars and Beyond [Television broadcast]. In *Disneyland.* Burbank, CA: Disney.

Kincaid, P. (2010). Against a definition of science fiction [Electronic version]. *World Literature Today, 84*(3).

Klein Dytham Architecture. (n.d.). *PechaKucha frequently asked questions.* PechaKucha 20x20. Retrieved from http://www.pechakucha.org/faq

Laprise, S., & Winrich, C. (2010). The impact of science fiction films on student interest in science. *Journal of College Science Teaching, 40*(2), 45-49.

Lowell, P. L. (1895). Mars. III. Canals. *The Atlantic Monthly, 76* (July 1895), 106-119.

Lowell, P. L. (1906). *Mars and its canals.* New York, NY. Retrieved from http://archive.org/details/marsitscanals00loweuoft

Markley, R. (2005). *Dying planet: Mars in science and the imagination.* Durham, NC: Duke University Press.

Mirisch, W. (Producer), & Selander, L. (Director). (1951). *Flight to Mars* [Motion picture]. United States: Monogram Pictures.

Mole, R. A. (2002). Terraforming Mars with four war-surplus bombs. In R. Zubrin (Ed.), *On to Mars: Colonising a new world* (pp. 134-137). Burlington, Ontario: Apogee Books.

Morrison, H. (Reporter). (1937, May 6). *Hindeburg disaster* [Radio broadcast]. Lakehurst, NJ: WLS Chicago. Retrieved from http://archive.org/details/SF145

National Academy of Sciences. (2013). *The science & entertainment exchange.* Retrieved from http://www.scienceandentertainmentexchange.org/

National Research Council. (1996). *National Science Education Standards.* National Academy Press: Washington D.C.

National Research Council. (2012). *A framework for K-12 Science Education: Practices, crosscutting concepts and core ideas.* National Academy Press: Washington D.C.

Pisaturo, R. (2002). First on Mars should own it. In R. Zubrin (Es.), *On to Mars: Colonising a new world* (pp. 211-216). Burlington, Ontario: Apogee Books.

Roach. M. (2010). *Packing for Mars: The curious science of life in the void.* New York, NY: Norton.

Robinson, K. S. (1993). *Red Mars*. New York: Bantam Books.

Roberts, A. (2005). *The history of science fiction*. New York, NY: Palgrave Macmillan.

Sagan, C. (1980). *Cosmos*. New York: Random House.

Sagan, C. (1985). *Contact*. New York: Simon & Schuster.

Sagan, C. (1996). A Message to Future Humans on Mars. Retrieved from http://www.carlsagan.com/media/GreetingSagan64k.mp3

Saul, E. W. (Ed.). (2004). *Crossing Borders in literacy and science instruction*. Arlington, VA: NSTA Press.

Schenck, A. (Producer), & Haskin, B. (Director). (1964). *Robinson Crusoe on Mars* [Motion picture]. United States: Paramount Pictures.

Silver, J. (Producer), Wachowski, A. (Director), & Wachowski, L. (Director). (1999). *The matrix* [Motion picture]. United States: Warner Bros. Pictures.

Strauss, M. (2012). Ten inventions inspired by science fiction. *Smithsonian*.com. Retrieved from http://www.smithsonianmag.com/science-nature/Ten-Inventions-Inspired-by-Science-Fiction.html

Suvin, D. (1979). *Metamorphoses of science fiction: On the poetics and history of a literary genre*. New Haven: Yale University Press.

Taylor, F. W. (2010). *The scientific exploration of Mars*. Cambridge, UK: Cambridge University Press.

Wallace, A. R. (1907). Is Mars habitable? A critical examination of Professor Lowell's book "Mars and its canals," with an alternative explanation. Retrieved from http://www.gutenberg.org/ebooks/10855

Wells, H. G. (1997). *The war of the worlds*. Mineola, NY: Dover Publications. (Original work published in 1898.)

Welles, O. (Director). (1938, October 30). *The war of the worlds*. [Radio broadcast]. New York, NY: CBS Radio. Retrieved from http://archive.org/details/OrsonWellesMrBruns.

Zubrin, R. (1996). *The case for Mars: The plan to settle the red planet and why we must*. New York, NY: Touchstone.

AARON PASSELL

3. SF NOVELS AND SOCIOLOGICAL EXPERIMENTATION

Examining Real World Dynamics through Imaginative Displacement

After years of schooling, I find that I have deeply internalized a distinction between reading for work and reading for fun. I'm a social scientist, so sociology, urban studies, political economy, geography, anthropology, etc., are all work. Fiction, by contrast, is fun. Of course, much of why I'm a social scientist is that I do enjoy and find myself engaged by my work reading (and part of why I chose not to study literature is that I didn't want to risk ruining the fun). I remain intellectually curious about empirically grounded explanations of a broad range of phenomena in the social world. Moreover, I read social theoretical phenomena into and out of the fiction I enjoy.

As a teacher, I feel it's my first task to encourage and inspire intellectual curiosity in my students. That requires, among other things, showing them that systematic inquiry can be fun. I try to lead by example, getting excited about conceptual innovation that reframes how I understand the world and drawing connections to everyday life to point out that we are all experts in it. But, I also bring stuff that I think is fun into the classroom—well-written ethnography, popular television, movies, music—science fiction novels!

"Wait, what?" I want them to say, "Science fiction in a sociology class?" Unfortunately, they mostly say something more like, "Hunh, I don't read sci-fi." As we forge ahead, some of them develop some interest in or affection for it, while others just learn to put up with it – instructive in itself, at least for me. In fact, many of them find the social science that I pair with the science fiction (SF) easier to manage, undermining entirely the work-fun distinction that I'm trying to leverage and pointing out how much it is a product of my educational formation and how subjective.

Nevertheless, they do get through the novels and, more than that, the novels open up broader, more speculative conversations than most of the focused works of social science that I teach. They enable us to talk about food security in a course primarily dedicated to images of the city, to take a recent example. As important, though, the novels I teach foster some emotional engagement with academic work. My students empathize with the characters or dislike them, admire them or revile them, but they feel something. If they can carry this feeling forward, this connection to the stuff of work—as well as any improvements in their approach to writing or knowledge about cities—that will count as success for me.

P. Thomas (ed.), Science Fiction and Speculative Fiction, 59–72.

AARON PASSELL

THE SF NOVEL AS SOCIOLOGICAL THOUGHT EXPERIMENT

SF novelists pose sociological questions. I don't know if that's what any of my favorite authors had in mind when they sat down to write, but they are doing so nevertheless. Is this true of all SF? More or less—or at least I provide you with lots of interesting examples below. The questions posed usually come in the form, "If this aspect of the world were different, what would our individual and collective lives be like?" (See also, Atwood [2011] on these points.) The answer is reached through stories about worlds that are sometimes only subtly different from our own.

Sociologists might describe this kind of question in terms of varying particular social phenomena while holding others constant: if we imagine that the humans in this alternate setting are roughly like the people we know and live among, but, for example, have access to technology that allows them to do something we can't, like settle Mars, how would they go about doing so? What would happen and what would result? Technology is not the only things SF novelists change: human abilities, politics, and history can all change too (and sometimes Earth gets invaded by aliens). A sociologist would note, though, that the more things change, the less clear it becomes how relevant any one of those changes is for the outcome (which argues for a subtle SF rather than a fantastical one and probably mostly indicates that sociologists shouldn't write or edit SF).

In varying some aspects of social life, then, while holding others constant, SF novels enable us to perform experiments more like those that our colleagues in the natural sciences do. We can hypothesize a relationship, we can create a model to test it (methods intricately worked out in the course of the narrative), and we can examine our results, considering whether they confirm, dispute, or inflect our original conception. The empirical world remains our control: for comparison's sake, we can refer to what the world looks like without alien invasion simply by stepping outside our door.

Of course, SF is, by definition, fictional. As a source for observations of real world dynamics it is fundamentally flawed. I'm not convinced that this poses quite as great a problem as it might seem, and I want to discuss this in some detail below, but to the degree that sociology is committed to scientific engagement with the empirical world, this is clearly a drawback. In addition, SF novelists are neither terribly likely to be trained in sociology, nor are they required to pose their seemingly sociological questions with explicitly sociological intent. They are not committed as a matter of discipline to varying some limited range of social characteristics while holding others constant, in the way that a sociologist would, to enable our distinguishing the influence of some kinds of changes from others.

Nevertheless, SF novelists are embedded in the social dynamics of their times. Accordingly, whatever it is they imagine, they are departing from and building in their own assumptions, criticisms, and idealizations of how the world works and of how it might be different. Other worlds tend toward utopia or dystopia and are frequently characterized by plenty, beauty, and lots of casual sex. The details of these worlds tell us quite a lot, in some general ways, about when they were imagined and by whom. I was fascinated to discover that my students, in an interdisciplinary class in which we read William Gibson's *Virtual Light* (1994), had never experienced the sense of foreboding that the Japanese might effectively colonize North America, at least economically, which is a foregone conclusion in Gibson and very much part of my childhood. (I will discuss this and other examples in more detail below.)

I began by stating that SF novelists pose sociological questions, but we should also recognize that sociologists need science fictional answers (or at least mechanisms). Sociologists need the opportunity for thought experimentation because we cannot perform on real people the experiments that we can imagine. And for good reason: while the ethics of professional research might sometimes overreach, researchers using human subjects have done problematic and horrible things to people in the pursuit of knowledge (see, for example, the Milgram Experiment (Milgram 1974), *The Tearoom Trade* (Humphreys 1970), or the U.S. Public Health Service Syphilis Study at Tuskegee). Furthermore, whether or not they are ethically possible, establishing the experimental conditions to test many of the questions sociologists might want to answer would require vast resources and the extensive control of the lives of many people for a long time.

To give you a sense of what I mean, consider a potential experiment: how would someone who grew up in the absence of the elaborate processes of racialization that we experience in the contemporary United States understand the phenotypic differences to which we attribute so much significance? What would people look like to us if we hadn't been taught to see their race and to associate it with characteristics that are presumed to be essential and essentially connected to their skin color? To test this, we would at least need to gather and isolate a diverse and extensive population of children, raise them in rigorously artificial circumstances, and then figure out how to ask them about distinctions we had raised them not to recognize. Comparative research (how attitudes vary in different places, for instance) accomplishes some of these goals, but it always falls short of ideal experimental conditions because we simply can't control all that we would need to.

SF can form the foundation of an intellectual process of discovering and interrogating the status quo, which is a good part of what we do when we teach sociological subjects. It can highlight how things *are* by imagining how things might be different, and it can point students to the excitement of identifying and describing social forces at work in their world. It can also be fun. Though aficionados of the SF genre are fewer and farther between in my classes than I had hoped, there are still some, and they enjoy the opportunity to read and discuss these works in an academic setting. For the rest, these books are often still more enjoyable than much scholarly work, and we should not underestimate the importance of that. A note of caution, though, SF seems to present particular challenges to students for whom English is not a first language, primarily because of extensive invented terminology.

In the remainder of this chapter I want first to identify SF novels that address particular sociological themes and then to suggest some pairings between SF novels and specific pieces of sociological literature. To conclude, I will return to the question of the relevance of fiction both for the teaching of sociology and for

AARON PASSELL

the discipline more broadly – why sociologists and SF need each other. I hope it is obvious that much of what I will argue about novels here might equally be said about SF movies and television shows, as my colleagues will demonstrate elsewhere in this volume.

SCIENCE FICTION NOVELS AND SOCIAL ISSUES

This section will examine a range of social issues that particular SF novels consider and discuss how they do so. This exploration should be understood as indicative rather than exhaustive—I will neither describe every possible use of any text nor include every possible text on a particular theme. The novels discussed here are, first and foremost, favorites of mine, and I hope my examination of them spurs readers to reconsider their favorite novels.

I want to begin with what I see as the low hanging fruit: novels that highlight and problematize contemporary assumptions about sex and gender, race and ethnicity, and human evolution. I group these together because all three are about the connections between bodies and social life that are commonly assumed to be natural, assumptions we challenge when we argue that these differences are socially constructed. Many of these novels suggest an optimistic future in which systems of difference and inequality have lost much of their force, but others exaggerate aspects of our current condition in ways that highlight precisely how damaging they are.

Sex and Gender

Ursula Le Guin's *Left Hand of Darkness*—In Le Guin's classic, *The Left Hand of Darkness* (1969), a man, serving as an emissary for a galactic empire arrives on a provincial planet where the inhabitants are apparently human, with one key exception: their bodies are not sexed except when they are reproductively capable, which occurs only periodically and for a limited time. Moreover, which reproductive role they take on (whether they become female or male) is determined by their contact with other reproductively capable people as they come into their period of fertility. The person coming into reproductive capability manifests complementary genitalia to the sexed person they encounter. Accordingly, the majority of the time, people are neither male nor female, but they have all been both at one time or another and many adults are both mothers and fathers, sometimes within the same long-term relationship.

This curious physiology is the bio-sexual background of a story of political intrigue involving rival nations in competition to forge the first alliance with the empire the emissary represents. Le Guin sets up fascinating, complex, and multi-layered interactions between her characters, but students' contemplation of the broader "what if" may be just as relevant for teaching purposes. I have assigned the task of writing about everyday activities from the perspective of another gender in connection with this book and been surprised by the thoroughness and thoughtfulness of the results. Both the novel and the assignment emphasize how sex and gender are frequently implicit in social relations explicitly dedicated to other interests or ends. Both also indicate how omnipresent they are as background conditions and how we reproduce gender differences in these everyday activities.

Neal Stephenson's *Diamond Age*—Stephenson's novel (1995) introduces a nano-technological future in which we can assemble materials at the molecular level. This makes for cool gadgets, but also the elimination of both hunger and the scarcity of basic necessities because they can easily be assembled from readily available elements. This future is also one in which cultural affinities have been played out so as to define exclusive, but elective, collectivities—the neo-Victorians are prominent, for example, characterized by their emphasis on grace and obedience in women, strength, probity, and honor in men, and their interest in material quality and craft. These collectivities occupy particular, bounded places (though they are present in many cities) and are frequently associated with privilege, but are elective in the sense that they ignore the ascribed characteristics around which we organize difference in the contemporary United States – race, ethnicity, and regional origin, in particular: if one has the commitment and the resources, one can join.

Gender enters the novel in the form of a book [spoiler alert]. An elite technician in Hong Kong designs an interactive book to function as the social and educational companion for the daughter of an "equity lord," but makes a secret copy for his own daughter. He loses his secret copy, which winds up with a poor, near-orphan girl, and, in his efforts to make another, he is discovered by an influential figure on the mainland who is concerned with the fate of Chinese girls who are being abandoned because of a preference for male descendants. The influential Chinese man agrees not to publicize the piracy of the book's design if the designer allows him to duplicate it for the abandoned girls he cares for.

The novel proceeds to track the development of the girl with the lost copy as she learns logic, computer programming, martial arts, and various other skills from the book, effectively taking on questions about cognitive abilities, gender, and education and resolving them as matters of education rather than innate ability. In the culmination of the story, the triumph of progressive forces over conservative, essentialist ones depends on the confidence and well-developed abilities of all the girls who have been raised by the book (so to speak). Stephenson successfully destabilizes a wide range of assumptions about gender, class, race, and culture (though potentially reproducing others through the representation of traditional Chinese culture).

Margaret Atwood's *The Handmaid's Tale*—Atwood (1985) imagines a dystopian future Republic of Gilead, in which women are comprehensively oppressed and substantially reduced to their reproductive roles, with some caring labor and cleaning thrown in for good measure. There exists a politically defined caste of women for whom breeding and housework are the primary purpose. Atwood's well-known novel (also a film and an opera, apparently) could be useful in studying the consequences of the construction of gender difference in its most extreme form (class and race also play key roles here).

The contrast with the real world seems stark, but some further investigation suggests important connections to empirical studies of the gendered division of labor and assumptions about essential differences connected to reproductive biology. The novel highlights, moreover, the oppressive potential of conservative Christianity. Atwood's invention is an exaggeration, but not completely discontinuous with the contemporary world.

Suzanne Collins's *Hunger Games* and Kameron Hurley's *God's War*—These books offer an interesting contrast to one another. *Hunger Games'* (Collins, 2008) main character is a tough, self-possessed young woman who is clever, strategic, driven, physically adept, and capable of violence. That this represents a radical departure from gender norms is explicit in the story, and, in fact, her success in the novel's action is represented as unexpected because she is "just a girl." The action in question involves a survival game, many of the details of which are quite graphic.

In *God's War* (Hurley, 2011), by contrast, we enter a world in the midst of a long-running war. As far as we can tell, all of the fighting is done by women, but unlike in Collins's novel, this is no surprise, simply the status quo. Women fight, kill, abuse substances, exploit sexually, plot, betray, worship, lead, all without question. There are men who also do these things throughout the novel, but most of them are wizards of questionable repute, servants, or sex slaves. Interestingly, all of the main characters are also Muslim, though that too is more a basic, background condition than anything worthy of comment internal to the world itself.

Neither of these is a great novel, by any measure, but the contrast of highlighting a non-normative performance of gender—"you go girl!"—with an even more elaborately non-normative performance that is the norm in the story itself is potentially fascinating. Moreover, because the *Hunger Games* series has been so popular, there is the potential to explore students' previous uncritical readings of the work.

Race and Ethnicity

Orson Scott Card's *Ender's Game* and China Miéville's *Perdido Street Station*—In my experience arguing with students about racial difference as socially constructed, it has proven important to acknowledge that the goal of that construction is to make the difference *seem* essential. These novels exaggerate that by presenting race as difference in speciation. Other races are critically alien, sometimes insuperably so. This representation of racial difference provides a mirror up to which we can hold the production of racial difference as natural in contemporary society.

Card's (1985) novel imagines an interspecies war and some part of the interest of the conflict arises from the way in which the enemy is constructed as other, not unlike how human enemies are routinely constructed in actual human conflicts. The "buggers" or formics (an adjective usually describing ants) are actually non-human in essence (unlike the Germans, Japanese, Vietnamese, Iraqis, or Afghans), nevertheless the hatred directed at them needs to be socially produced and, to some degree, the conflict needs to be pursued under false pretenses.

This process of producing hatred is similar in nature, if neither in intensity nor scale, to contemporary processes of inscribing difference, an extreme version of everyday "otherizing" along racial lines. Not only does Card's novel indicate the manner in which racial difference can be constructed as species difference, but his story also reminds us of the potential role for political ideology, here liberal individualism, in reifying difference. The formics are governed by a "hive mind," a kind of collective consciousness that values the group above the individual, not unlike the contrasts frequently drawn in the American media between China and the U.S.

China Miéville (2000) provides a remarkable contrast to Card in that, while Card's others are very distant, at least in the first book in the series, Miéville's others are in constant contact. The world of *Perdido Street Station* includes many non-human humanoids and prominently involves inter-species sexuality (which may make the book inappropriate for younger readers—it also involves some pretty graphic horror). Importantly, inter-species sexuality is not normal in this world and seems to be widely, if informally, sanctioned, so the characters involved both conceal their relationships and reveal shame in relation to them. This opens the possibility of highlighting sexuality as at the paradoxical center of historical racist concerns: the key trigger for lynching young Black men, while female slaves were routinely raped by their White owners, for example.

Human Evolution

Bacigalupi's *Windup Girl* and Greg Bear's *Darwin's Radio* and *Darwin's Children*—SF novels that take up human evolution raise questions again about natural differences and socially constructed ones by suggesting that genetically different humans might also be socially different – they might interact in the world in novel ways. For example, the new humans in Bear's *Darwin's Radio* (1999) and *Darwin's Children* (2003) represent the next step beyond *homo sapiens sapiens* in a punctuated human evolution. In these novels of public health and political crisis, what initially appears to be a disease ultimately proves to be part of a process of activating inactive elements of human DNA that produce humans who have improved communication abilities. Physical differences in their bodies facilitate their empathic abilities in ways that initially appear telepathic. These new humans are imprisoned at first and treated as dangerous deviants, though their superiority is conspicuous to the reader.

Bacigalupi (2009) works questions of sexuality into explorations of evolution and bodily difference by introducing us to a "new human" sex worker (this novel also involves significant sexuality and sexual violence). New humans are genetically engineered and optimized for specific tasks. The major new human character in the story is designed for work as a geisha: slender and attractive, predisposed to obedience (dog genes, apparently), stylized elegance, and perfect skin. Though we never meet them, other new humans are mentioned, including many-armed, non-thinking factory workers and gigantic, super-strong warriors.

The key difference in Bacigalupi's work [spoiler alert] is that new humans are *better* than regular, old humans, representing an evolutionary step forward (if not through a natural process). Even the geisha is stronger, faster, smarter, less susceptible to disease, and better at languages than the people she lives among. Like Miéville, though, sexual desire for her is constructed as taboo-violating exoticism and this is part of reconstructing her as other. She is the title character of a story that is substantially about the risks of genetically modified organisms and environmental depredation in a post-global warming Thailand.

In framing difference as improvement, Bear and Bacigalupi reflect on an aspect of racialization that is sometimes difficult to draw out. Like with the conception of Asian Americans as a model minority, difference as improvement still locates the accomplishments of those in question *in the different essence*, rather than with individual effort or structural factors. My students often struggle initially with the idea that saying "Asian Americans are better at math" reproduces a racialized distinction that is the same as the negative ones involved in discrimination against Latinos or Black Americans. We might point out, using Bacigalupi or Bear, that Asian Americans' success is not because they are genetically engineered for academic success or further evolved, not because racialized groups are biologically different, but rather because of broad, complex social conditions and history.

Briefly, Richard K. Morgan, in a series that includes *Altered Carbon, Broken Angels,* and *Woken Furies* (2002, 2003, 2005), separates human consciousness from bodies entirely. These novels are primarily hard-boiled detective stories in a fantastic future world, which critically involves the ability to transmit human consciousness over trans-galactic distances and download it into a body when it arrives at its destination. Accordingly, the same person can appear in differently bodies, depending on circumstances that are primarily related to wealth. The main character's name, Takeshi Kovacs, constantly reminds readers that this is a post-racial world.

Other Themes

Sex and gender, race and ethnicity—all raising questions about how bodies are caught up in social life—are perhaps the sociological themes that are best explored through SF. There are many other themes possible, though, and I want to mention just a few. The "what-ifs" operate variously in the books below, some highlighting real world conditions by their proximity to them (as if they followed from them), others by their radical distance (historical reversals).

Climate change, bioengineering, and pandemics.   A number of SF novels take as their setting, if not as their focus, a world substantially altered by human interference with nature: processes of climate change continuous with ones we are already witnessing and unintended consequences of genetic engineering of organisms and diseases. The already apparent reality of these threats and the politicization of the issue make these works particularly compelling.

Bruce Sterling's *Heavy Weather* (1994) is about storm chasers hypothesizing about and hunting for a transcendent, paradigm-shifting storm that would pose a permanent threat to life in the United States. It also touches on contemporary medical issues, like antibiotic resistant bacteria, and political economic problems related to inequality. Bacigalupi's *Windup Girl* (discussed above) is set in a future Bangkok that is only kept from be submerged under a rising sea by continuously operating pumps. The world's food supply is uncertain, moreover, because of deadly crop diseases that seemingly emerge from the laboratories of competing agri-business empires. Moreover, most energy is kinetic energy: humans and beasts of burden store usable power by winding springs, transforming calories into joules. Atwood's *Oryx and Crake* (2003) takes place in a virtually post-human world, ravaged by a pandemic that has spared genetically engineered humanoids. Finally, most of the thoughtful zombie novels (*Zone One* [Whitehead, 2011], *World War Z* [Brooks, 2006]) locate the emergence of zombification in environmental change or the evolution of disease.

Alternate political histories.   Philip K. Dick's The Man in the High Castle (1962) is an archetypal example of alternate history: the Axis powers won World War II, invaded North America, and have divided it into spheres of influence. This is not the exclusive focus of the novel, but much of it is dedicated to the developing a sense of a totalitarian, Fascist America.

Michael Chabon's *Yiddish Policemen's Union* (2008) is also based in events around World War II playing out differently: European Jews are resettled in Alaska, many of them thereby spared the Holocaust, and the nascent state of Israel is destroyed in 1948. The action of the novel takes place in the early 2000s and involves issues of cultural collision with native Alaskans, the evangelical Christian-led continental United States, and covert, catastrophic Zionism, all interwoven into a humorous detective story.

Interestingly, a number of important, early to mid-1990s novels—Gibson's *Virtual Light*, Stephenson's *Snow Crash* (1992)—presume the realization of widely-feared Japanese economic imperialism. This opens the opportunity to discuss race and nationality, political economy, and media obsessions of various eras, since the contrast between the memory of that fear for this author and the contemporary reality of the Japanese economy and global political profile is fascinatingly stark.

Capitalism and economic inequality.　　Many SF novels are set in a future in which capitalism has run its course to one exaggerated degree or another. In *Snow Crash* (mentioned above), government has been privatized and even residential developments are franchised. In *Virtual Light*, capitalism still exists as such, but elaborate informal economies have developed among the poor. Both of these and Ian McDonald's *Brasyl* (2007) involve significant mention of radical inequality as a driving social force. *Virtual Light, Snow Crash*, and the recent *Ready Player One*, by Ernest Cline (2011), also emphasize the digital divide, alluding to how the differential access to virtual spaces might reinforce economic inequality.

Butler's *Parable of the Sower* (1995), by contrast, foresees the collapse of the contemporary political economy in broad terms, predicting the end of government and capitalism. Butler's novel does a number of other things too, taking up spirituality and youth in a way few others manage. Butler herself deserves mention, furthermore, for the distinction of being a successful Black woman in a genre dominated by White men.

Miscellany: Human Relationships

There are a few works that do not fit into any of the above categories and, moreover, don't accomplish something particularly relevant for the sociology classroom in any focused fashion, but deserve mention nevertheless. First among these is the sociological experiment extraordinaire that is Kim Stanley Robinson's *Mars* series (1993, 1994, 1996). The "what-if" here is a big one: if you were going to colonize a new planet, who would you send and what would happen? Robinson writes a good story that reiterates the significance of nationality, political-economy, religious tolerance, and environmental stewardship, among other things, while exploring human relationships.

Similar in its attention to human relationships, but different in almost every other respect, is Colson Whitehead's *Zone One* (2011). Zombies have overrun North America. The main character of this humorous, if apocalyptic, story looks back on life before zombies and his travels to reach the relative safety of Manhattan through the lens of his relationships with family and friends and how quickly they can change when familiar and significant people in your life try to eat you.

Note of caution: most of my examples above are from particular favorite novels of mine that take up a conspicuously progressive orientation toward questions of social equity (at least that's how I prefer to read them). SF, as a broader body of literature, is also full of work that would serve better as examples of precisely the ideas we are trying to problematize in a sociology classroom. Classic authors like Robert Heinlein (and probably some contemporary ones too), frequently feature women as little but sexual objects in their stories. And there remains the problem of interpreting the human-alien difference in regard to racialization. It is frequently the case the positive human-alien relations mimic aspects of racialized distinctions reproduced in the real world (I am thinking here particularly of White Captain Kirk and his unemotional, analytical (Asian?) counterpart Spock and White Han Solo and his loyal, brutal, simple sidekick Chewbacca). Acknowledging species differences as parallel in SF stories risks making race essentially different too.

PAIRING SF NOVELS WITH SOCIAL RESEARCH

The next step in understanding how we can make SF novels relevant at least in the sociological classroom, if not also in sociological practice, is pairing. By pairing, I mean simply reading SF and sociology together, interspersing chapters and theoretical essays or alternating between a novel and an ethnography. I want to argue that pairing accomplishes a number of things, prominent among them a critical reflection on compelling narrative across genres and a heretical reconsideration of epistemology.

Straightforward thematic pairing can be quite fruitful. Reading Le Guin's *Left Hand of Darkness* (1969), in which the connections between biological sex and the performance and perception of gender are radically destabilized, alongside West and Zimmerman's seminal "Doing Gender" (1987), gives us both theoretical tools for discussing what we see in the novel and further descriptive examples of what the theorists assert. I would also recommend either Schleifer's "Make Me Feel Mighty Real" (2006) or Pascoe's *Dude, You're a Fag* (2007), both of which fold sexuality in with West and Zimmerman's concern with the performance of gender difference. A pairing like this can also emphasize that social theorizing bears some resemblance to the thought experiment quality I attribute to SF novels, suggesting that a degree of abstraction from the empirical should not discount the force of an argument.

Further examples abound: Miéville's *The City & the City* (2009) is all about socially reproduced boundaries and the internalization of social control. One could read it against Foucault's *Discipline and Punish* (1975/1977) or classic theory like Mead's conception of the self (1972). Le Guin's *Dispossessed* (1974) and Robinson's *Red Mars* (1993) both concern metropole-province relations could profitably be read against scholarship on colonialism and nationalism like Anderson's *Imagined Communities* (1983/1991), Calhoun's *Nationalism* (1997), or even Mamdani's *Citizen and Subject* (1996). Miéville's *Perdido Street Station* (2000), with its interspecies sexuality, might work with Judith Butler on bodies and difference. As noted above, stark economic inequality appears in various novels and much recent journalism and scholarship attends to growing wealth inequality and racial wealth gaps.

More exciting are the pairings that bring the form of the writing into focus. Reading skillful and compelling ethnography in conversation with a SF novel highlights the importance of narrative in social science. This kind of pairing emphasizes the recreation of setting and scene through the text and the communication of character, calls attention to how the authors of both kinds of work accomplish this, and reveals similarities in the way that they do. This focus on compelling narrative also raises questions of how we know what we know.

I have had significant success pairing Jeffrey Kidder's *Urban Flow* (2011), a recent, smart ethnography of bike messengers, with both Gibson's *Virtual Light,* which has an important bike messenger character, and Stephenson's *Snow Crash*, which has an important skateboard messenger character. Interestingly, both are young women. Students find Kidder's work engaging and accessible, and it explicitly theorizes the experience of messengering, something both messenger characters also make clear. Kidder then goes beyond the idea of *flow* to explain more broadly social interaction with the city as a physical environment and the production of meaning, which, in turn, can be read back into the novels in interesting ways.

While ethnography is well established in sociology, it also remains methodologically marginalized by those most concerned with sociology as a science. Compelling ethnographic accounts are sometimes smeared as *journalism*, and students often wish for *numbers* to support data that they perceive as anecdotal. This suspicion of ethnography isn't totally unjustified: generating knowledge about the empirical world rigorously and systematically through the application of qualitative methods is really hard. It is very time consuming and effectively un-reproducible, but even the most devoted quants recognize the immediacy of research based in human experience.

And here is where we perhaps wander into the heretical. Both in my formation as a sociologist and in my teaching, I have found that we frequently learn more from books that are fun to read. Acknowledging the subjective experience of the consumption or synthesis of knowledge takes us well outside the scientific aspirations of sociology, but embraces the significance of experience in a way that we regularly do in our research. *Scientifically*, it shouldn't matter how it feels to read a book or article, but it does. Moreover, this question of enjoyment re-emphasizes the importance of narrative across genres, since storytelling and flow are frequently the basis of enjoyment. Of course, this also returns us to some questions about what is *fun* with which I began this chapter.

The pairing of SF novels with ethnography helps us see that some of what we know comes from a sense of the world that is profoundly shaped by its skillful evocation in narrative (feeling leading to knowing) and that this can occur similarly, if not equally, in fiction and scholarship. There are scenes in books ranging from *Harry Potter and the Chamber of Secrets* (1999) to Michael Burawoy's classic ethnography of factory work, *Manufacturing Consent* (1979), that inform how I engage with the world, both as a sociologist and as a human being, in an ongoing fashion. My students, particularly readers of ethnography, refer to enduring images from those works to explain sociological phenomena. Reading SF alongside ethnography gives us a lever to work on loosening that key element of the experience of a text, because we know we are supposed to value images in the novels and the similarity of fiction to ethnography inspires the recognition that we might do the same in the sociological work.

MUSINGS ON THE NOVEL'S RELATION TO TEACHING SOCIOLOGY MORE GENERALLY

SF novels' refusal to leave the world alone, to observe it without first altering it, makes them particularly important as examples of sociological thought experiments. But non-SF can accomplish something similar when it takes the form of "imagine that ...." Non-SF fiction, like SF, fulfills the role of fun for me too and can, of course, similarly destabilize the assumption that we know about the world based on "true" empirical research, while fiction is merely artistic.

In terms of non-SF "what ifs," I have in mind literary fiction like Jeffrey Eugenides's *Middlesex* (2002): imagine that you were a person with ambiguous genitalia (not science fictional, but real), what would your life be like? Of course, this is both obvious and not unique to stories of radically marginal experience – the act of reading a novel is frequently that of imagining that one was someone else. Junot Diaz, for example, in *The Brief Wondrous Life of Oscar Wao* (2007), makes me imagine that I were a Dominican-American boy from Newark, something I am not (or in his more recent short fiction, a Dominican-American Harvard professor (2012), something I'm not either).

Fiction can do other things too that can highlight the ways in which traditional sociological accounts of the world fall short. My own research is caught up in questions of the relationship of social life to space and place, a connection that sociologists have recognized and still struggle to figure out what to do with. That said, I don't think anyone has done a better job of evoking that relationship than Annie Proulx in *That Old Ace in the Hole* (2002). The landscape of the particular corner of northern Texas in which the novel takes place is more important, in my reading and rereading, than any of the human characters around which the story is organized and, while I've never been there, I "know" something about it in a way that has changed me.

I want to risk stepping off the deep end, if I haven't already, with a couple of concluding thoughts and examples. Neither Sherman Alexie nor Haruki Murakami are normally characterized as SF authors (though works of each might qualify). In fact, they're both difficult to characterize at all. These two very different contemporary writers claim in their work that introducing some measure of the fantastical is necessary to evoke the world and our experience of it. This is not to argue for the magical imaginary in sociology, but rather to say that we need to remain concerned with the compelling evocation of the world that surrounds us and that authors like these are so accomplished at doing so, that we can't afford to ignore their approach—the defamiliarization of the everyday through the fantastical can be the best way to bring it into focus.

REFERENCES

Anderson, B. (1983/1991). *Imagined communities*. London and New York: Verso.
Atwood, M. (1985). *The handmaid's tale*. Toronto: McClelland and Stewart.
Atwood, M. (2003). *Oryx and Crake*. Toronto: McClelland and Stewart.
Atwood, M. (2011). *In other worlds: SF and the human imagination*. New York: Nan A. Talese/ Doubleday.

71

Bacigalupi, P. (2009). *The windup girl*. San Francisco: Night Shade Books.

Bear, G. (1999). *Darwin's radio*. New York: Ballantine.

Bear, G. (2003). *Darwin's children*. New York: Random House.

Brooks, M. (2006). *World war Z*. New York: Crown.

Burawoy, M. (1979). *Manufacturing consent*. Chicago: University of Chicago Press.

Butler, J. (1990). *Gender trouble*. New York: Routledge.

Butler, O. (1995). *Parable of the sower*. New York: Warner.

Calhoun, C. (1997). *Nationalism*. Minneapolis: University of Minnesota Press.

Card, O. S. (1985). *Ender's game*. New York: Tor.

Centers for Disease Control and Prevention. (2011). *U.S. Public Health Service syphilis study at Tuskegee*. Retrieved from http://www.cdc.gov/tuskegee/timeline.htm.

Chabon, M. (2008). *The Yiddish policemen's union*. New York: HarperCollins.

Cline, E. (2011). *Ready player one*. New York: Crown.

Collins, S. (2008). *Hunger games*. New York: Scholastic.

Collins, S. (2009). *Catching fire*. New York: Scholastic.

Collins, S. (2010). *Mockingjay*. New York: Scholastic.

Diaz, J. (2007). *The brief wondrous life of Oscar Wao*. New York: Penguin.

Diaz, J. (2012). The cheater's guide to love. *The New Yorker*, July 16, 2012.

Dick, P. K. (1962). *The man in the high castle*. New York: Berkley.

Eugenides, J. (2002). *Middlesex*. New York: Farrar, Straus and Giroux.

Foucault, M. (1975/1977). *Discipline and punish*. London: Penguin.

Humphreys, L. (1970). *The tearoom trade*. Chicago: Aldine.

Hurley, K. (2011). *God's war*. San Francisco: Night Shade Books.

Kidder, J. (2011). *Urban flow*. Ithaca: ILR Press.

Le Guin, U. (1969). *Left hand of darkness*. New York: Ace Books.

Le Guin, U. (1974). *The dispossessed*. New York: Harper and Row.

Mamdani, M. (1996). *Citizen and subject*. Princeton: Princeton University Press.

McDonald, I. (2007). *Brasyl*. Amherst, NY: Pyr.

Mead, G. H. (1972). *Mind, self, and society*. Chicago: University of Chicago Press.

Miéville, C. (2000). *Perdido Street Station*. New York: Ballantine.

Miéville, C. (2009). *The city & the city*. New York: Macmillan.

Milgram, S. (1974). *Obedience to authority*. New York: Harper and Row.

Morgan, R. K. (2002). *Altered carbon*. New York: Random House.

Morgan, R. K. (2003). *Broken angels*. New York: Random House.

Morgan, R. K. (2005). *Woken furies*. New York: Random House.

Pascoe, C. J. (2007). *Dude, you're a fag*. Berkeley and Los Angeles: University of California Press.

Proulx, A. (2002). *That old ace in the hole*. New York: Scribner.

Robinson, K. S. (1993). *Red Mars*. New York: Random House.

Robinson, K. S. (1994). *Green Mars*. New York: Random House.

Robinson, K. S. (1996). *Blue Mars*. New York: Random House.

Rowling, J. K. (1999). *Harry Potter and the chamber of secrets*. New York: Scholastic.

Schleifer, D. (2006). Make me feel mighty real: Gay female-to-male transgenderists negotiating sex, gender, and sexuality. *Sexualities, 9*(1), 57-75.

Stephenson, N. (1995). *Diamond age*. New York: Random House.

Stephenson, N. (1992). *Snow crash*. New York: Random House.

Sterling, B. (1994). *Heavy weather*. New York: Random House.

West, C., & Zimmerman, D. H. (1987). Doing gender. *Gender & Society, 1*(2), 125-151.

Whitehead, C. (2011). *Zone one*. New York: Doubleday.

JENNIFER LYN DORSEY

4. "PEEL[ING] APART LAYERS OF MEANING" IN SF SHORT FICTION

Inviting Students to Extrapolate on the Effects of Change

Punk rock and science fiction (SF) both played a huge role in shaping my identity as a teen. The two seem incongruous, I know, at least if you think about the stereotypical depiction of each. Punk rock was all about nonconformity, angst, and mohawks. SF, on the other hand, was all about nerds, glasses, and pocket protectors. And yet, both offered something the rest of my life and education lacked. They asked questions. Questions that confronted and explored the essence of reality presented to me as Truth at home and at school; questions that forced me to think and examine my stances regarding the nature of society, government, and my role in both.

In the song "The Answer," Bad Religion sings about how science evolves notions of truth and asks the listener to remain skeptical when given answers as truths. They proclaim, "don't tell me about the answer/ cause then another one will come along soon. /I don't believe you have the answer, /I've got ideas, too. /But if you've got enough naivety, and you've got conviction, /then the answer is perfect for you." Conviction combined with faith makes people believe ideas presented as truths, but since truths change as we learn more, perhaps the only answer is suspended disbelief. Similarly, legendary SF writer Robert A. Heinlein discussed the infallibility of logic depicted as truth by illustrating how "[l]ogic proved that airplanes can't fly and that H-bombs won't work and that stones don't fall out of the sky. Logic is a way of saying that anything which didn't happen yesterday won't happen tomorrow" (Glory Road, 1963, p. 120). Think for yourself, question truths, ponder what could be—these are the things I learned from punk rock and SF, and these are the abilities I believe, more than ever, students who live in a world where truths change and evolve at an astronomical rate, need today.

CRITICAL LITERACY IN A CHANGING SOCIETY

In *Teaching as a Subversive Activity*, Postman and Weingarten (1969) point out the need for a pedagogy that develops students capable of dealing with change, an inherent feature of our modern world. They argue such a student would be an "actively inquiring, flexible, creative, innovative, tolerant, personality who can face uncertainty and ambiguity without disorientation, who can formulate viable new meanings to meet changes in the environment which threaten individual

P. Thomas (ed.), Science Fiction and Speculative Fiction, 73–93.

and mutual survival" (p. 218). Today's students are born into a world where an information tsunami exists on demand via the Internet and technology. In this world educational success no longer depends purely on knowledge. Students now need to be able to navigate the flood waters of available knowledge. Because "the heart of critical thinking and problem solving is the ability to ask the right questions" (Crowe & Stanford, 2010, p. 36), the compass they need is the ability to think critically and evaluate (Crowe & Stanford; Wagner, 2008). Facts, students learn early on, are not reliable. After all, today's young people have grown up in a world where at a touch of a button they can find co-existing, yet paradoxical facts, affirming and refuting major scientific concepts like global warming. They spend their days on Facebook, where the paradoxes presented are so ubiquitous, posts are even made mocking the fact, as shown in the picture (Koranek, n.d.):

Growing up enmeshed in postmodernity, even the heroes young people admire, like Doctor Who, and the shows they watch, like *Game of Thrones (GoT)*, both described in the picture as being "awesome," demonstrate the complexity of rightness and knowing and truth. Doctor Who, a SF program, uses a character imbued with power over time itself to explore the potential shifts and effects in power and world structures, as well as the ethical ramification surrounding the use of such power. *GoT*, a fantasy series based on fantasy novels, deals with people's uses and misuses of power in a world in flux. Both portray complex worlds wherein everything is painted in shades of grey, and both force viewers to confront difficult ethical questions.

SF AND CRITICAL THINKING

The global community these students will enter will be a world continually evolving into one even more complex, one in which "yesterday's answers won't solve today's problems," a world where they will be expected to confront the challenge of doing "things that haven't been done before" (Wagner, 2008, p. 21). However, despite the growing body of research indicating the need for critical thinking skills, it is rare for a classroom to teach a student how to think (Wagner) and even rarer for a classroom to provide a forum where students can pose questions aimed toward transformation, questions that critique existing power structures and strive to find a better way.

Even if an educator would like to find a forum for student exploration into notions of T(t)ruth, finding an effective medium can be problematic. Many traditional literary and non-fiction works are laden with polarizing, socio-political undertones and, as a result, make it difficult for students to step outside their ethics and engage in effective discussions of the issues posed. Because speculative literary forms take the big issues and questions out of their potentially polarizing cultural contexts, speculative fiction is an excellent medium for developing this kind of critical thinker. In his essay, "My Definition of Science Fiction," Dick (1995) writes that for a piece of fiction to be SF, it must present a distinctly new idea, and for it to be *good* SF,

> the conceptual dislocation—the new ideas, in other words—must be truly new (or a new variation on an old one) and it must be intellectually stimulating to the reader; it must invade his mind and wake it up to the possibility of something he had not up to then thought of. (p. 77)

Good SF confronts the nature of reality and forces readers to engage with philosophical questions in a creative way by thrusting them out of their comfort zones and into worlds that operate according to different rules and structures. This makes SF an "ideal literature for rethinking the world through words" (Zigo & Moore, 2004, p. 88). The words used to rethink the new/shifted worlds presented even operate differently in SF.

Since SF deals in "worlds of if" (Evans et al., 2010, p. xvi), language can likewise be used speculatively taking on new nuances. For example, Bradbury uses the word "firefighters" in Fahrenheit 451 to depict people who are dedicated to extinguishing knowledge through fire instead of extinguishing fire itself. Moreover, SF's popularity is increasing astronomically, a fact that is understandable considering that SF is the fiction of change, one that helps us "view change as both natural and inevitable" (Tymn, 1985, p. 41). Therefore, the genre offers students an engaging way for them to explore the nature, causes, and consequences of change.

SHORT SF AND CRITICAL THINKING

That being said, introducing new literary forms, regardless of the worth, into curriculum already laden with required reading, standards, and testing can be a challenge. Novellas and short stories are both accessible and easier to integrate than full-length works, and as this chapter will show, offer just as much depth and complexity. Furthermore, the strictures inherent in the short form create stories geared towards posing provocative questions as opposed to providing answers, stories geared at interacting with readers causing them to become the meaning makers. Because the focus in SF short stories is ideas, many do not have a hero, and some lack human characters all together. Individual characters matter less (Shippey, 1992). They operate more as representative of social forces often symbolizing power, oppression, and marginalization. The stories serve to explore T(t)ruths and how truths affect people and society.

This chapter will begin by discussing the origin of modern science fiction in the short story, evolving from its early roots in pulp magazines into the "fiction of change" (Zigo & Moore, 2004, p. 88). After discussing the trajectory of the SF short story, the chapter will explore the ways in which "SF invites readers to peel apart layers of meaning and interrogate subjective positions within our current techno-global existence, prodding us to ask who develops technology, who has access to technology, who benefits from technology, and who is oppressed by technology" (p. 88). And it will do so, by positing a question as a theme at the beginning of each section as a backdrop for learning (Marzano, Pickering, & Pollock, 2005).

Complex questions require reconfiguring and restructuring knowledge in new forms. Such questions force the reader to develop the "questing-questioning" (Zigo, 2004, p. 86) stance to make new meanings with the text. Analysis questions, for example, call for learners to separate topics into smaller pieces. This requires the reader "to cognitively process a complex idea into simpler more manageable parts helps them see relationships and generalize learning," and "[e]valuative questioning often is used to characterize and appraise opinions, facts, propaganda, and thoughtful insight" (Crowe & Stanford, 2010, pp. 39, 40). Critical questions are useful for helping readers develop and justify their own points-of-view. Questioning that engages this type of thinking is key in English class, as literary analysis and essay writing tasks often require students to take their understanding or comprehension of a material and analyze, synthesize, or evaluate the material in order to create a new understanding.

The early works by SF's Grand Masters developed the querying nature of the genre by asking readers to consider: *what ethical issues surround the uses and misuses of technology?* Recurrent dystopian and post-apocalyptic themes explore relationships among power, society, and technology as well as how power is engrained and embedded in our selves and our societies (Foucault, 1980). These stories ask readers to ponder: *how is humanity shaped by power structures?* SF doesn't always look at how society and science can wrongly evolve. In fact, some of the best short SF confronts notions of *self* and society and explores issues regarding marginalization making readers wonder: *how could the definition of humanity evolve?*

HISTORICAL ORIGINS OF THE SF SHORT STORY

There is much dissent regarding where SF originated with opinions ranging from the satirical works of Lucian of Samosata in ancient Greece to the fantastic voyages written in the Romantic Age to the Industrial Revolution and even Darwinism. Regardless of where the ideas originated, the genre came together in a coherent form as a short story due to the work of Hugo Gernsback, who coined the term "science fiction," originally called "scientifiction." He created the first magazine dedicated to the form, *Amazing Stories* in 1926. Gernsback's steadfast promotion of SF contributed greatly to the growth in the field through the 20's and 30's as more pulp magazines arose and the genre became more popular. A key turning point for the genre came when John W. Campbell took the helm at *Astounding Stories* in 1937. A SF writer himself, Campbell sought out writers with scientific backgrounds, writers who were willing to write with more style and who could incorporate more sophisticated ideas.

Under Campbell's leadership *Astounding*'s writers "were encouraged by Campbell to tap psychology, philosophy, politics, and other soft sciences and areas of specialization" (Tymn, 1985, p. 46). Campbell believed the science and ideas explored in SF were possible and believed writers and editors could hasten the coming using the power of words. At times Campbell and his writers showed a Wellsian prescience lessening readers' incredulity over time conditioning them to accept technological change and how it leads to social change (Shippey, 1992). Under Campbell's leadership *Astounding* became one of the premiere SF magazines, and although the name was changed in the 60s to *Analog*, it survives today as one of the field's leading magazines. Because of Campbell's prominence in the early years of the field, writers would seek him out for advice, rewrite stories for him, and considered him their primary audience. His voice had tremendous power in the market, and under his guidance "science fiction matured, and entered what fans refer to as its 'golden age' roughly from the period from 1938-1950" (Tymn, p. 46).

JENNIFER LYN DORSEY

WHAT ETHICAL ISSUES SURROUND THE USES AND MISUSES OF TECHNOLOGY?

"Knowledge is not made for understanding; it is made for cutting"
~Foucault

Four of SF's Grand Masters gained prominence during this golden age: Robert A. Heinlein, Isaac Asimov, Arthur C. Clarke, and Ray Bradbury. These men's work has been tremendously influential to today's authors and the genre overall. From the beginning of their careers, these forerunners to modern SF wrote future histories that challenged readers' beliefs and notions regarding philosophical concepts considered unanswerable by science. Foucault (2010) claimed "history has a more important task than to be than to be a handmaiden of philosophy, to recount the necessary birth of truth and values .... Its task is to become a curative science" (p. 90). Similarly, histories of the future should do more than explain truth and values. Texts should look at events as symptoms and use the events to diagnose and critique truths and values. These authors do exactly that showing how nothing, not death, creation, or even faith, is exempt from technology's reach and force readers to consider the boundaries of what technology can and should do. Contrasting beginnings and end points, faith and destruction, the stories stipulate how forces work to define humanity.

Creators and Creations

Nietzche expressed concern that the death of God would lead to life lacking significance for man leading to a "sense of the utter bleakness of life and the devaluation of all values" (Kaufman, 1974, p. 101). This philosophical pondering is a central theme in both Clarke's "The Star" (1967) and Asimov's "The Last Question" (1956), both of which present ideas regarding the ramifications of technological development on faith. The two tales also explore Clarke's notion that "any sufficiently advanced technology is indistinguishable from magic" (Evans et al., 2010, p. 241) by looking at technology on a galactic level.

"The Star," originally published in 1955, predicts what might happen when the magic is exposed by presenting the reader with a crisis of faith that demonstrates the power science has to reveals holes in faith and induce doubt in the faithful. Technology discovers the origin of Christianity has a scientific explanation when an astrophysicist discovers the brilliant star signaling people to the birth of Christ as described in Matthew and Luke, the Biblical Star of Bethlehem, was a supernova from a distant galaxy. The text depicts technology's power to destroy faith and explores the effects on humanity using the character of the doubting astrophysicist priest as a vehicle. Throughout the story, the priest wonders how the destruction he discovered could "be reconciled with the mercy of God" (Clarke, 1967, n.p.), and he wonders how his discovery will effect other people of faith. "The Last Question" expounds on the possibility of science answering and overcoming one of the big questions—what happens when time ends as a result of entropy. The text positions an evolved computer, Multivac, as The Creator described in *The Bible*. In "The Star" and "The Last Question," events deemed magical and inexplicable are explained by "sufficiently advanced technology." In one, the Star of Bethlehem, a magical light symbolizing the birth of Christ, is transformed into a scientifically verifiable destruction. In the other, the biblical phrase, "Let There Be Light," stated by God during the moment of creation, is transformed into a program stated by a computer who has computed a means of reversing entropy.

Characters in both are merely vehicles for exploring these concepts. Clarke's only character is the doubting scientist priest, and the story focuses solely on the priest's discovery and subsequential faith crisis to explore how God's death might affect humanity's faithful. While there are people in Asimov's story, they are only used to illustrate man evolving and expanding across space and continually striving to stop the universe's inevitable decline. Technology symbolized by Multivac evolves along with man and keeps striving to find a solution to man's question. In both, characters symbolize man's quest for meaning, and in both the characters find answers in science. Foucault (2010) held that "knowledge was made for cutting" (p. 88), and these stories force readers to wonder how deep knowledge can cut and what the implications for such knowledge might be.

Death and Destruction

Science's capacity for cutting is also explored in Heinlein's and Bradbury's stories, but these tales focus more on technology's capacity for misuse than its potential to transform. Heinlein's "Life-Line" (1987), first published in 1939, looks at how technological developments can shift economic and social forces, even when the technology deals with events we consider nonnegotiable like death. Bradbury's 1950 story "There Will Come Soft Rains" (2010) speculates on humanity's ultimate destruction through nuclear war.

"Life-Line" looks at the ethics surrounding death—and not just how death affects us as individuals, but death's role in society and how all too often, technology represents an economic force. In the story, one man's invention, a machine that predicts death, shifts powers in society away from the life insurance salesmen who fight to main control over the death industry and the discourse surrounding death. Bradbury's story also deals with death, but instead of death's economic role, the story is concerned with humanity's potential for genocide via technology. In the story, nuclear war has wiped out humanity, and the balance of power has been shifted back into the natural world.

Characters are used in both stories to symbolize power/ knowledge relationships. In Heinlein, Pinero, the machine's inventor, symbolizes progress and new ideas, while the insurance men represent the establishment. The story focuses on the arguments and arrogances as both forces strive to control the discourse surrounding death. Intriguingly, Pinero shifts from being a force to a person when death is removed from the realm of technology. He is affected by death when his machine reveals an innocent young couple who requested his services will both die that day. Although he had claimed his knowledge is absolute, he tries to forestall the couple to save them. Even to Pinero, the cynical little scientist, when death becomes personal, the issue ceases to be a rhetorical matter and moves into the realm of ethics.

Bradbury's (2010) story juxtaposes two kinds of technology: the helpful and the destructive. The former is portrayed by the story's main character, a personified house, and the latter is symbolized by humanity's lack of presence and voice. Technology's potential for good is shown through the helpful little house struggling to maintain normalcy with a "mechanical paranoia" (p. 236) right along with all of its potential for evil shown through the family's remains: five spots of paint, silhouetted on the charcoal covered outer wall like a macabre painting. As alluded to in the eponymous Sara Teasdale poem, nature ultimately prevails over both helpful and destructive technology. Fire rips down the earnest little home leaving behind only "smoke and silence" and a natural world full of creatures who would not mind "if mankind perished utterly" and "would scarcely know that we were gone" (p. 238). Technology's misuse brings about our downfall, and despite our arrogant assumption that the world exists for us alone, it continues on— growing and evolving once more without us. More than any other presented here, this story begs the reader to ponder if humanity should limit how technology is developed and whether the potential for protection outweighs the potential for destruction.

HOW IS HUMANITY SHAPED BY POWER STRUCTURES?

"In individuals, insanity is rare; but in groups, parties, nations,
and epochs, it is the rule."
~Nietzsche

Foucault (1980) wrote about the role and nature of power in society. Power, he believes, is inseparable from people and "reaches into the very grain of individuals, touches their bodies and inserts itself their actions and attitudes, their discourses, learning processes and everyday lives" (p. 39). Power as threat and lure is evident in a host of post-apocalyptic and dystopian works, a subgenre developed in the wake of World War II. The devastations dealt during WWII war led to society worrying about the Cold War and threat of nuclear war, while writers pondered the consequences of advancement on humanity and the possibility that people could "become the victims of our owns creations" (Tymn, 1985, p. 46). The expansion of SF writing into post-apocalyptical and dystopian realms lead to a greater degree of integration of sociocultural and social sciences into SF stories. SF text's form privileges social theory by basing the social arguments around worlds constructed for the purpose of discussing social practices, and the best SF requires a sophisticated understanding of the antagonisms inherent between social and economic classes (Freedman, 2003).

Science as a Threat and Lure

Power's catastrophic potential can clearly be seen in "The Brief History of the Dead" (Brockmeier, 2003), which like Bradbury's "There Will Come Soft Rains," explores cataclysmic loss of life via science, but examines the ramifications of viral genocide on the after life. While apocalyptical destruction is an old yarn in SF, Brockmeier posits a unique idea by pointing out that the consequences of genocide might reach beyond this life.

Set in The City where people wake after dying, the story's structure is journalistic. Told in a decidedly neutral tone, instead of having a main character, the story consists of snippets of stories from the various residents who came to The City from locations across the globe. The multiplicity of voices interviewed reflects the lived experiences of the billions of residents and illustrates the myriad of ways people died and then lived again because "that was what the living did: they died" (Brockmeier, 2003, n.p.). Each person interviewed is given a unique character and voice, and each represents a different life. This personalizes the tale; the characters become people not faceless masses.

Because each resident eventually disappears, the residents believe they only exist in The City as long as they are remembered by the living. No one knows where they go. Recently, however, the city had been filling more rapidly, and just as rapidly, the city dwindled. Interviews with new residents reveal an engineered virus has been sweeping over the Earth. Each character interviewed eventually disappears, leaving the reader to ponders the fate of each, expanding the scope and reach of the story's pathos. In the end, the city became silent, and one resident ponders, "What would happen, he wondered, when that other room, the larger world, had been emptied out" (Brockmeier, 2003, n.p.)? Global eradication in the living world leading to eradication in the next.

The weapons by which we wound each other aren't always dramatic, but that doesn't make them any less devastating. "'HELLO,' said the stick" opens Swanwick's (2007, p. 25) ironic little tale of a unique way weapons can wreck havoc during war. This technologically enhanced talking stick, lying innocuously on the ground, is speaking to a soldier on his way to join his troop. The soldier is cognizant enough to ask why a technologically imbued stick was lying around when technological weapons were banned. But it is the cynical stick who knows that it exists because "the technology is there, even if it's not supposed to be used. So they cheat. Your side, the other side. Everybody cheats" (p. 30). The worse a war goes, the more both sides cheat. The stick's comments speak to how man's quest for power is seldom limited by rules. Too often people convince themselves that the ends justify the means.

The seemingly helpful stick itself turns out to be a trick, which the soldier discovers when he gets ill and the stick claims the illness is "radiation poisoning, I expect. I operate off a plutonium battery" (Swanwick, 2007, p. 33). Filled with rage, the soldier rants about the cruelty in killing a man via illness, but the savvy stick posits, "Is this crueler than hacking a man to death with a big knife?" (p. 34). The stick has a good point. The means do simply seem trickier and more clever, not more cruel. Man used his intelligence and his technology to find better ways to kill—ways that sort of-kind of follow the rules imposed by society. The irony is exacerbated when the stick admits the man might not die if runs to the medics on his side, since the soldier does more damage alive consuming resources than dead. The man drops the stick and hurries for help. A few days later, another soldier comes along, '"'Hello,' said the stick" (p. 34). And the cycle continues.

Using the character of a wise and cynical technologically enhanced stick that is able to dupe men into picking up the object of their own destruction emphasizes how power operates behind man's back. The average man here is portrayed as ignorant of technology's scope; he doesn't know how those in control cheat; he lacks the understanding of power structures to realize how he is being manipulated. The stick does. The science knows more than the man, and even when the stick explains things to him, the soldier still doesn't understand.

Swanwick's (2005) stories of the ways humans use and distort their resources and powers aren't always so amusing. Sometimes, they are out right disturbing. "The Dead" is set in a world where zombies are used as high-end workers and peddled as "Postanthropic biological resources" (p. 344), a luxury commodity that is in the process of breaking into the blue-collar market due to a technological breakthrough. Zombies, the product, can now be offered for "the factory-floor cost of a subcompact" a price that is "way below the economic threshold for blue-collar labor" (p. 344). The enormous reduction in cost for businesses is projected to overcome the revulsion factor that had been holding the market back. Swanwick's language evokes political speak. The dead are called "postanthropic biological resources," not zombies or corpses, terms connoting disgust and decay. They are discussed as a means of "competing in a dwindling consumer market" (p. 344) since corpses require no benefits or sick days. The effects on the workers the zombies replace is only discussed by the protagonist, who sees the workers becoming the walking dead, worth more dead than alive. The parallels to American corporate economics is clear: reducing cost while increasing productivity is the name of the game—never mind if the money is made at the cost of other's tragedies.

Throughout the story, the protagonist, Donald, is recruited to join the burgeoning postanthropic market. Yet after accepting the job, he is troubled, hallucinating that the world was "a vast necropolis," thinking about how the millions who would lose their jobs would hate them, sitting there powerless to do anything, helpless against the economic power and force of the corporations. Donald fully realizes the lives he and the others in power will destroy and looks out upon the masses and considers how "there were so many of them and so few of us. If they were to all rise up at once, they'd be like a tsunami, irresistible. And if there was so much as a spark of life left in them, then that was exactly what they would do" (Swanwick, 2005, p. 351).

Constructed as a sales pitch to a desirable executive, and narrated from his perspective, the form emphasizes the moral ambiguity in the situation. Donald describes his uncertainties in joining the death market and his distaste for using corpses as a commodity. Using a man in the crux of joining the powerful or masses internalizes the issue and shows how when power moves to fill a vacuum, each of us is forced to become an Us or a Them, one of the powerful or powerless.

"A spark of life" Donald claims is all that is needed. If people are not dead inside, they will revolt. Maybe. He hopes. Indicating the degree of oppression it takes for people to rise up against the Powers That Be. Many today distrust the amount of power held by corporations in America and are dismayed by the ever-increasing disparity in wealth. Swanwick forces the reader to wonder if he too is dead inside.

Power as a Threat and Lure

Thoreau states in "Civil Disobedience" that most men "serve the state" as "machines" and "wooden men" whose will and purpose can be controlled as well (as cited in Ellison, 2010, p. 368). He believed few have the spark needed to regain power and control over their destinies; these few "heroes, patriots, martyrs, reformers" (p. 368) possess the capacity to serve the state with their consciences as well. It is one of those few who serves as the subject for Harlan Ellison's 1967 story "'Repent, Harlequin!' Said the Ticktockman" (2010), which ponders the control of the masses for the greater good of society through "an allegory of civil disobedience set in a cartoonishly vivid dystopian future" (p. 368). Ellison's story is told in a form as anarchical as its main character, starting in the middle, jumping back to the beginning, leaping back and forth between Harlequin's tale and the tale of how a society structured on time and order developed. Through the chaotic unstructured structure, Ellison speculates if there is virtue, at times, in embracing anarchic change. The vehicle for Ellison's supposition is the comedic Harlequin, a character who darts about in a jester costume wrecking havoc by dumping jellybeans in the machinery and taunting the workers calling them "ants" and "maggots" that "hurry and scurry" ordered about by the Time Lords.

In Harlequin's society, the old adage that time is money has been taken to a whole new level. Time, in his world, is not just money in the metaphorical sense, but a commodity payable through hours of your life. To make society function smoothly, tardiness was deemed a crime, a crime punished by losing minutes of life. Therefore perpetual tardiness could result in a person being "turned off," like a faulty piece of machinery (Ellison, 2010, p. 373). The overly order-ridden society is described in language that is equally order ridden: "the single driving force was order and unity and equality and promptness and clocklike precision and attention to the clock, reverence of the gods of the passage of time" (p. 371). Order rules. Time is God. Harlequin's disorder was disastrous. He told the masses, "Don't be slaves of time, it's a helluva way to die, slowly by degrees" (p. 376), using language as disorderly as his actions.

To the governmental leader's dismay, Harlequin had "become a *personality*, something they had filtered out of the system many decades before." He had become what the masses need "their saints and sinner, their bread and circuses, their heroes and villains, he was considered a Bolivar; a Napoleon; a Robin Hood; a Dick Bong (Ace of Aces); a Jesus; a Jome Kenyatta" (Ellison, 2010, p. 369). He was one of Thoreau's few whose conscience would not let him serve Order and spoke up asking others to stand up as well. A role model, if only his society's people possess the spark Swanwick suggests is necessary to rise up. But as quickly as a spark can ignite, it can be extinguished. Harlequin is caught and instructed in how to conform. Yet, Ellison concludes Harlequin's loss was worth it and "you can't make an omelet without breaking a few eggs, and in every revolution a few dies who shouldn't, but they have to, because that's the way it happens, and if you make only a little change, then it seems to be worthwhile" (p. 378). The change, in this case, seems to be in the Ticktockman, who in the end, runs late himself…and even seems amused by the fact—another spark being lit, perhaps. This time in a person with the power to enact change. And maybe that is part of the issue. People need to possess not just the initiative but the power to enact change. That is, unless the masses can be persuaded to rise up. Masses use force of numbers behind them. Single voices need power and privilege.

While Swanwick and Ellison's stories portray the ways the masses of men are held down for the greater good, Orson Scott Card's "Unaccompanied Sonata" (1979) looks at how individual talents can be exploited. Structured as a traditional coming of age/ identity quest tale, Card uses the example of a musical prodigy, Christian Haroldson, to force the reader to reckon whether "preserving the world that made the world, for the first time in history, a very good place to live" was worth the destruction of the few. The system worked "for practically everyone" (n.p.) but the misfits tend to be the extraordinary, those with gifts surpassing society's capacity to placate.

Each person is assessed and given the job he would love best, but if, and only if he follows the rules. To ensure his music is unique, Christian is isolated as a small child and forbidden to listen to the music of others, but his longing to hear other musicians is too great and he listens to Bach and is ruined. He becomes "derivative." So The Watchers, overseers who notice when "someone acted madly" or against the role given, make Christian a truck driver and forbid him to make music. According to this society Christian is Mad and needs to be fixed. Individual choice is deemed madness in this society, a disease to be eradicated for the greater good.

Years passed, but the lure of music is always too great for Christian. He keeps creating songs of such sadness and wonder they infect all who hear them with his madness, and so he keeps losing pieces of himself: his fingers, and finally, his voice. After losing his voice, Christian is made a Watcher himself, charged with overseeing the system that kept "almost everyone happy" (Card, 1979, n.p.). Those beyond redemption, like Christian, are eventually charged with watching other dissenters and systematically squashing individuality out of society.

Reading the tale of a prodigy being destroyed piece by piece so that society overall can function better forces the reader to critique whose rights matter. If order and happiness for most is maintained, is it worth the loss of the da Vincis and the Einsteins? Moreover, it confronts whether this level of control is good—and if attempts to control and extinguish outliers even works. Near the end of his life, Christian discovers his songs being sung by teens who say the songs have to be sung because they were "written by a man who knows." Christian's gift couldn't be silenced no matter how hard the authorities tried.

"Unaccompanied Sonata" looks at how music speaks to people and communicates an intangible/ indefinable aspect of being human and binds people together. Butler's (2005) 1983 story, "Speech Sounds," also looks at what binds us together as people and a society. Through exploring communication issues readers see how tenuous mankind's hold is on the very things that make us human. All too easily, everything we built can be taken down, and disintegrated, and it takes a special extremely strong individual to fight back.

In Butler's story, civilization, not humanity is destroyed by means of a mysterious virus that leaves survivors with specific, stroke-like after effects impairing language skills and cognitive abilities as well. The way speech and language are harmed is highly individualistic, so two people may end up having no way to communicate. This inability to communicate brings out all the darker sides of human nature, rape and beatings had become common, and those who struggled less with language were frequently targeted for attack. The story, therefore, contains almost no dialogue and is narrated by a third person narrator from the perspective of one woman who learns to fight the destruction while she travels attempting to find her family.

Butler's (2005) warrior in the war to regain communication and humanity is a woman named Rye who had been an author before the illness. To her devastation, the language skill she lost was reading and writing leaving her with "a houseful of books that she could neither read nor bring herself to use as fuel" (p. 573). This loss leaves her—like the other people in this world with a bitter resentment for those who can do what she lost. Due to the lack of communication and surplus of anger and frustration simple things like travel had become huge ordeals. People can only communicate by body language and gestures and these are often misunderstood. Miscommunication leads to confrontation and often to violence. Showing the reader the many means by which literacy binds society together, and what happens when the bindings are torn apart.

During the journey, Rye finds two small children whose mother was just murdered, children who can speak fluently. Children who symbolize hope. The kind of hope all too readily destroyed by the hopeless, driven by despair and vengeance. But while Rye is also struck by evidence of the children's skills, a stronger feeling exerts itself, awe.

"She had been a teacher. A good one. She had been a protector, too, though only of herself. She had kept herself alive when she had no reason to live. If the illness let these children alone, she could keep them alive" (Butler, 2005, p. 578)—so she reveals that she, too, can speak clearly. She reaches out, and the story ends with this little glimpse of humanity's goodness and instinct to survive and rebuild, rising out of the devastation. Maybe this story shows kindness can overcome, and maybe we are more than our instincts, even in the face of devastation. In Butler's tale, the character does matter as much as the message if only to emphasize how individuals do matter.

HOW COULD THE DEFINITION OF HUMANITY EVOLVE?

"When you light a candle, you also cast a shadow."
~Ursula K. Le Guin

Besides confronting the interwoven relationships between technology, power, and society, much of SF confronts notions of *self* and society and even asks the reader to explore notions of what it means to be human, all of which are key features of a critical literacy that "connects the political and the personal, the public and the private, the global and the local, the economic and the pedagogical, for reinventing our lives and for promoting justice in places of inequity" (Shor, 1999, p. 1). Related to the notions of identity and society, SF stories also challenge readers through exploration of our notions of "other" and marginalization never fearing to address issues like race, gender, and sexuality.

Evolving/Redefining Humanity

Like several of the previous stories, Gunn's (2005) 1988 funny and odd story, "Stable Strategies for Middle Management," discusses the relationship between individuals and corporations, but from the angle of individual ambition. Gunn's story depicts "how bioscience may someday make possible career-advancement ploys far more bizarre than any that are possible today" (p. 152). Today, people worry about getting the appropriate education and possessing the skills corporations are looking for, while corporations urgently push educators to instill "21st century skills" in students believing we live in revolutionary times requiring new abilities (Rotherman & Willingham, 2009).

However, the new abilities envisioned by corporations now are nothing compared to those pushed by companies in this future world where employees volunteer for bioengineering and agree "to let the B-E staff mold you into a more useful organism"(Gunn, 2005, p.156). Structured to show one individual's quest for career advancement set on a single day at work, the story depicts Margaret's attempts to mold herself into "a successful competitor for a middle-management niche" (p. 158). Margaret's only problem is that while "you can truly be anything you want to be" (p. 156), you have to cooperate, and Margaret's engineering isn't agreeing to mold itself safely into the social insect she believed would situate her properly for advancement. Instead, her inner competitor comes out in an extreme fashion when she discovered she is being pushed aside and she, quite literally, bites a co-worker's head off. But in this dog, or bug-eat-bug world this is all too normal and she simply calls the assistant and reports, "Mr. Samson and I have come to an evolutionary parting of the ways. Please have him re-engineered. And charge it to personnel" (p. 161). Although the story parodies the corporate world, it does evoke images of ambition in an advanced scientific environment. Mediated by science, companies can design perfect workers, and it's not hard to imagine how far ethical boundaries could be pushed, especially if the workers are willing.

Bear's (2005) 1983 story, "Blood Music," straddles the border between science and fiction while implying how wildly different—and far from human—the future could be in a nanotech story that explores how "the true frontiers of exploration may not lay Out There, but rather deep inside" (p.1) depending on how far science is willing to push. Like always, the danger seems to lie in the nature of the person holding the power, and Bear's tale asserts Frankenstein-esque images of advancement gone far astray. Bear's Dr. Frankenstein is embodied in Vergil, a microbiologist who has been experimenting on himself after he was fired by his company for going off on tangents they felt were "premature." Vergil asks his old doctor friend Edward to give him a physical that reveals Vergil is "being rebuilt from the inside out" (p. 4) by biochips he inserted in bacteria and then into his body.

The chips kept evolving, clustering, rearranging, and cooperating till each group became as smart as a small child, and as the chips evolve and improve, they make improvements to Vergil's body. If this seems a little too bizarre to be possible, science is rapidly proving the fiction Vergil was correct. In 2012, *Scientific American* published an article discussing the potential for "engineering microorganisms to ferry nanoparticles" citing bacteria as a logical choices because they know how to maneuver around a body and "can sense changes in their environment and adapt" genetically (Jabr, 2012, p. 2). This seems like a good idea, letting technology help the body help itself, but once again, ethical boundaries get fuzzy when man's quest for knowledge and self-betterment is thwarted by rules. Rules are made to be broken, from time to time, if the greater good is served—at least some believe. The problem becomes determining when the rules should be broken, and under what circumstances, and when rules are broken without regard for the consequences, the results can be dire.

Bear's (2005) story pushes the boundaries of possibility to show how dire the consequences of experimentation can be when the chips don't stop evolving and start talking to each other within his body, which Vergil says is their universe. They are growing and making cities of cells, and these expanding colonies send out scouts. Edward finds Vergil in a bath full of pinkish water—the scouts, not blood, sitting there waiting and trying to decided if he should flush them down the drain. Terrified, Edward electrocutes Vergil and his trillions of little bioteched beings. Unfortunately, he didn't do it fast enough. Edward is also infected and so is his wife, Gail. Within hours they melt and merge growing together while filaments grow out across the room. Eventually, they look like cells, and as time goes on, their "individuality declines," and they have been completely taken over. Even more troubling, the infection has spread throughout their building. New creatures are coming, and Edward is left with only one question: "How many times has this happened, elsewhere? Travelers never came through space to visit the Earth. They had no need. They had found universes in grains of sand" (p. 18). Unnatural evolution transforming humanity, melding it into something new, resulting in utter loss of self—for us at least. The interesting thing here is how many more lives and identities were created in the process leading the reader to ponder the lives created in humanity's ultimate evolution and if the new evolution could be defined still as being human.

Redefining Notions of Self and Society

The question of boundaries and identity is also the topic of Michael Resnick's (2005) "Kirinyaga," first published in 1988, which considers preservation and loss of identity on a cultural level. Historically many marginalized groups like Native Americans worried about identity loss when their people were transformed from being "savages" through education, "civilized," and integrated into modern society. While some of the Indians "were thankful for the education" many worried about the little pieces of "self" lost—language, traditions, religions (Enoch, 2008, p. 74). Eventually, the groups wonder if they have an identity separate from the mainstream any more. Efforts to reclaim minority identity can be met with skepticism and resistance, especially when so many feel the new and larger norms are better.

In Resnick's (2005) future, identity concerns cause a group of space colonies to be created as utopian experiments where marginalized groups could reclaim their cultural identities. One such colony uses an ancient Kenyan tribe, the Kikuyu, as a model. This culture's norms include practices such as infanticide and "leaving the old and the feeble out for the hyenas" (p. 168) that outreach the ethical boundaries considered acceptable even by the colonies. Yet, the Kikuyu feel these practices are an inherent part of their identity. When colony authority's come to question the strangling of a baby, Koriba, the priest, insists the baby had to die. It was born feet first and was therefore a demon

The representative tries to be responsible and claims they can accept the elderly being left to die because they can consent, but an infant cannot. Identity is not the issue to the representatives from the majority—ethical treatment is. But whose ethics? To Koriba "it is not murder to put a demon to death" (p. 169). He and his people do not equate this child as being normal and deserving of concern. To them, it is a harbinger of evil. Furthermore, Koriba goes on to explain that if the Kikuyu turn their backs on their customs and beliefs, they will be just as bad as the modern Kenyans on earth—so where should the boundaries be drawn? Koriba insists his people's beliefs must be respected:

> Our society is not a collection of separate people and customs and traditions. No, it is a complex system, with all the pieces as dependent upon each other as the animals and vegetation of the savannah. If you burn the grass, you will not only kill the impala who feeds upon it, but the predator who feeds upon the impala, and the ticks and flies who live upon the predator, and the vultures and marabou storks who feed upon his remains when he dies. You cannot destroy the part without destroying the whole. (Resnick, 2005, p. 174)

That night Koriba takes the young men of the tribe to the wood saying to himself that he will "administer a hideous oath and force you to do unspeakable things to prove your fealty" (p. 176). The tribe does not know this, but war is upon them, and the reader is left believing Koriba will use any means possible to ensure the safety of his people's cultural identity and wondering where cultural identity lines should be drawn.

Gender and sexual identity are the core of Le Guin's (2005) 1995 tale, "Coming of Age in Karhide," which is set in the same world as her best-known novel, *The Left Hand of Darkness*. Her tale explores a common concern, the difficult transition to adulthood, but what makes this story intriguing is the extent gender and sexual identity concerns are universalized when the story is set in an Alien world, full of intelligent beings who develop in different ways then humans. Their young people still struggle with the changes brought on by growing up—and the changes in this world are even more complicated since most people possess the potential to be either sex. Gender here is not inherent but changeable each time a person comes into kemmer, the time of fertility. Sexual roles shift, since each person can kemmer male or female during a fertility cycle. Therefore, who you are as a person, is distinctly different than your sex, which is not constant.

Interestingly, the baseline androgyny of these people makes storytelling in English, and even describing the story in English, difficult. English has only gendered pronouns, while the language of Karhide has gender neutral pronouns called "somer pronouns" (Le Guin, 2005, p. 331). Le Guin's narrator admits the trouble and to compensate makes sex choices for some characters based around the sex the person was last or becomes most frequently. The first person narration aides in this as well, since it allows the main character, Sov, to say "I," thus avoiding the "he/she/it" quandary. "It," when referring to sentient beings, feels derogatory, as if implying the characters are things, not people.

The language difficulties are even more intriguing since the fourteen-year-old Sov is facing coming of age, as they call it, coming in kemmer. "Until we come of age we have no gender and no sexuality, our hormones don't give us any trouble at all" (Le Guin, 2005, p. 332). The time and process of reaching gender they call kemmer. Sov comes from a large family, with lots of "sibs", but no father—since people can be either sex, the sperm donor is simply the "getter." Sov is raised and educated with sibs in what is described as a happy home. Kemmer is all that worries Sov as it is quickly approaching and causing all kinds of grief. A grief Sov describes in a way that resonates human adolescence saying, "It did not feel like my body, like me. It felt like something else, an ill-fitting garment" (p. 333). While Sov feels like an alien, all the adults seem to be amused, this is after all completely normal. They welcome Sov throughout the process and the family all goes to the kemmerhouse together. There Sov kemmers for the first time as a woman and is iniated into the arts and acts of love by a friend who kemmers as a male, and she learns "love is love," even when she/he isn't in kemmer. The story carries a strong message about the nature of love, sex, and gender when acts of love are completely separated from a person's sexual identity. This makes worrying about a person's sex feel petty, and begs readers to consider their own notions of love, self, and sexual identity.

"When it Changed," written by Joanna Russ (2010) in 1972, explores gender, sexuality, and identity by examining the effects of gender loss. The story takes place on the colony of Whileaway, "a lost earth colony populated exclusively by women—all the men having perished in a shadowy plague" (p. 507). Despite the lack of men, the women manage to run society and raise children, a fact that shocks the male explorers who "rediscover Whileaway after six centuries of women-only rule" (p. 508). In many ways, this makes the encounter a first contact story— neither sex knows what to make of the other—and their cultures wildly clash.

The men expect the women to be thrilled to see them and shocked to find the women are repulsed by their big and hairy appearances, and really, just don't know what to make of them, especially since the men declare Whileaway's culture "unnatural." One of the men explains how he believes in instincts and that the women, who claim to be a couple, should somehow feel there is something missing and insists "men must come back to Whileaway" (Russ, 2010, p. 513). These misunderstandings lead to struggles between the sexes. The men believe they know how women should be and act, objectify the women, and assume the women here would want to assume traditional gender roles if given the opportunity. Whileaway's women are simply put off and repelled by the hairy creatures who make no attempts to accept or understand the single gendered society and go about asking disrespectful questions such as which of the women plays the role of man.

But the men are coming, and so the narrator ponders if future generations will look back on Whileaway as a curiosity, "quaint but not impressive" (Russ, 2010, p. 515) and reflects back on the original name, changed by the women after the men died as being too painful and says, "I find it amusing, in a grim way, to see it all so completely turned around. This too shall pass. All good things must come to an end. Take my life but don't take away the meaning of my life. For-A-While" (p. 515).

Both Le Guin and Russ's stories speak to sexual identity issues explored by feminist scholars who feel "we need now to ask not only how sexual difference works in history but also how it matters in relation to other kinds of mapping in the universe. And we need to interrogate and historicize our own desires, subjectivity, and ideological practices" (Dubois, 1988, p. 7). While these stories do not function in a historical context, they do ask the reader to question how sexual differences work in society, And whether ideological practices reflect society's treatment of gender issues.

WHY THESE QUESTIONS MATTER

After being condemned to death for corrupting the youth of Athens by asking questions that challenge them to explore their beliefs, Socrates was asked by the court to offer a counterproposal. Most in his circumstances would have countered with exile. Socrates, however, refused exile saying he would rather die than give up philosophy because "an unexamined life is not worth living." Socrates believed questioning and speculating on the nature of man and society was "the greatest good there can be for a mortal man" (Plato, 2001, p. 315) because it is only through examination can truth be revealed. Socrates wasn't wrong. The Athenian court system was. In ancient Greece, the Socratic method was an invaluable tool for examining and defining ontological, metaphysical, and epistemological T(t)ruths, and today more than ever interrogating our selves and our positions is required to reimagine the world of now into the worlds that might be. As the fiction of change, SF's inherent nature and form works to teach the skills needed for success in an ever-changing society. In fact, Card (2011) claims the point of SF is

> to show how humans adapt and change to deal with whatever the future brings. The skills that sci-fi readers practice are adaptability, resourcefulness, calmness in the face of change and stress. When we read, we practice extrapolation—if this changed, then these other things would have to change as well, but this and that might remain the same. What is at the core of human nature, and what can change according to the winds of fashion or culture. (n.p.)

Because SF takes important issues out of their inherent sociopolitical contexts and places them in speculative settings, the genre offers a way to alleviate the polarizing undertones and enables "critique of the hegemony of dominant texts in relation to diverse cultural and sociopolitical resources" (Wohlwend & Lewis, 2011, p. 188) opening the issues for classroom discussion and debate. More than any other form, short SF forces students to extrapolate on the effects of change. As demonstrated throughout this chapter, short stories pose questions and introduce provocative situations, but force the reader to answer the questions. This process of meaning making helps students see they've *got ideas too*, ideas that matter and merit our consideration.

REFERENCES

Asimov, I. (1956). The last question. *Experimental Life*. Retrieved from http://www.arunchinna chamy.com/isaac-asimov-the-last-question-analysis/

Bear, G. (2005). Blood music. In G. Dozois (Ed.), *The best of the best: 20 years of the year's best science fiction* (pp. 1-18). New York, NY: St. Martin's Griffin. (Original work published 1983.)

Bradbury, R. (2010). There will come soft rains. In A. B. Evans, I. Csicsery-Roney Jr., J. Gordon, V. Hollinger, R. Latham, & C. McGuirk (Eds.), *The Wesleyan anthology of science fiction* (pp. 234-241). Middletown, CT: Wesleyan University Press. (Original work published 1950.)

Brockmeier, K. (2003, September 8). The brief history of the dead. *The New Yorker*. Retrieved from http://www.newyorker.com/archive/2003/09/08/030908fi_fiction?currentPage=all

Butler, G. (2010). Speech sounds. In A. B. Evans, I. Csicsery-Roney Jr., J. Gordon, V. Hollinger, R. Latham, & C. McGuirk (Eds.), *The Wesleyan anthology of science fiction.* (pp. 566-579). Middletown, CT: Wesleyan University Press. (Original work published 1983.)

Card, O. S. (1979). Unaccompanied sonata. Retrieved from http://janlowman.escuelacampoal egre.wikispaces.net/file/view/Card,+Unaccompanied+Sonata.pdf

Card, O. S. (2011, October 3). Orson Scott Card on science fiction. FiveBooks interviews. Retrieved from http://fivebooks.com/interviews/orson-scott-on-science-fiction

Clarke, A. C. (1967). The star. *Nine billion names of god: The best short stories of Arthur C. Clarke*. Retrieved from http://www.uni.edu/morgans/astro/course/TheStar.pdf (Original work published 1956.)

Crowe, M., & Stanford. P. (2010). Questioning for quality. *Delta Kappa Gamma Bulletin, 76*(4), 36-44.

Dick, P. K. (1995). My definition of science fiction. In L. Sutin (Ed.), *The shifting realities of Philip K. Dick: Selected literary and philosophical writings*. New York, NY: Vintage Books. (Original work published in 1981.)

Dubois, P. (1988). *Sowing the body: Psychoanalysis and ancient representation of women*. Chicago, IL: University of Chicago Press.

Ellison, H. (2010). Repent, Harlequin! said the Ticktockman In A. B. Evans, I. Csicsery-Roney Jr., J. Gordon, V. Hollinger, R. Latham, & C. McGuirk (Eds.), *The Wesleyan anthology of science fiction*. (pp. 234-241). Middletown, CT: Wesleyan University Press. (Original work published 1965.)

Enoch, J. (2008). *Refiguring rhetorical education: Women teaching African American, Native American, and Chicano/a students, 1865-1911*. Carbondale, IL: Southern Illinois University Press.

Evans, A. B., Csicsery-Roney Jr., I., Gordon, J., Hollinger, V., Latham, R., & McGuirk, C. (Eds.). (2010). *The Wesleyan anthology of science fiction*. Middletown: Wesleyan University Press.

Freedman, C. (2003, July). The strongest link: SF as social register. *Science Fiction Studies, 30*(2), 176-178.

Freire, P., & Macedo, M. (2001). *Literacy: Reading the word and the world*. London: Routledge.

Foucault, M. (1980). *Power/knowledge: Selected interviews and other writings 1972-1977*. New York, NY: Pantheon.

Foucault, M. (2010). Nietzsche, genealogy, history. In P. Rabinow (Ed.), *The Foucault reader*. New York, NY: Vintage Books. (Original work published 1977.)

Graffin, G. (1992). The answer. On *Generator*. United States: Epitaph Records.

Gunn, E. (2005). Stable strategies for middle management. In G. Dozois (Ed.), *The best of the best: 20 years of the year's best science fiction* (pp. 152-161). New York, NY: St. Martin's Griffin. (Original work published 1988.)

Heinlein, R. A. (1987). Life-line. *The past through tomorrow* (pp. 3-14). New York, NY: Ace Books.

Heinlein, R. A. (1963). *Glory road*. New York: Tom Doherty Associates, LLC.

Jabr. F. (2012, March 29). Microbial mules: Engineering bacteria to transport nanoparticles and drugs. *Scientific American*. Retrieved from www.scientificamerican.com/article.cfm?id=microbial-mules

Kaufman, W. (1974). *Nietzsche: Philosopher, psychologist, antichrist* (4th ed). Princeton, NJ: Princeton University Press.

Koranek, I. (n.d.). In Facebook [George Takei]. Retrieved from http://www.facebook.com/georgetakei?fref=ts

Le Guin, U. K. (2005). Coming of age in Karhide. In G. Dozois (Ed.), *The best of the best: 20 years of the year's best science fiction* (pp. 328-341). New York, NY: St. Martin's Griffin. (Original work published 1995.)

Marzano, R. J., Pickering, D., & Pollock, J. (2005). *Classroom instruction that works: Research-based strategies for increasing student achievement*. Upper Saddle River, NJ: Pearson.

Moylan, T. (2003, July). "Social" versus sociopolitical. *Science Fiction Studies, 30*(2), 174-175.

Plato. (2000). *Selected dialogues of Plato* (B. Jowett, Trans.). New York, NY: Modern Library.

Postman, N., & Weingarten, C. (1969). *Teaching as a subversive activity*. New York, NY: Dell Publishing Co., Inc.

Resnick, M. (2005). Kirinyaga. In G. Dozois (Ed.), *The best of the best: 20 years of the year's best science fiction* (pp. 162-176). New York, NY: St. Martin's Griffin. (Original work published 1988.)

Rotherman, A. J., & Willingham, D. (2009, September). 21st century skills: The challenges ahead. *Educational Leadership*, 15-21.

Russ, J. (2010). When it changed. In A. B. Evans, I. Csicsery-Roney Jr., J. Gordon, V. Hollinger, R. Latham, & C. McGuirk (Eds.), *The Wesleyan anthology of science fiction* (pp. 507-515). Middletown, CT: Wesleyan University Press. (Original work published 1972.)

Shippey, T. (Ed.). (1992). *The Oxford book of science fiction stories*. Oxford: Oxford University Press.

Shor, I. (1999). What is critical literacy? In I. Shor & C. Pari (Eds.), *Critical literacy in Action: Writing words, changing worlds* (pp. 1-30). Portsmouth, NH: Boyton/Cook.

Swanwick, M. (2005). The Dead. In G. Dozois (Ed.), *The best of the best: 20 years of the year's best science fiction* (pp. 342-351). New York, NY: St. Martin's Griffin. (Original work published 1996.)

Swanwick, M. (2007). "Hello!" said the stick. *The dog said bow-wow* (pp. 3-8). San Franciso, CA: Tachyon Publishing.

Tymn, M. B. (1985, April). Science fiction: A brief history and review of criticism. *American Studies International, 23* (1), 41-66.

Wagner, T. (2008, October). Rigor redefined. *Educational Leadership*, 20-24.

Wohlwend, K. E., & Lewis, C. (2011). Critical literacy, critical engagement, and digital technology: Convergence and embodiment in glocal spheres. In D. Lapp & D. Fisher (Eds.), *Handbook of research on teaching the English language arts* (pp. 188-194). New York, NY: Routledge.

Zigo, D., & Moore, M.T. (2004, November). Science fiction: Serious reading, critical reading. *English Journal, 94*(2), 85-90.

JOHN HOBEN

5. READING ALIEN SUNS

Using SF Film to Teach a Political Literacy of Possibility

Education is often seen as being about content transmission or the acquisition of marketable skills. Yet, in a world where scientific management has turned many human institutions into systems governed by an alienating instrumental logic, the ability to read and reclaim cultural space is an increasingly indispensable one for all citizens. Far more important in today's world, I would suggest, is a notion of education that promotes the creation of the types of safe, open and creative environments where human beings can interact in ways that are at once meaningful and transformative. Since cultural space is where human meaning making happens, such digital media literacies allow cultural readers to begin the process of making authentic human connections within highly regulated and alienating institutions.

In contrast to an education system that makes students reluctant witnesses to a world that is not of their own making, SF film offers the opportunity for civic education to take on a more immediate, imaginative and popular form. This is because the genre, especially in its dystopian manifestations, forces the viewer to consider the ways in which we are shaped by particular cultural and political spaces. SF Film offers a powerful representation of alienation in action providing ways for viewers to identify and redeploy mechanisms of control against the claustrophobic architecture of oppression. Consequently, the medium yields uniquely accessible texts for civics and literature teachers, as students come to ask themselves fundamental questions about the cultural impact of technology and the role of democracy in striking a balance between human and virtual worlds.

Education in this sense becomes a way of understanding where and who we are and of using this knowledge to reimagine our connection to the spaces we inhabit. This is a theme explored in Ridley' Scott's *Prometheus* (2012), a film that opens with panoramic shots of majestic mountains on an early earth. The audience soon views a tall hooded figure at the edge of a raging waterfall. As he casts off his robe we see that he is pale, heavily muscled, with intense black eyes, but despite this, almost human in appearance. After drinking a strange black concoction with a space ship hovering over him he disintegrates into the falls, the camera following the fragments of this seemingly noble but tormented figure, as they morph into DNA molecules that flow through a vast primeval earth. The movie title then transitions us to 2089 on the stark and magnificent landscape of the Isle of Skye where a group of archeologists exploring a rocky mountainside find a prehistoric cave. Here, the excited group led by Dr. Elizabeth Shaw finds a star map written on the cave wall along with images of tall alien beings and strange objects in the sky.

P. Thomas (ed.), Science Fiction and Speculative Fiction, 95–117.

The audience is quickly taken four years into the future to the closed futuristic spaces of a space ship journeying far from earth to the destination identified on the prehistoric star map. Here we encounter a tall, fair-haired android named David who looks after the mission's passengers who are suspended in hyper-sleep while he monitors the ships progress. Peculiarly, David passes the time playing basketball, listening to classical music, learning languages and watching old movies. Through a devise called a "neuro-visor," David can see the dreams of Dr. Shaw sleeping in suspended animation and we see her as a young girl deep in a jungle watching a funeral procession of "natives" with her father:

Elizabeth: What happened to that man?

Father: He died?

Elizabeth: Why aren't you helping them?

Father: They don't want my help; their god is different from ours.

Elizabeth: Why did he die?

Father: Sooner or later everyone docs.

Elizabeth: Like mommy?

Father: Like mommy.

Elizabeth: Where do they go?

Father: Everyone has their own word. Heaven. Paradise. Whatever it's called, it's someplace beautiful.

Elizabeth: How do you know it's beautiful?

Father: Because that is what I choose to believe. What do you believe, Ellie? (Scott, Giler & Hill, 2012)

Before we can hear Elizabeth's answer David leaves the hyper-sleep chamber to eat in the ship's mess while watching *Lawrence of Arabia* (1961), another film that explores the themes of identity, distance and place. David seems enthralled by the film and we see him repeating the lines from a particular scene where Peter O'Toole snuffs out a match with his fingers, seemingly without any pain. When his companion, Potter, tries to do the same he cries out "bloody hell that hurts," to which Lawrence replies "certainly, it hurts." Potter promptly asks "what's the trick then?" And a smug Lawrence quickly replies, "the trick William Potter is not minding that it hurts" (Lean, 1962). The scene closes with David repeating these lines over and over to himself as he moves toward the ship's bridge to view the crew's final destination.

In the space of a few short minutes, then, *Prometheus* (2012) has raised the issue of human origins and the question of how we make sense of the past, suggesting that the trick to living in a dehumanizing and alienating world requires more than simply pretending that it is anything but deadening and hurtful. Despite the fact that these films are rarely taken seriously by curriculum specialists and academics, SF Film offers today's educators a space where a cultural-ecological literacy can employ critical thinking in solving issues that connect personal experience and curriculum.

SF FILM AND A NEW MODE OF CRITICAL LITERACY

As *Prometheus* (2012) illustrates in dramatic fashion, though popular culture is often seen as low status knowledge, it is replete with narratives that are timely, socially relevant, enduring and powerful. In this sense, science fiction (SF) film offers a model of public life as a web of unexplored possibility, and an anticipatory *space*, positioned between the human and the virtual. Despite the best efforts of many scholars to trivialize SF film, the genre/medium provides us with countless questions for ethical dialogue as we consider just how to uphold Adorno's urging for a new categorical imperative—a cultural and ethical critique that will help us ensure that Auschwitz never happens again. In this way, SF forces us to challenge a version of the world and future as "bare life" defined by brute sovereign power (Agamben, 1998, 2005), and to consider the narrative dimensions of critical thought. Whether the crime is the Empire's destruction of Alderaan, the overthrown of the Old Republic by the Sith, or the latter's cosmic war of extermination against the Jedi, SF film offers us countless texts to consider the intersection of the political and the ethical as part of a broader ongoing struggle for social justice (Lucas, 1977, 2005).

Although SF film is replete with portrayals of brutal Hobbesian cultures, equally ubiquitous are stories of epic moral struggle, where otherwise ordinary characters strive to retain some semblance of human dignity in a world gone bad. These are themes we find in post apocalyptic SF films like *On the Beach* (1959), *Escape from New York* (1981), *Waterworld* (1995), *I Am Legend* (2007), *The Postman* (1997), *The Book of Eli* (2010), and *The Road* (2009). In the stark lifeless terrain we find in *The Road* (2009), we see a dark but ultimately hopeful portrayal of a man and his young son striving to survive in a post-apocalyptic America. In a despairing existence where people have turned to cannibalism the boy's mother commits suicide rather than carry on living. As the father and son move south before the approaching winter the landscape they move through is cold, ashen and barren and they are driven by the father's desperate determination to find a way to help his son survive. Although the father eventually dies, his son remembers his message that they are "the good guys" who are "carrying the fire," a lesson that he communicates to the seemingly caring family that adopts him at the film's end. In *The Road* (2009), the fire is a faith in love and the power of goodness to help us to endure an existence that is often bereft of any kindness or hope.

When we think of the future, we are quite often contemplating the meaning of human life and the terrain that it occupies; in other words, the ability to explore the possibilities inherent alternative conceptions of life-in-space. The infamous 1938 radio broadcast of HG Well's *War of the Worlds* (1898) revealed much about contemporary American society and its fear of the outsider and the unknown, just as the theme of alien invasions in 1950's SF (e.g. *Earth vs. The Flying Saucers* [1956], *Invasion of the Body Snatchers* [1956], *Them!* [1954], *Invaders from Mars* [1953]) reflected the red scare that gripped much of post war America. As Frederic Jameson (2007) notes, we have forgotten the "far more complex temporal structure [of SF]: not to give us images of the future … but rather to de-familiarize and restructure our experience of our own present" (p. 286). In this sense, by describing cultures that are radically removed from our own in time and/or space these films cause us to question fundamental presuppositions about the "proper" or "natural" order of human societies. In a dark age, SF film offers "an apprenticeship in living beyond despair … a receptivity to it—a way of endowing despair with meaning [as] … artistic creation allows the ego to assume an existence on the basis of its very vulnerability to the other" (Kristeva, 1987, p. 17).

Yet, despite the fact that students live in a world of unprecedented technological change, contemporary curricula often lack any sense of how human communities can create ways of life that are attuned to the ever represent realities of ecological crisis and human conflict. In contrast, the SF film genre provides teachers and students with repeated warnings of the potentially apocalyptic ramifications of our failure to create more accountable forms of political organization. Like Charlton Heston's character Taylor in the *Planet of the Apes* (1968)—a human astronaut who finds himself stranded on a strange planet—SF film audiences encounter countless examples of the dangers of a single minded belief in the scientific rationality. Indeed, the film presents us with the stubborn Dr. Zaius, the Ape's Minister of Science, who refuses to acknowledge Taylor's intelligence as much out of pride as a self-interested desire to maintain the current caste structure. Taylor is filled with indignation at the injustice of Ape society until he discovers at the film's end that the planet he has found himself on is actually the remnants of a post apocalyptic earth. In many ways, then, both Taylor and Zaius share a similar flaw: the inability to imagine a better world, one unexpectedly connected with their refusal to recognize the full nature of the reality around them. Both Taylor and Zaius are prisoners to their lack of knowledge implying that perspective taking is essential to combining critical and imaginative capabilities in order to fully understand the social realm in which individual action is given meaning.

Although the apocalyptic and post-apocalyptic genres offer ways for educators to explore many pressing social issues including war, population control, nuclear disarmament, and climate change, dystopian SF also allows the educator to challenge students to see society as a reality that is continually in process. It is not too hard to imagine, for instance, that the blindness of the populace in *Day of the Triffids* (1962) is a metaphor for society's inability to contextualize social experience in ways that promote meaningful forms of social solidarity. In many ways SF represents a revolt against the deterministic view of human society, articulated by the slave trader Haskell Moore says in *Cloud Atlas* (2013) who said: "There is a natural order to this world, and those who try to upend it do not fare well." For all these reasons,

> [SF's] deepest vocation is to bring home, in local and determinate ways and with a fullness of concrete detail, our constitutional inability to imagine

Utopia itself: and this, not owing to any individual failure of imagination but as the result of the systemic, cultural and ideological closure of which we are all in one way or another prisoners. (Jameson, 2007, p. 289)

The future tense, then, becomes emblematic of our inability to create the temporal and spatial conditions of a more humane, just and fulfilling social community (Freedman, 2006). More often than not, these moral conflicts play out within the space of the subject (Atwood, 2011). As Lacan (2006) has described the problem

it is clear that the promotion of the ego in our existence is leading, in conformity with the utilitarian conception of man that reinforces it, to an ever greater realization of man as an individual, in other words, in an isolation of the soul that is ever more akin to its original dereliction. (p. 99)

Lacan here identifies a central irony in scientific fiction: namely that the more society perseverates on technological resolutions to tensions inherent within the ego-structure, the more society's problems become manifested as psychic or spiritual in nature. This, for Lacan, necessitates a new psychological analysis of space and the "kaleidoscopic" structure of "human space" (p. 99). Indeed, SF films such as *Star Wars* (1977), *Fifth Element* (1997), *Signs* (2002), *Event Horizon* (1997), *Flatliners* (1990), *Minority Report* (2002), *Dune* (1984), *Avatar* (2009), *The Adjustment Bureau* (2011) and *Cloud Atlas* (2013) hint at the idea that there is a powerful, often ignored, spiritual dimension to human existence. Quite simply, the amoral "god of biomechanics"—to use Roy Batty's phrase—provides us with no easy answers to the question of human purpose or origins (Scott & Deeley, 1982).

In similar fashion, dystopian SF also reminds us of the threat of social collapse: an event that often comes through some fatal moral flaw—dispositions that are also often reflective of deep shortcomings inherent in modern culture. These moral failings, often set against fantastic technological cityscapes, remind us that technology is no miraculous *deus ex machina*. As David Harvey (2006) has argued, "thinking through the different ways in which space and space-time get used as a key word helps define certain conditions of possibility for critical engagement. It also opens up ways to identify conflicting claims and alternative political possibilities" (p. 139). I am thinking for example of Katniss Everdeen in the *Hunger Games* (2012), a young girl who lives in a totalitarian society that punishes rebel districts by requiring them to put forward its young people as tributes for annual Hunger Games. Although Katniss seems remarkably heroic when she steps in to replace her little sister in the Selection, she also finds herself troubled by the reality that in order to survive she must pander to the whims of the show's television audience and perhaps even kill her friends in the arena. Eventually using her newfound mass popularity to become the figurehead of a political rebellion, Katniss also serves as a telling reminder that agency is complex and often difficult.

By presenting protagonists coming to terms with transformative realizations encoded in the broader culture (Freire, 2000), the SF film forces learners to critically consider the meaning of, and possibilities inherent in, human agency. Other genre protagonists are great problem solvers; they possess the ability to unlock solutions to seemingly impossible problems. Doctor Who and Captain Kirk are archetypical examples of this—protagonists who combine great intellect with a capacity for action and a deep sense of the importance of character and friendship. We see this for example with Kirk's penchant for disobeying orders to protect his crew or to save his friends as he does in *Star Trek III* (1984) or the opening scenes of *Star Trek Into Darkness* (2013). Similarly, like Kirk, the enigmatic and quirky Dr. Who is also a character who operates on high ethical principles but who is sometimes willing to bend the laws of time to serve some higher end, or again, to save a friend as he battles Daleks, Cybermen and Zygons. Although he is more powerful than Kirk, the Dr.'s personal foibles and his compassion for the suffering mark him as being at once heroic and very much "human."

Both Kirk and Dr. Who have a high regard for the need for laws as well as for the institutions that create them even though at times they may be willing to break certain rules to further the "greater good" or simply to save a friend. By doing so they combine the active and contemplative life, in a way, that provides a model for the good life in an age dominated by rational-instrumentality. Somehow, far from living god like in serene isolation, these heroes humanize these otherwise cold and distant technological spaces through the act of reaching out beyond themselves into the lives of others. As one scholar put it, "One of the contradictory impulses at the heart of the genre is the desire for stories to happen on a grand scale ... but also a need to follow human actions, to humanize the events" (Bould, 2008, p. 89). Such SF heroes reaffirm the value of the human by acting in ways that often combine intuition and rationality and that reveal "a diversification of moods – a spectrum of sadness, a refinement of grief or mourning – [that] is the hallmark of my humanity; assuredly not triumphant but subtle, combative and creative" (Kristeva, 1987, p. 8).

Technology's ability to reduce life into bare productive power probes a realm where the boundaries between the spiritual and the scientific are blurred. This is true, for example, in the horror genre where we see dark seemingly inscrutable forces at play or in movies that raise the issue of human origins. In Ridley Scott's *Prometheus* (2012), for example, even though it is clear that the human species is engineered by another race that has for unknown reasons decided to destroy it the main character, archaeologist Elizabeth Shaw, still hangs on to her faith in some higher power that has created the Engineers, though she is increasingly unsure what that power looks like. As the replicant Roy Batty says in *Blade Runner* (1982), "it's not an easy thing to meet your maker," suggesting it is misguided perhaps to pretend that technological mastery of the world will somehow magically resolve the mystery of human existence. Indeed, the search to reduce consciousness into an anemic object of technological power hints at a soul-destroying technology that disrupts our capacity to remember and to choose and further reveals a split subject in search of its home-in-the-world, a quest that remains frustratingly elusive.

The dangers of technology are also illustrated by genre films that portray androids and genetically altered humans who represent the sterility of a life lived pursuing empty modernist values of efficiency and progress, as we find, for example, in films like *Gattaca* (1997) or Frank Oz's *The Stepford Wives* (2004).

But even within the most highly controlled environments we find protagonists who somehow manage to retain some semblance of free will. Such movies address two major themes: again, the mystery of human consciousness, and, the threat of forms of consciousness that are disruptive to the idea of human community. In the SF-horror genre, for example, like *The Andromeda Strain* (1971), *Alien* (1979) or *The Thing* (1982), *28 Days Later* (2002), *Resident Evil* (2002), *Screamers* (1995), *Species* (1995), *I am Legend* (2007), or, to cite earlier examples, *Invasion of the Body Snatchers* (1956) and *It Came from Out Space* (1953) we have a hidden Other that threatens to destroy the community from within. More than a simple allusion to the Freudian tension between Eros and civilization, this formula hints at the dangers inherent in radical alterity as well as the bankrupt nature of a utilitarian vision of technological progress. These versions of reality are far removed from what Augusto Boal (2002) has called "*spaces of liberty* [emphasis in original] where people can free their memories, emotions, imaginations, thinking of the past, in their present, and where they can invent their future instead of waiting for it" (p. 5).

Yet, Lacan (2006), following Hegel, also warns us of what he terms "the very delusion of the misanthropic beautiful soul, casting out into the world the disorder that constitutes his being" (p. 93). Defining freedom and responsibility within the space of the human is a theme we find explored in films that center around villains or protagonists that are near human androids or trans human such as *A.I. Artificial Intelligence* (2001), Screamers (1985) *Blade Runner* (1982), *Cargo* (2009), *Moon* (2009), or *2001: A Space Odyssey* (1968). Is there, these films ask, really a ghost in the machine or can we simply define the human by its formal and functional equivalents? At what point does instrumental rationality rob us of our human dignity and our libidinal attachments to the familiar? Many of these movies suggest that what it means to be human is not simply a matter of function, form or simple genetic constitution. "Having extended our grasp," Lacan (2006), asks, "to the farthest reaches of matter, won't this realized space—which makes the great imaginary spaces in which the free games of the ancient sages roamed seem illusory to us—thus vanish in turn in a roar of the universal ground?" (p. 100). Collectively, these films hint at the tension between utopian visions and their negation (Jameson, 2007), and in doing so, they explore the types of losses that abound in contemporary human spaces. By encouraging a "literacy of transience in place" (Kelly, 2009, p. 3), they enable use to come to terms with the modern condition of what Glenn Albrecht terms solastalgia: "a register of the profundity of human distress resulting from displacement and loss ... by which places are traumatized to the point that they can no longer provide solace and sustenance" (Kelly, 2009, p. 2).

NOETIC SPACE AND THE FUTURE

Quite often then, SF film presents us with the twin deserts of an alienating virtual world and of a natural world that has been destroyed by runaway technology. Sometimes the virtual world is used to augment or escape a dysfunctional world that has been effectively destroyed, a motif we find, for example, in *Existenz* (1999), *The Matrix* (1999), *Cargo* (2009) or the *Terminator* (1984). In this way the virtual and the embodied become uniquely interdependent meaning that agency cannot come unless we have a full sense of both realms. In other movies, like *Total Recall* (1990), *Eternal Sunshine of the Spotless Mind* (2004), *The Lawnmower Man* (1992), *Dark City* (1998), *Vanilla Sky* (2001), the *13th Floor* (1999), *Solaris* (2002), the lines between the virtual and "the real" are blurred to create a dissonance that can at once augment and trouble an unsettled self. This mental triangulation of self, time and place mirrors the type of contextualization that is required by critical thinking, one that is often accompanied by a profound sense of displacement,. As Zizek (2004) puts it:

> we can never cut the links from our real body and float freely in the cyberspace; since, however, our bodily self-experience itself is already-already "virtual," symbolically mediated, this body to which we are forced to return is not the constituted body of the full self-experience, of "true reality," but the formless remainder, the horror of the Real. (Zizek, 2004, p. 67)

This identity problematic reflects the realization that any utopia must allow for both the entropy of play and the constant iterative striving of will and desire. Like the android David in *A.I. Artificial Intelligence* (2001) who wants desperately to be human, desire motivates us to refashion the world and ourselves. Though David is continually frustrated by his inability to become real, it is perhaps his insistent refusal to abandon his desire to be loved that mark his most human like moments. We see this from his request to spend one final day with his long dead human owner, a wish granted by the highly evolved Mecha who reanimate him after rescuing from the frozen ocean's depths. This act of love provides us with insight into SF's scaffolding of conscious agency, using the parameters established by historical and cultural conditions. But where do such transformations occur? To extend the metaphor of space we have been using, I want to allude to the concept of noetic space described by Belleau and Johnson (2008) in their essay on law, language and dissent, originally developed by Amsterdam and Bruner (2000):

> We therefore propose to conceive of culture as an interplay of the two—a dialectic between the canonical ways laid down by a society's institutional forms and the possible worlds generated by the rich imaginations of its members, who nonetheless must remain dependent to a large extent upon the society's institutional arrangements. In some deep sense, a culture's canonical ways are brought into question by the products of its collective imagination of the possible—its noetic space, as we call it. Yet the culture tolerates those possible worlds in noetic space; they are been nurtured by such 'marginal' institutions as theater, novels, dissenting political movements, styles of gossip and fantasy; some of them come in time to gain more solid support; and a few may eventually co-opt or replace institutions at the core of the society's canon. The "dialectic" of culture, as we see it, is a kind of ying-and-yang tension that produces continual small shiftings and

occasional large readjustments in the balances among a society's institutions and imaginings, its actualities and its possibilities. (pp. 15, 16)

Amsterdam and Bruners' (2000) concept of noetic space brings to mind perhaps Roger Simon's (1992) idea of social forms and human capacities, or even on another level, George Herbert Mead's (2009) theory of the social self—they are theories that explain human agency in terms of social conditions that shape and are shaped by perspective taking and critical thought. The interdependence that lies at the heart of the social experience explains why the monstrous or the alien function, in the words of Kearney (2003) to "signal borderline experiences of uncontainable excess, reminding the ego that it is never wholly sovereign" (Kearney, p. 3). SF film allows its audience to contemplate these "canonical ways laid down by a society's institutional forms" (Belleau & Johnson, 2008, p. 15) within the noetic space necessary for fashioning a new participatory politics of the present.

To cultivate a participatory critical literacy, then, educators need to understand how power shapes space. Nomadic noetic space is a type of digital space that science fiction allows learners to enter, by merging the horizons between the real and the virtual. Like Plato's famous cave dweller, the SF protagonist's rarely has an easy journey into a world of authentic freedom (Zizek, 1999). Indeed, once the prisoner has escaped the closed confinement of the cave he is confronted with the awe inspiring but initially painful experience of seeing the sun and a world he did not even imagine. This outside world is what Zizek calls the "desert of the real" and what Plato saw as the sentient power of a knowledge-larger than the conscious self. Indeed for Zizek (1999) this dichotomy between the virtual and the real is a false one that ignores the significance of our psychic attachments. And yet it is important to remember that Plato's prisoner decides to risk capture to return to the cave to free his compatriots, an act of compassion that represents a second epiphany whereby the prisoner realizes that he needs a community to make sense out of this new outside space. Since in some mysterious way the prisoners' being is interconnected by this unseen web of mutual need and moral responsibility, the task of this new community is to build a language with which they can experience the new shared reality of this alien sun.

Echoing SF scenes such as Thx 1138's escape from the underground prison city to stand in front of a literal sun, Neo's escape from the Matrix (Zizek, 1999), or the workers escape from the underground factories of the Metropolis, Plato's cave also reminds us how space conditions the possibilities for human agency. Most famously the theories of Gilles Deleuze and Felix Guattari (2009) parse space into smooth and striated space. Smooth space is the space of the nomad; it is the open, free space of possibility and generation. It is the space of the war machine that thwarts the authoritarian and repressive organization of the state from growing up within nomadic culture (Reid, 2003, p. 64). Striated space, in contrast, is the sedentary space of hierarchy and control, that has been subjected to human design and will, and has been demarcated and transformed into something quantified and mapped. As Deleuze and Guattari describe it, "there is a significant difference between the spaces: sedentary space is striated, by walls, enclosures, and roads between enclosures, while nomad space is smooth, marked only by 'traits' that are effaced and displaced with the trajectory" (p. 381).

Space, then, is more than a simple backdrop for the film's action. Rather, SF often portrays the plight of the lone protagonist who is caught between the striated space of the state and the smooth nomadic space of the war machine, revealing subjects that are split, wounded or driven to look behind appearances in search of something frustratingly reclusive. Space in this sense represents the possibility of continuity. It reveals the imprint of the consciousness that inhabits it, and in this sense it is a type of collective cultural memory that bears the traces of souls.

Recreating space and studying its mysteries, these films suggest, is often a means of recreating ourselves. Many characters in SF films, for example, Kevin Flynn in *Tron* (1982), Allegra Geller in *Existenz* (1999), Joe in *Looper* (2012), Chris Kelvin in *Solaris* (2002), Ariadne in *Inception* (2010), deal with the ability of a symbolic order to create secrets or for the protagonist to unlock them by resignfiying reality. This process of defining one's self through the act of signifying is often the catalyst that unlocks a character's agency, like Joel Barish, one of the quirky lovers in *Eternal Sunshine of the Spotless Mind* (2004), who attempts to erase his memory of his girlfriend only to rediscover the value of their relationship. In *Looper* (2012) this self exploration involves a conflict between a characters past and future selves, one where the life of a boy and his mother lie in the balance. While in *Cloud Atlas* (2013) a young lawyer's efforts to save a slave stowaway becomes the catalyst for a chain of events whereby the same slave saves his life, causing him to question his own participation in the slave trade. But, of course, these ethical choices only have meaning for us because of the possibilities for perspective taking opened up for us by the narrative structure and visual power of film. SF asks the spectator to suspend belief and enter a world of fantasy and then to step back and to consider the uncharted trajectory of the present (Atwood, 2011; Freedman, 2006).

The future, then, like Agamben's (1998) description of the concentration camp as a metaphor for an alienating modern world, provides a "space where 'everything is possible' but where not everything should be possible" (p. 170). Agamben's camp represents the dangers of creating social spaces governed by an organizing ethos of technical efficiency that treats the human as simply another instantiation of the objective. The camp is a dystopia that is placeless and faceless, a principle of dehumanizing order that represents the totalizing logic of technological instrumentality turned against the human capacity to imagine. As a representation of the desire to dominate and control, the camp is the antithesis of human love and the creative impetus that it generates—it is an insidious underworld of the modern soul's own making.

This feeling of dread of some sort of horrifying inevitability beneath the surface reality of things is a common theme in science fiction. Sometimes in film it is expressed in a film's mood, its setting and imagery. This hint of a dark ontological mystery is the type of unease that one gets from Plato's descriptions of the demiurge in the *Timaeus* or from contemplating the nature of his puppeteers working feverishly in his dark cave. We get a similar sense of awe and dread perhaps from the scene in which the prodigal son Roy meets his creator Tyrell in the film *Blade Runner* (1982), from the precogs in the *Minority Report* (2002), the phantom-like Old Georgie from *Cloud Atlas* (2013) or from the inscrutable otherness of the monolith in *2001: A Space Odyssey* (1968). In some way these questions about origins are important because identity itself is relational—meaning that others and the way they are signified places some sort of demand on us rooted in the imaginary and the metaphorical.

As Augusto Boal (2002) once said, "space is infinite; my body is finite. But around my body is my territory, which is subjective" (p. 161). Space and territory often imply a subjectivity of frustrated agency that threatens to break through into awareness, as we see in the gritty sparseness of the cityscape in *They Live* (1988) or the surreal cyber noir aesthetic we find in *Dark City* (1998). Another classic example of space conditioning human subjectivity and existential freedom can be found in Richard Fleischer's *Soylent Green* (1973), where the closed, grungy, claustrophobic spaces of the urban masses serve as the setting for a clash of human desire for a better world and an instrumental rationality that creates a population control plan that sees consuming humans as a logical response to an environmental crisis. Although the full truth about Soylent Green is not revealed until the film's end, the audience does see the personal costs of daily survival in an overpopulated world as the wealthy businessman's servant is forced into selling her sexuality and a policeman reduced to petty pilfering. Eventually, however, Shirl, the former maid/concubine of a murdered director of the Soylent Corporation, is willing to move beyond her comfortable confines to live with Robert Thorn, a burnt out cop, who refuses to be silenced about the ultimate secret about the food crisis. Yet, the truth about Soylent Green proves too difficult to bear for Thorn's close friend, Solomon Roth, who decides to enter a state euthanasia clinic where he terminates his life amid moving scenes of a lost world of natural beauty. Indeed, the older Roth, unlike Thorn, is able to remember the world that now exists only in the form of a moving spectacle that is nonetheless unable to provide any lasting consolation. At the end of the film, after being wounded while breaking into one of the Soylent Corporation's production facilities, the gravely injured Heston tells the truth about the population crisis to an honest policeman named Hatcher. Despite this revelation the film itself leaves us only with a dark knowledge, a vision of the horror of a totalitarian rationality that destroys human life and the warning that knowledge, like ignorance, has a cost that we must be willing to pay.

The most interesting aspect of the future, then, rather than anything technological is its psychic terrain. Another SF film classic, Kubrick's *2001: A Space Odyssey* (1968), explores the theme of humanity's evolution and its relation to the imaginary. In this case, the nature of consciousness is explored right from the opening scenes that move quickly from images of stone-age man to those of modern space-faring satellites. It is in this setting that we are introduced to the narrative of the flight of a space crew to Jupiter to explore the mystery of the monolith, and, subsequently, the conflict of the main protagonist Bowman with the supercomputer HAL. Yet, this test merely precedes a more fundamental shift in our perception of human existence, as Bowman has a terrifying encounter with the monolith in Jupiter orbit during which he appears to move through space, time and the phases of his own life to become a star child floating in near-earth-space. Bowman, then, seems to have an experience of the other that shatters his old concepts of place and self. Consequently, the monolith functions as a boundary that is also a portal; it marks the outer limits of the old self that must be cast off if consciousness is to evolve beyond its existing sticking point. In this sense, the monolith represents a place that is also the self; it is a sign for the Real that eludes representation and threatens to undo any neat distinctions between the imaginary, language and the subject. Like the monolith, the star child has an origin and a purpose that is ambiguous but deeply symbolic of the possibility of radical transformation outside of the boundaries of the known and the familiar.

The monolith as a touchstone is also a repository of human memory that seems inscrutable but that can, by placing oneself at great risk, and by allowing the dissolution of old conceptions of the self, be unlocked. Death, for all forms of consciousness represents a form of erasure, a loss of memory, and an inability to maintain some coherent sense of self through recollecting fragmentary experiences. As Roy Batty the hybrid-replicant says as he dies in one of the final scenes of *Blade Runner* (1982): "all those moments will be lost in time, like tears in the rain." Death, Batty teaches us, occurs whenever we occupy a space without any ability to set to work at making experiences coherent and meaningful. The monolith then, represents a type of unseen vertical power that contains a desire to dominate that we encounter as alien or other, but that really springs from deep inside ourselves. As Carrol (2003) emphasizes,

> these image patterns and visual metaphors document the true meaning of the word "Odyssey" in the title-an evolutionary journey from beast, to technology, to a stage of evolution transcending the physical realm and also underscore a central theme of the film: the limits of technology and the nature of humanity. (p. 333)

These twin questions of evolution and survival resonate with us, and, more importantly, cause us to question the value of modern ideals of competition and progress. Again, the film also uses a functional critical aesthetic to explore the problem of defining an ethos of freedom-as-responsibility that all too often is lacking in the contemporary world. Bowman achieves a kind of transcendence but never any real semblance of home—he is exiled-to-transcendence, one might say..

Home, then, is often defined as a dialectic of alienation and belonging. For Agamben (1998), the concentration camp irrevocably alters the interconnected fabric of human life and community meaning such that it became "the hidden matrix and *nomos* of the political space in which we are still living" (p. 166). This dark future vision of life without life, is a reminder of the fact that the alien suns of science fiction are libidinal in nature. Indeed, in films like *Children of Men* (2006)*, Fahrenheit 451* (1966), *1984* (1984), *Fortress* (1992), *The Hunger Games* (2012), *The Road* (2009), *Blade Runner* (1982), *Thx 1138* (1971), *Cloud Atlas* (2013) and *Oblivion* (2013), we are confronted with dystopian versions of the future in which human freedom and social community are seriously disrupted—to the point even, where much of the action within the movies is focused around the attempt to forge new social bonds on the margins of ruined societies. These are films where most succumb to the temptation of bad faith: to live a life that is not defined by authentic responses to the demands of human will and desire. In some ways, even characters like Katniss Everdeen from *The Hunger Games* (2012)—to cite a recent popular example—remind us of the value of human freedom in a world where technology has made most human relationships shallow and instrumental. In this sense, the alienated body enhanced, adorned or immersed in technology becomes emblematic of the way in which technology and capitalism isolate, fragment and dislocate humans from the ethical and emotive possibilities inherent in human community.

This question of ethical standards is often connected to late capitalism's insistence that social relations are necessarily devoid of any responsibility for the other. As we are reminded by films like Fritz Lang's *Metropolis* (1927) or Lucas' groundbreaking *THX 1138* (1971), this is because, "Today a law that seeks to transform itself wholly into life is more and more confronted with a life that has been deadened and mortified into juridical rule" (Agamben, 1995, p. 187). Agamben's notion of a lawfulness that is tantamount to lifelessness is often associated with societies such as the one portrayed by Lucas in *Thx 1138* (1971) where technology and mass consumerism are the governing ethics of a Spartan world where citizens are continuously drugged, sexual activity is carefully regulated and the state prohibits any individual differentiation. We see a similar theme of death-giving-order portrayed in *Serenity* (2005) where a drug that is given to the populace to make them compliant also renders them incapable of defending themselves just as it also creates psychotic and violent Reavers who prey on the unsuspecting citizens. Such films remind us that human freedom, while often arduous and sometimes unpleasant, is the only way that we can experience meaningful authentic lives.

According to dystopian SF film, then, just who controls technology and towards what end frequently determines the degree of social freedom that may exist in a given culture Often, as we see in *Gattaca* (1997), *Blade Runner* (1982), or *Logan's Run* (1976), this theme is associated with the extension of corporate control over the genetics of the body itself to reduce human life to a sterile and alienated existence. Yet, despite this immense power, human beings often defy the odds by finding tactics that enable them to resist. In *Repo Men* (2010), for example, a future is described in which an immensely powerful company, The Union, charges exorbitant fees for genetically engineered organs. The repo men are contractually given the right to repossess the organs once the buyer fails to make payment, a process that often results in the person's death. In a strange twist of fate, one of the repo men, Remy, eventually requires a new heart after suffering a cardiac arrest during a repo-operation and finds himself on the run with another organ buyer, Beth. The dramatic irony of the situation is compounded by the repo man is now trying to protect his newfound love interest from Jake, his former partner. Eventually, Jake finds the pair, but after a physical confrontation in which Jake hits Remy in the head, Beth stuns their assailant, and they manage to escape. After this incident, in a desperate attempt to find lasting freedom, Remy and Beth manage to gain access to the company mainframe, clear their accounts and then destroy the computer. The movie ends with Jake, Remy and Beth laughing and drinking on a tropical island while sharing a copy of Remy's bestselling autobiography. Soon, however, the scene flickers and cuts to a scene of Remy being wheeled away in a vegetative state as we learn that Remy in fact suffered brain damage in his fight with Jake who subsequently purchased a neural net implant that let his friend live out the rest of his life in a dream like fantasy. Perhaps like a society in terminal decline, death is metaphoric, representing here a life of distraction where all existential choices are essentially superficial and meaningless.

HOMO SACER AND BEHAVIORIST EDUCATION: KUBRICK'S DARK KOAN

Rather than simply being another form of "amusing ourselves to death" (Postman, 1985), SF film as "an artistic system of languages, or…a system of images of languages" (Bakhtin, 1981, p. 416), represents texts that offer an opportunity for the development of a transformative public imagination. By combining narrative and spectacle (Bould, 2008) to explore what Eco (2004) calls "the beauty of provocation," speculative SF film provides today's learners with an evocative imaginative terrain. Just as the camp "is a piece of land placed outside the normal judicial order, but is nevertheless not simply an external space" (Agamben, 1998, p. 170), SF deals all too often with a dark future that is looked upon as both a representation of current society and as a lived possibility. Moving beyond our present disenchantment (Curle, 2008, p. 348), this question of how educators can provide conceptual, social, and physical spaces where we can utilize the imagination to begin the process of re-enchantment lies at the heart of any productive engagement with speculative fiction.

Finding space in which one can be fully human is also, these films suggest, a question that is ultimately cultural and historical since societies themselves, create the conditions that enable people to be more or less human. Many SF films challenge a deterministic view of human existence in an increasingly authoritarian world. *Gattaca* (1997), for example, offers an inspiring portrayal of human agency in a tightly ordered techno-bureaucratic world, and a single individual's dream of escape from a rigid world of genetic discrimination. In a society where people are genetically engineered into rigid caste systems, Vincent, an employee of Gattaca Aerospace Corporation steals the identity of man injured in a car accident as he works to meet standards set for a higher genetic caste to become part of a manned mission to Titan. Eventually succeeding against seemingly insurmountable odds, Vincent once again is representative of a hero-figure working from the margins to grasp a world transformed by imagination and love. He is awake in a way that becomes a burden, but he also feels a sense of agency and direction so strong that it impels him toward action, even in the face of possible exile. This is agency as re-enchantment in an oppressive authoritarian world where the instrumentally defined burden to be perfect is at odds with the desire for a more purposeful human existence.

Indeed SF reminds us that societies themselves make similar defining choices. In Stanley Kubrick's film adaptation of Anthony Burgess' *Clockwork Orange* (1971), we find a dystopian society that has a very violent and disconnected youth culture that it deals with by behaviorally reprogramming offenders. The film portrays a culture that allows a type of freedom based in sensual indulgence and recklessness until it becomes a true threat to the social order. In Kubrick's film (1971), we see there is a complete lack of nurturing space, even as the bond of friendship within Alex's gang is constantly undermined by the threat of violence. Alex, who is both outside of the law and a threat to civil society, is infatuated with the Dionysian life force he finds in sexuality, music and bloodletting. However, this rebellious daring youth is soon replaced by a soulless, compliant citizen who has been psychologically conditioned to associate thoughts of violence with unbearable nausea. The moral climax of the novel occurs with the self-abasement of Alex as he kisses the boots of the scientist who has reformed him: a scene that underscores the importance of Burgess' film as a modern day morality tale about the dangers inherent in failing to take freedom and its concomitant burdens – social as well as individual – seriously.

Alex, I would suggest, is reduced to a state of what Agamben (1998) calls "bare life" by the state's violent and dehumanizing educational apparatuses. In the technocracy in which he lives, he is an example of the power of the sovereign, "the point of indistinction between violence and law, the threshold on which violence passes over into law and law passes over into violence" (pp. 31, 32). Whereas throughout the movie Alex and his gang appeared to be deeply transgressive, his re-education reveals the lawlessness of the state itself, a force that is roused only by a meaningful threat to its sovereign power. The murder of a high society woman that causes Alex to be incarcerated, symbolizes the power of the law over the body, and foreshadows Alex's own loss of dignity. In doing so, Kubrick presents us with a stark fable of a future in which we all live in the space of the camp, one that we are called upon to actively guard against in an age that has already seen the advent of the state of exception. Particular ways of orientating oneself to space, Kubrick suggests, is a powerful tool for shaping human lives and communities.

Blade Runner (1982) is another film that shares this sense of a society's structure being premised on defining the manifestation of a particular form of difference. In this case they are the android and the human: modes of life distinguished primarily by their capacity for free will. Yet the events depicted in the film forces the audience to challenge our preconceptions regarding the nature of freedom. Inexplicably, after trying to kill Deckard, the replicant Batty suddenly decides to save him from falling to a certain death in one of the final scenes of the film. Strangely, this act of mercy precedes the end of Batty's own artificially shortened lifespan by minutes. Perhaps Roy senses that Deckard is in some way closer to him than anyone else because he has witnessed the meaninglessness of bare life, and understood the modern alienation that has made them both less than human. Indeed the similarities do not end there: as Roy had done in the off world Deckard polices the boundaries of the camp, keeping it orderly—ensuring things are in their place until, like Roy, he realizes the need to seek new spaces for a different kind of life, where the possibility of love exists. As Deckard muses at the end of the film:

> I don't know why he saved my life. Maybe in those last moments he loved life more than he had ever before. Not just his life-anybody's life; my life. All he'd wanted were the same answers the rest of us want. Where did I come from? Where am I going? How long have I got? All I could do is sit there and watch him die. (Scott & Deeley, 1982)

Behaviourism in this sense misplaces the capacity for empathy and love that are one of our most defining human attributes. Like Batty, Kubrick's anti-protagonist is *homo sacer*: the exile who is marked as less than human and set off for punishment but who is unfit for ritual sacrifice. Alex, as he is reduced to the spectacle of punishment warns us of the state's overarching power over daily existence. Diversions, it seems, are fine as long as lawlessness does not set itself against the state and it's primary power—namely the ability to define laws and their exceptions. As Agamben (1998) points out:

> the biopolitical body that constitutes the new fundamental political subject is neither a *quaestio facti* (for example, the identification of a certain biological body) nor a *quaestio juris* (the identification of a certain juridical rule to be applied), but rather the site of a sovereign political decision that operates in the absolute indiscretion of fact and law. (p. 171)

By taking over Alex's body the state signifies its own obsessive desire to monopolize the parsing of public space. Alex, once free and full of desire, by the end of the film, lacks any psychic defences to an authoritarian rationality that cuts off any possibility of resuscitating a life that promises wholeness, acceptance and affection. Like Bowman, he is removed from the realm of the symbolic and thus we are forced to reassess his fundamental humanity in a way that troubles our preconceptions of self and society.

Indeed there are similarities between Alex and Deckard that also shed light on the meaning of bare life and the metaphor of the camp. Like Alex, Deckard as a Blade Runner represents someone who embodies the paradoxical ability of the law to define the rule and its exception. He is also set apart by his status as an instrument of the state, a status that is threatened by his growing love for another replicant, Rachel. Yet, despite this, Deckard's loneliness is the result of his own existential choice, just as Roy's decision to return to Tyrell to seek more life and his decision to save Deckard define his most human like qualities. Indeed, we see the opposite tendency in *A Clockwork Orange* (1971) as Alex becomes increasingly dehumanized, until at the end of the film, he also becomes a symbol of life without any experience of the imaginary. In this sense, Alex's exile is far more complete, and far more terrifying than any other we have encountered. Alex represents a complete alienation of the self as the self is subsumed by the social— just as perhaps Bowman is subsumed by the Real. Kubrick reminds us the sovereign sphere is the sphere in which it is permitted to kill without committing homicide and without celebrating a sacrifice, and sacred life— that is, life that may be killed but not sacrificed—is the life that has been captured in this sphere. (Agamben, 1998, p. 83)

Agamben, then, shows us how power sets apart and even reveres the things it wants to control. There is a certain way of parsing human life he warns that makes it particularly vulnerable to alienation and brutalization. This perhaps is the significance of the camp since such spaces are constituted by the state from categories of persons whose difference can only be addressed through violence and containment. Neither the camp nor the sacred can exist without the other, they are the shadow side of the same dehumanizing desire, a desire that somehow draws us to the distancing and objectification that resides in the state's technological striated spaces. Heroic action in many SF films, consequently, functions to reveal the contradictory nature of the sovereign sphere and the false necessity that it uses to justify the inherent indignity of the modern human condition. In some ways the factory of *Metropolis* (1927), the pods of the Matrix, the recycling factories of neo-Seoul in *Cloud Atlas* (2013), or the prison-like city states of *Logan's Run* (1976) or *Thx 1138* (1971) are all modeled after this central organizing trope of the camp.

To return to Agamben,

if the essence of the camp consists in the materialization of the state of exception and in the subsequent creation of a space in which bare life and the juridical rule enter into a threshold of indistinction, then we must admit that we find ourselves virtually in the presence of a camp every time such a structure is created, independent of the kinds of crime that are committed there and whatever its denomination and specific topography. (p. 174)

Technology itself then, can never solve those fundamental questions of existential authenticity—questions closely aligned to the educational process of defining our own individual, but socially mediated versions of the good life. Neither the genius Tyrell in *Blade Runner* (1982) nor the behavorial scientists of *A Clockwork Orange* (1971), can offer any neat clean solution for humanity's vexing spiritual questions. Ultimately spaces and institutions that pretend to manage these problems or to absolve us of the responsibility for this aspect of our humanity resemble the camps that Agamben so earnestly warns us against—they use the illusion of technological mastery over nature to effectively manage us to death. What would we do, Kubrick seems to be asking us, if we knew the future was a camp being prepared for us, and the momentum of the present pushed us along like some dark infernal train?

A HOME IN ANTICIPATORY SPACE? RE-TERRITORIALIZING THE FUTURE

When we imagine the future it is important to realize that we are making some sort or claim on cultural spaces, for as David Harvey (2006) has pointed out, "it is only when relationality connects to the absolute spaces and times of social and material life that politics comes alive" (p. 148). As Klaatu realized in *The Day The Earth Stood Still* (1951), rather than technology mastery over the world, deep and lasting social change first requires some way to hold humankind's collective attention. The value of SF, as Jameson (2007) suggests, is not so much in the worlds that it portrays but in the associations it creates between the world of here-and-now and the possible worlds that exist as holes in time's dark fabric. Film grabs hold of our imaginations in a way that is uniquely vivid, immediate and engaging as it draws us out of the world to confront us with startling and provocative fictions.

If education is a way of making worlds, film is a medium that uses moving spectacle to create a language of space, thereby creating a uniquely evocative and powerful mode of expression. For Agamben (1998), "[i]t is on the basis of these uncertain and nameless terrains, these difficult zones of indistinction, that the ways and the forms of a new politics must be thought" (p. 187). Like the chained prisoners in Plato's Cave, movies like *The Matrix* (1999), *They Live* (1988), *Cargo* (2009) and *Inception* (2010) present us with dystopian societies where a type of insistent detachment prevents us from seeing the exploitative and utterly unjust nature of the world. Yet, for some reason, the audience, like Plato's prisoner, is forced to come to grips within this seemingly overpowering truth in a manner where

> the unease produced by the text is capable of bleeding off the page and shaking the reader's reality, much the way the angst produced by a terrifying film can follow the reader out of the theatre and into the night. (Frost, 2012, p. 156)

Despite the terror of the Real and the angst it engenders, SF film teaches citizens that our responses to the world must be constantly re-evaluated to ensure they are sufficiently flexible to function in a space constantly threatened by modernity's imperialistic logic. In another sense perhaps, SF at once represents the threat of anarchy and a frightening sort of dystopian power that lays claim to the territorialization of space itself. As Agamben (1998) noticed: "It has often been observed that the juridico-political order has the structure of an inclusion of what is simultaneously pushed outside" (p. 18). Thus, he argues, "The particular 'force' of law consists in this capacity of law to maintain itself in relation to an exteriority. We shall give the name *relation of exception* to the extreme form of relation by which something is included solely through its exclusion" (p. 18). As we have seen then, many of the films above explore the relation of exception and the threat of bare life as they are both manifested in striated space.

As William Gibson (2012) reminds us, technology cannot replace the need for critical imaginative engagement with the world since "upon arriving in the capital-F Future, we discover it, invariably, to be the lower-case now" (p. 41). I am thinking here of an ideal of the type described by Larkin (2012) in his eerily beautiful poem "High Windows" that describes an aesthetic of the incomprehensible amidst a human world of lies, senseless rules, aging, mute violence and fading desire: "And immediately/Rather than words comes the thought of high windows:/The sun-comprehending glass,/And beyond it, the deep blue air, that shows/ Nothing, and is nowhere, and is endless" (p. 73). The high windows Larkin talks about are both architectural and metaphorical. This misguided but strangely satisfying effort at creating an architecture of the sublime, like the furtive "fucking" that Larkin describes, takes place within the fractious confines of human communities. It is politics, consequently, that represents the temptation of using these impulses to control and use us, just as it is politics that represents a possible way of organizing spaces to make more of these moments of transformative comprehension possible.

All of the films I have discussed in some way remind us of the dangers of a rationality that refuses to live with wonder. "Belief in the significance of architecture," says Alain De Botton (2006), "is premised on the notion that we are, for better or for worse, different people in different places—and on the conviction that it is the architect's task to render vivid to us who we might ideally be" (p 13). The deep blue air Larkin (2012) describes, for me, is a type of space that undoes space, it is visible but somehow strangely unreachable, simply because it is a totality (all air) that is only glimpsed from a specific position—a definite here and when. We can see this space as an analogue but it does not exist in the way other things exists, and our encounters with it are strange albeit it deeply authentic and connective. Glass does not comprehend but minds do and it is the latter that conceptually animates the glass and holds it in place against the surrounding air. This is as close to any understanding of the sun, of being, as we can reach, a creaking broken ladder of metaphors and intuitions that allow us glimpses of awe inspiring love and the infinite.

As we see the increasingly glaring failings of conventional schooling, it becomes necessary to "envision the institution itself as a learner over time" and to "create environments and experiences that bring students to discourse and construct knowledge for themselves, to make students members of communities of learners that make discoveries and solve problems" (Barr & Tagg, 1995, p. 2 & p. 4). We are most vulnerable to authoritarian power when we experience a kind of cultural vertigo that renders us unable to put in motion tactics that help us to continue our unending war of symbolic position against the repressive state. "The sovereign power," says Agamben (1998), "is this very impossibility of distinguishing between inside and outside, nature and exception, *physis* and *nomos*" (p. 37). Space in this sense represents possibility even from a position of relative or absolute marginality. Space is where relation exists. Indeed, in many SF dystopian films we see power attempt to make the body into a striated space that can be completed mapped, segmented, controlled, and, in some cases, as in the case of Burgess' (2012) sacrificial A-*lex*, this power extends to consciousness itself.

"Imagination," says Raymond Williams (2010), "has a history … a structure, at once grammatical and historical, in tenses of past, present and future" (p. 115). Wonder, I want to suggest, offers us with a means of escaping the everyday and of engaging the familiar in a more meaningful and sustained manner. In other words, it is something to be taken seriously, to be carefully studied and mapped, to be entered, enjoyed and emulated like an analogue of creation, of birth and a doorway beyond the self, hinting at something larger than ourselves, the finite world around us, and perhaps, even—perhaps—death. What is unique about SF is that this prospect of radical alterity is not an excuse for disengagement, but a motive for finding an alternative space, a new horizon, in which imagination and critical thought become a uniquely playful, yet powerful, combination, a future that comes like the sound of laughter in thunder. This is more than mere diversion—it is an exemplary mode for a model of education in the 21st century that moves beyond bricks and mortar, pencil and paper into a more daring and imaginative world, the pale fire of this strange invention—this wandering ageless sun.

REFERENCES

Abrams, J. J. (Director). (2013). *Star Trek into darkness* [Motion Picture]. Hollywood, CA: Skydance Productions

Agamben, G. (1998). *Homo sacer: Sovereign power and bare life.* Stanford, CA: Stanford University Press.

Agamben, G. (2005). *State of exception.* Chicago, IL: University of Chicago Press.

Alvart, C. (2009). *Pandorum.* [Motion Picture]. Beverly Hills, CA: Overture Films.

Amsterdam, A. G., & Bruner, J. S. (2000). *Minding the law.* Cambridge, MA: Harvard University Press.

Anderson, P. (Director). (1997). *Event horizon.* [Motion Picture]. Hollywood, CA: Paramount Pictures.

Anderson, P. (Director). (2002). *Resident evil.* [Motion Picture]. Munich, DE: Constantin Film.

Anderson, M. (Director). (1976). *Logan's run.* [Motion Picture] Beverly Hills, CA: Metro-Goldwyn-Mayer.

Arnold, J. (Director). (1953). *It came from outer space.* [Motion Picture]. Universal City, CA: Universal Studio

Atwood, M. (2011). *In other worlds: SF and the human imagination.* New York, NY: Nan A. Talese/Doubleday.

Bakhtin, M. M. (1981). *The dialogic imagination: Four essays.* Austin, TX: University of Texas Press.

Barr, R. B., & Tagg, J. (November 01, 1995). From teaching to learning—A new paradigm for undergraduate education. *Change, 27*(6), 12-25.

Belleau, M. C., & Johnson, R. (2008). I beg to differ: Interdisciplinary questions about law, language and dissent. In L. Atkinson & D. Majury (Eds.), *Law, mystery, and the humanities: Collected essays* (pp. 145-166). Toronto, ON: University of Toronto Press.

Besson, L. (Director). (1997). *The fifth element.* [Motion Picture]. Culver City, CA: Columbia.

Boal, A. (2002). *Games for actors and non-actors.* London, UK: Routledge.

Boyle, D. (Director). (2002). *28 days later.* [Motion Picture]. London, UK: DNA Films

Bould, M. (2008) Film and Television. In E. James & F. Mendlesohn (Eds.), *The Cambridge Companion to Science Fiction* (pp. 79-96). Cambridge, UK: Cambridge University Press.

Burgess, A. (2012). *A clockwork orange.* New York, NY: W.W. Norton & Co.

Cameron, J. (1984). *The terminator.* Beverly Hills, CA: Metro-Goldwyn-Meyer.

Cameron, J. (Director). (2009). *Avatar.* [Motion Picture]. Los Angeles, CA: Twentieth Century-Fox.

Carpenter, J. (Director). (1981). *Escape from New York.* [Motion Picture]. Boston, MA: Avco Embassy Pictures.

Carpenter, J. (Director), & Foster, D., Turman, L., Stark, W., Cohen, S. (Producers). (1982). *The thing.* Universal City, CA: Universal.

Carpenter, J. (Director), & Franco, L. J. (Producer). (1988). *They live.* [Motion Picture]. Universal City, CA: Universal Studios.

Carrol L. (2003). From technology to transcendence: Humanity's evolutionary journey in *2001: A Space Odyssey. Extrapolation: A Journal of Science Fiction and Fantasy, 44*(3), 331-343.

Costner, K. (1997). *The postman.* [Motion Picture]. Burbank, CA: Warner Brothers.

Cronenberg, D. (Director). (1999). *Existenz.* [Motion Picture]. Toronto, ON: Alliance Atlantis

Crowe, C. (Director). (2002). *Vanilla sky.* [Motion Picture]. Hollywood, CA: Paramount.

Cuarón, A. (Director), & Abraham, M. (Producer). (2006). *Children of men.* [Motion Picture]. Universal City, CA: Universal Studios.

Curle, C. T. (2008). The re-enchantment of the world? Max Weber, Ernst Troeltsh, and human rights. In L. Atkinson & D. Majury (Eds.), *Law, mystery, and the humanities: Collected essays* (pp. 347-370). Toronto, ON: University of Toronto Press.

De Botton, A. (2006). *The architecture of happiness.* New York, NY: Pantheon Books

Deleuze, G., & Guattari, F. (2009). *A thousand plateaus: Capitalism and schizophrenia.* Minneapolis, MN: University of Minnesota Press.

Donaldson, R. (Director). (1995). *Species.* [Motion Picture]. Beverly Hills, CA: MGM

Douglas, G. (Director). (1954). *Them!* [Motion Picture]. Burbank, CA: Warner Brothers.

Duguay, C. (Director). (1995). *Screamers.* [Motion Picture]. Culver City, CA: Triumph Films

Eco, U. (2004). *History of beauty.* New York, NY: Rizzoli

Engler, I., & Etter, R. (Prod.). (2009). *Cargo.* [Motion Picture]. Ebikon, SUI: Atlantis Pictures: Atlantis Pictures.

Fleischer, R. (Director), Seltzer, W., & Thacher, R. (Producers). (1973). *Soylent green.* Burbank, CA: Warner Entertainment.

Freedman, C. H. (2006). *Critical theory and science fiction.* Middletown, CT: Wesleyan University Press.

Freire, P. (2000). *Pedagogy of the oppressed.* New York, NY: Continuum.

Frost, G. (2012). Reading the Slipstream. In E. James & F. Mendlesohn (Eds.), *The Cambridge Companion to Fantasy Literature* (pp. 154-165). Cambridge, UK: Cambridge University Press.

Gibson, W. (2012). *Distrust that particular flavor.* New York, NY: G. P. Putnam's Sons.

Gondry, M. (Director). (2004). *Eternal sunshine of the spotless mind.* [Motion Picture]. Universal City, CA: Focus Features.

Gordon, S. (Director). (1999). *Fortress.* [Motion Picture]. Burbank, CA: Dimension Films.

Harvey, D. (2006). *Spaces of global capitalism.* London, UK: Verso.

Hillcoat, J. (Director), Wechsler, N., Schwartz, P. M., & Schwartz, S. (Producers). (2009). *The Road.* [Motion Picture]. Culver City, CA: Dimension Films.

Hughes, A., Hughes, A. (Directors.). (2010). *The book of Eli.* [Motion Picture]. Burbank, CA: Warner Brothers.

Jameson, F. (2007). *Archaeologies of the future.* New York, NY: Verso Books.

Johnson, R. (Director). (2012). *Looper.* [Motion Picture]. Culver City, CA: Tristar Pictures.

Jones, D. (Director). (2009). *Moon.* [Motion Picture]. Culver City, CA: Sony Pictures.

Kearney, R. (2003). *Strangers, Gods, and monsters: Interpreting otherness.* London, UK: Routledge.

Kelly, U. (2009) Learning to Lose: Rurality, Transcience and Belonging. *Journal of Research in Rural Education, 24*(11). Retrieved from www.jrre.psu.edu/articles/24-11.pdf

Kosinski, J. (Dir). (2013). *Oblivion.* [Motion Picture]. Universal City, CA: Universal Pictures.

Kramer, S. (Director). (1959). *On the beach.* [Motion Picture]. Santa Monica, CA: MGM.

Kristeva, J. (1987). On the melancholic imaginary. *New formations, 3,* 5-18.

Kubrick, S. (Director & Producer). (1968). *2001, a space odyssey.* [Motion Picture]. Beverly Hills, CA: MGM.

Kubrick, S. (Director & Producer). (1971). *A clockwork orange.* [Motion Picture]. Burbank, CA: Warner Bros. Pictures.

Lacan, J., Fink, H., & Fink, B. (2006). *Ecrits: The first complete edition in English.* New York, NY: W. W. Norton & Co.

Lang, F. (Director). (1927). *Metropolis.* [Motion Picture]. Berlin, DE: UFA.

Larkin, P. (2012). *The complete poems* (A. Burnett, Ed.). New York, NY: Farrar, Straus and Giroux.

Lawrence, F. (Director). (2007). *I am legend.* Burbank, CA: Warner Brothers.

Lean, D. (Director). (1962). *Lawrence of Arabia.* [Motion Picture] Culver City, CA: Columbia Pictures.

Leonard, B. (Director). (1992). *The lawnmower man.* [Motion Picture]. Los Angeles, CA: New Line Cinema.

Lisberger, S. (Director). (1982). *Tron.* [Motion Picture]. Burbank, CA: Walt Disney Studios.

Lucas, G. (Director). (1971). *THX 1138*. [Motion Picture]. Burbank, CA: Warner Brothers.

Lucas, G. (Director). (2005). *Revenge of the Sith*. [Motion Picture]. San Rafael, CA: Lucasfilm.

Lucas, G. (Director), & Kurtz, G. (Prod.). (1977). *Star Wars*. [Motion Picture]. Los Angeles, CA: Twentieth Century-Fox.

Lynch, D. (Director). (1984). *Dune*. [Motion Picture]. Universal City, CA: Universal Pictures.

Mead, G. H. (2009). *Mind, self, and society: From the standpoint of a social behaviorist*. Chicago, IL: University of Chicago Press.

Menzies, W. C. (Director). (1953). *Invaders from Mars*. [Motion Picture]. Los Angeles, CA: Twentieth Century-Fox.

Niccol, A. (Director), DeVito, D., Shamberg, M., Sher, S., & Lyon, G. (Producers). (1997). *Gattaca*. [Motion Picture]. Culver City, CA: Columbia Pictures.

Nimoy, L. (Director). (1984). *Star trek III: The search for Spock*. [Motion Picture]. Hollywood, CA: Paramount.

Nolan, C. (Producer & Director). (2010). *Inception*. [Motion Picture]. Burbank, CA: Warner Bros. Pictures.

Nolfi, G. (Director). (2011). *The adjustment bureau*. [Motion Picture]. Universal City, CA: Universal Studios.

Oz, F. (Director). (2004). *The Stepford wives*. [Motion Picture]. Hollywood, CA: Paramount Pictures.

Perez, G. (2000). Towards a rhetoric of film: Identification and the spectator. *Society of Cinema Conference*, Issue 5. Retrieved from http://sensesofcinema.com/2000/5/rhetoric2/

Postman, N. (1985). *Amusing ourselves to death: Public discourse in the age of show business*. New York, NY: Viking.

Powers, W. (2010). *Hamlet's Blackberry: A practical philosophy for building a good life in the digital age*. New York, NY: Harper

Proyas, A. (Director). (1998). *Dark city*. [Motion Picture]. Los Angeles, CA: New Line Cinema.

Radford, M. (Director). (1984). *1984*. [Motion Picture]. Los Angeles, CA: Twentieth Century-Fox.

Reid, J. (2003) Deleuze's war machine: Nomadism against the state. *Millennium Journal of International Studies*, *32*(1), 57-85.

Reynolds, K. (Director). (1995). *Waterworld*. Universal City, CA: Universal Pictures.

Ross, G. (Director), Jacobson, N., & Kilik, J. (Producers). (2012). *The hunger games*. Santa Monica, CA: Lions Gate.

Rusnak, J. (Director). (1998). *The thirteenth floor*. [Motion Picture]. Culver City CA: Columbia Tristar.

Sanders, S. (2008). *The philosophy of science fiction film*. Lexington, KY: University Press of Kentucky.

Sapochnik, M. (Director), & Stuber, S. (Producer). (2010). *Repo men*. [Motion Picture]. Universal City, CA: Universal.

Sax, G. (Director). (2005). *White noise*. [Motion Picture]. Universal City, Calif.: Universal Studios

Schaffner, F. J. (Director). (1968). *Planet of the apes*. [Motion Picture]. Los Angeles, CA: Twentieth Century-Fox.

Schumacher, J. (Director). (1990). *Flatliners*. [Motion Picture]. Culver City, CA: Columbia Pictures.

Scott, R. (Director), & Carroll, G., Giler, D., Hill, W. (Producers). (1979). *Alien*.[Motion Picture]. New York, NY: Twentieth-Century Fox.

Scott, R. (Director), & Deeley, M. (Producer). (1982). Blade runner. [Motion Picture]. United States: Warner Bros.

Scott, R. (Director & Producer), Giler, D., & Hill, W (Producers). (2012). *Prometheus*. [Motion Picture]. Beverly Hills, CA: 20th Century Fox.

Sears, F.F. (Dir). (1956). *Earth vs. The Flying Saucers*. [Motion Picture]. Culver City, CA: Columbia Pictures.

Sekely, S. (Director). (1962). *Day of the triffids*. [Motion Pictures]. Los Angeles, CA: Allied Artists.

Shyamalan, M. N. (Director). (2002). *Signs*. [Motion Picture]. Burbank, CA: Touchstone Pictures.

Siegel, D. (Director). (1956). *Invasion of the body snatchers*. [Motion Picture]. Los Angeles, CA: Allied Artists Pictures.

Simon, R. I. (1992). *Teaching against the grain: Texts for a pedagogy of possibility.* New York, NY: Bergin & Garvey.

Soderbergh, S. (Director). (2002). *Solaris.* [Motion Picture]. Beverly Hills, CA: 20th Century Fox.

Spielberg, S. (Director), Kennedy, R., Spielberg, S. & Curtis, B. (2001). *Artificial intelligence, A. I.* [Motion Picture] Warner Bros. Entertainment.

Spielberg, S. (Director). (2002). *Minority report.* [Motion Picture]. Los Angeles, CA: Twentieth Century-Fox.

Truffaut, F. (Director). (1966). *Fahrenheit 451.* [Motion Picture]. Universal City, CA: Universal Pictures.

Tykwer, T., Wachowski, A., Wachowski (Dirs). (2013). *Cloud atlas.* [Motion Picture]. Burbank, CA: Warner Brother.

Verhoeven, P. (Director). (1990). *Total recall.* [Motion Picture]. Culver City, CA: Tristar Pictures.

Vonnegut, K. (1994). *Slaughterhouse-five, or, The children's crusade: A duty-dance with death.* New York, N.Y: Delacorte Press/Seymour Lawrence.

Wachowski, A., Wachowski, L. (Directors), & Silver, J. (Producer). (1999). *The matrix.* Burbank, CA: Warner Bros. Pictures.

Wells, H. G. (1898). *The war of the worlds.* New York, NY: Harper & Bros.

Whedon, J. (Director). (2005). *Serenity.* [Motion Picture]. Universal City, CA: Universal Pictures.

Williams, R. (2010). *Tenses of imagination: Raymond Williams on science fiction, utopia and dystopia.* (A. Milner, Ed.). New York, NY: Peter Lang.

Wise, R. (Director). (1951). *The day the earth stood still.* [Motion Picture]. Beverly Hills, CA: Twentieth Century Fox.

Wise, R. (Director). (1971). *The Andromeda strain.* [Motion Picture]. Universal City, CA: Universal Pictures

Zizek, S. (1999). The matrix, or, the two sides of perversion. In *International Symposium at the Center for Art and Media*, Karlsruhe. Retrieved from http://www.lacan.com/zizek-matrix.htm

Žižek, S., & Schelling, F. W. J. (2004). *The abyss of freedom.* Ann Arbor, MI: The University of Michigan Press.

LEILA E. VILLAVERDE AND ROYMIECO A. CARTER

6. SINGULARITY, CYBORGS, DRONES, REPLICANTS AND AVATARS

Coming to Terms with the Digital Self

In this chapter we propose engaging the premise that technology is the new opiate of the masses. Transhumanism as a movement has provided the science fiction (SF) genre with an internal scaffolding of fear, power, and paranoia in the blinding light of progress. There is a long list of films throughout media history, from the 1916 silent epic *20,000 Leagues under the Sea* to the 2012 remake of *Total Recall* that serve as examples. These fictitious technology-driven futures offer thought-provoking discussions on singularity and the social manifestation of the digital self. SF sets the stage for the proleptic, the convergence of past, present and future through an interrogation of the border between fiction, reality, and progress. We explore *The Island* (Bay, Bates, & Parkes, 2005), *Logan's Run* (David, 1976), *Minority Report* (Molen, Curtis, & deBont, 2002), *Ghost in the Shell* (Mizuo, Matsumoto, Ivadomi, & Ishikawa, 1995), and *In Time* (Niccol, Abraham, Israel, Laiblin, & Newman, 2011) as contemporary representations of this.

These films explore the intersection of cloning, reality, class, the body, work, time, and wealth with scarcity and fate as conceptual themes. SF cinema embraces opportunities that verge on the unthinkable or perhaps at the unimaginable for a moral or ethical culture. This genre of film provides a *free* space to consider what defines humanity, how emotions and logic traverse the biological and inanimate, and what consequences are left when the rules of governance fail to maintain control. This opens the door and awakens us to how we might more cautiously consider both the assimilation and use of technology into our lives. In addition, of critical concern are the ways in which these films address knowledge production, the nature of knowledge and power's pervasiveness in lived experience.

So we regard SF film as augmenting media literacy in general, providing an increased awareness and critical analysis of the production of media and possibility of identity development. SF has historically always studied the interaction between human and machine / demon and angels / technology and magic, raising ethical questions both of imminent concern and forecasting issues to ponder. As a genre it offers challenging narratives that should be used as pedagogical tools to critically shift what we consider curriculum and learning to be, as well as where it resides.

P. Thomas (ed.), Science Fiction and Speculative Fiction, 119–131.

PROGRESS AS A PLEA FOR A TRANSHUMANIST FUTURE

During the 2012 London Olympics the IAAF, the governing body of track and field, deliberated whether Oscar Pistorius had an unfair advantage because of his two cheetah flex-feet. Aimee Mullins, athlete, model, activist and double amputee gave a stirring TED talk in 2009, "It's Not Fair Having 12 Pairs of Legs," where she challenged limited conceptions of disability, identity, aesthetics and function. She reconceputalized "disability" as both augmentation and new forms of identity. Both Mullins and Pistorius were subject to the strange, but real jealousy from so called able-bodied individuals who remarked, "I wish that I had blades to run that fast" or as Mullins gracefully states women found it unfair that she could change her height by altering the length of the prosthetic limbs.

In the immediate, these comments appear to be insensitive and of the simple-minded. However, given more thought and consideration, these requests for physical augmentation are not relative to what was lost, rather from what one stands to gain. Progress through the lens of what we stand to gain is intertwined with thoughts about what types of experiences and interactions we want from those around us. The space to flex and change the conditions in which we live is both stimulating and stressful. Why would the ability to change the speed in which we move our bodies or the ability to change our height be desirable? We are told in polite company that we should be happy with the bodies that we were given. However, we spend much of our time and money making minor socially acceptable adjustments to this *perfect carriage*. Many of who choose to change an eye color or insert fat into wrinkles in the hopes to preserve *youth* are doing so as a testament to a sense of control in a world where this very mechanism of control is enacted on the everyday. Others who need to extend the reach of their shrinking bodies due to disability, heredity, or act of nature use technologies from eyeglasses to pacemakers to push back against time and physical limitation. These biotech advances are considered necessities, products, and proof of human progress and ability to provide a better life through technology.

The premise that intellect when exercised on technology assures a *better life* appears as an established norm for the medical, computer, and car industries. We know that these companies spend billions of dollars to forecast and build the currents of desire within society. So what role does SF play for these multi-billion dollar industries of progress? Under the veil of entertainment and envy we are presented with what may seem as impossible challenges to the human condition, yet what has repeatedly taken place is that these remarkable fictions become social, political, and cultural realities.

"Ready or not here we come" are words that are delivered as a warning on the playground, as a threat in sporting arenas, and now through a performance sports brand who is committing to technology and science (factual) fiction to secure its market share and future. Under Armour through its latest "I Will" ad campaign announced that they will deliver the next level of biotech performance enhancement apparel. In a television ad spot that aired during the 2013 NBA All-Star Weekend, Under Armor did something special. This global ad campaign cuts through the media noise by telling anyone who is listening, "Our job is to make you better ...." After a short montage of good old fashioned running, lifting weights, and rep training, they proceed to tell you that "the next great athletic innovation is not available yet ... but it's being built at Under Armour right now." It is fair to assume some company is always working on the next big deal and innovation. Under Armour is making a commitment of integration between the athlete and apparel technology. The interface between the body and its tech is amplified and monitored in order to improve physical performance. As we struggle to balance desire, jealousy, and fear, the ability to augment our body for health, vanity, or performance will remain an innovation platform in sports, popular culture, and medicine.

It isn't only our own bodies that we wish to alter, but those of the unborn. Prenatal care provides a series of tests parents can consent to or opt out of to make *informed* decisions about their unborn child, introducing genetic counseling through a variety of rationalized ways. The reality is many of us rely on technologies for not only punctuated decisions, but also everyday to see, hear, walk, breathe or pump the right amount of blood to our hearts. Cars, phones, and houses talk to us; control lights, air temperature, security; and provide a personal digital assistant. The consensual encroachment of technologies in our lives, some would say, gives way to our already cybernetic experience.

The future portrayed in many SF films, series, and text is here. As a society we are titillated by the in-between of progress and ethics. We are enamored by an improved quality of life, a longer life, and one of minimal effort. We clamor to our smart phones, tablets, or laptops and interact with the ether (or cloud) in numerous urgent ways. "Are we there yet" is becoming "been there, done that." There is no sacred line between human and machine, at least not for the sake of progress. Fekete (2001) reviews Freedman's *Critical Science Fiction* and states:

> Meanwhile, the future, though factually less set than the past, exists for the sake of the present as "a locus of radical *alterity* to the mundane status quo, which is thus estranged and historicized as the concrete past of potential future" (55). Freedman takes this idea from Jameson, for whom it serves in fact as a melancholy reminder of a contemporary waning of historicity and an *inability* to imagine the future and, by extension, the inability to *imagine* utopia ("Progress" 152). Jameson also argues that even the ability to *imagine* the present as history through the imaginary future is no longer available because, he contends, everyday habits of futurology and speculation about future scenarios prefigure the experience of the future and forestall "any global vision of the latter as a radically transformed and different system" (Political 285). (p. 88)

What the present already forecloses in the future or what SF might, requires further contemplation; we don't believe our imagination or innovative inclinations are as fragile as one might be led to believe by both Fekete and Freedman above, but it does warrant some critical analysis. The relationship between past, present, and future is proleptic; no doubt these are related and impact each other. Nonetheless, how these impact or influence the other is the differential pivot. In large respects this pivot is what we hope to dwell in as we discuss transhumanism and the various films.

TRANSHUMANISM AS A MOVEMENT

In the late 1990s two prominent organizations were established to bring scholars, writers, and interested groups together to discuss the legitimacy and necessity of transhumanism to scientific inquiry and policy. In 1998, The World Transhumanism Association (WTA) was launched and a year later they published its manifesto. The WTA was such till 2009 when it changed names to Humanity+ and became a slightly more left-centered organization. Humanity+ (n.d.) defines transhumanism as taking:

> A multidisciplinary approach in analyzing the dynamic interplay between humanity and the acceleration of technology. In this sphere, much of our focus and attention is on the present technologies, such as biotechnology and information technology, and anticipated future technologies, such as molecular nanotechnology and artificial general intelligence. Transhumanism seeks the ethical use of these and other speculative technologies. Our theoretical interests focus on posthuman topics of the singularity, extinction risk, and mind uploading (whole brain emulation and substrate-independent minds).

The WTA casts a wide net of interests and responsibilities in establishing its authority within the discipline. There were other prominent organizations existing parallel to WTA, The Extropy Institute and The Institute of Ethics and Emerging Technologies. We mention these briefly to situate how ethical and theoretical discussions of the existence and potential of technology have been disciplined.

Hefner (2009) illustrates the movement and its discipline through an important distinction, capital letter (T)ranshumanism and lower case (t)ranshumanism. The former regarded in many ways as an ideology which largely focuses on the posthuman and the latter "is a central element of American culture today" (Hefner, 2009, p. 160). Lower case (t)ranshumanism is the movement we feel is of note and much more powerful as the layman movement, the one where popular culture increases the reception of what is and will be possible as humanness and technology intersect as well as merge. The pervasiveness and commonness of our acceptance is what makes it most powerful, we invoke the spirit of SF and transhumanism as we desire a clone of ourselves, more time, do overs, turning to services and gadgets to make our lives *easier* and more *efficient*. We displace our agency, our ability to be present in our own outcomes, so slowly and surely we hand over this influence over the trajectory of our lives, eroding our self-confidence and skill-set. We hope to bring pause and awareness to the ways we've accepted science, fiction, and technology into our everyday.

MASS CULTURE AND NEW MEDIA: THE OPIATE OF DYSTOPIA

SF films have illuminated the possibilities of the future. Some of which are cautionary tales that ask us to reflect on the outcomes of our current behaviors and choices. Cloning, genetic-splicing, social-tracking, surveillance, sustainability, communication, identity, race, class, and mortality are some themes that are presented to the public as tales of promise that hang over us like the Sword of Damocles. We are asked to question our desires and maybe sacrifice our thirst for the new in order to stave off the impending collateral damages of change.

It is said that we are hardwired to reject pain and see it as undesirable. Similarly we chant there is no growth without pain. Growing pains are physical manifestations that help us understand a social and psychological decentering when the conditions of our interactions change. The narratives within SF as a genre illustrate the presumed necessity of growth within a society. If a society must grow intellectually, economically, scientifically, politically, geographically, and creatively then the social pains that accompany the growth should not only be expected, but also accommodated within the same order. SF carefully shows us our failure to consider the painfulness of progress. Through its scenarios and conditions SF provides the virtual space for discussion and preparation in order to better accommodate whatever movement is being made.

This evolution of thinking is often quite difficult to see as a singular object of study. It is like watching the hands of a clock, you know they move, but you find it difficult to witness by simply staring at it with the naked eye. The certainty of time passing allows us to accept the relocation of the hands on the watch, yet once we glance away and look back to find a new orientation we often question what we see (is it really that late? where did time go?). Questioning the validity of time is not a normal practice outside the halls of the academy. To question time in the activities of a regular day places all progress in jeopardy. The uncertainty and contradiction questioning creates holds us in place as if someone pulled the pin on our watch and made our mark of time stand still. If we take the question "does time exist?" and place it in the narrative structures of SF, then the question not only accelerates with possibilities, but also multiplies itself into new concepts of time.

The hands on the face of the clock don't just continue on its fixed flat rotation. They rotate and turn on themselves as sphere. The potential for new axes and locations of logic are set in motion by the narrative illustrations of SF. We are fascinated when these ruptures to our thinking take place. Let's take for example the James Bond, 007, gadget called the rebreather. This SF idea where humans can recycle their breath has been on scientists' minds since the early 1800's. However when moviegoers went to see the 1965 James Bond action blockbuster *Thunderball,* they saw an apparatus called the "rebreather" that inspired new ways of thinking about the size and potential freedoms of breathing underwater without use of an airbag or large tanks of compressed air. This small device in the film had enough SF power to convince the Royal Corps of Engineers to ask the film's production designer how long a man could use the device underwater (Cork, 1995). This instance is important in illustrating how SF is a subgenre of fiction in the macro-sense and how it is located within other ideas and narratives, as in the James

Bond action series. The rebreather is a product of SF because it is born in the logic and rationale of science, yet wedded to the possibilities of fiction. The genre has a distinct richness because of its ability to be truth and abstraction simultaneously, to be here in the moment while also being in another dimension, waiting for someone to prove or disprove its existence (Cork).

This contradiction between certainty and uncertainty is how film narrative is utilized as a rich conduit for philosophical discussions. The object of imagination created by uncertainty is defeated by the representations of certainty working itself out page-by-page and frame-by-frame. As we witness the conditions we previously believed to be the *frozen* uncertainty, the fear and stillness melts away to possibilities and theory. The audience has a safe space to ponder the unthinkable. They are no longer held in place by uncertainty. They are collectively witnessing new forms of being and through the narrative accepting these as real where otherwise these would remain unknown, unjudged, and unvalued. We can only really speculate what society might tolerate, so film constructs a good space for experimentation. SF provides both catalysts and promises for social and cultural change.

Daniel Burrus (2013) says uncertainty simply doesn't give the world any confidence so there is little desire to move on possibilities. Possibilities are realized through cycles and these cycles are how SFs writers and designers are able to present familiar images to us of our future. For your run of the mill SF narrative this appears to be an easy and clear way to gain that security of certainty, but what about those narratives that escape the cycle. What happens when we continue to feel that uneasiness because the narrative does not resemble a familiar history? For example *Star Wars, Tron, E.T., Cocoon, Invasion of the Body Snatchers*, and *Blade Runner*—these films are narratives that at best offer subtle glimpses of a cycle, though not enough to see ourselves reflected in it. We bond with these narratives for an entirely different reason. These SF narratives offer us another structure in which to see the future. Burrus (2011) calls this linear change, one that exhibits simply a better way. Burrus notes once you have a smartphone you will never go back to a dumb one.

Since these films illustrate better ways to understand what it means to live, we then grasp the validity of the images we are given and begin to move on the variables embodied in new future representations. The range of representation, bending of time, tangible degrees of immortality, infinite intelligence available, and disassociation of the body all increase the decentering of *man* which for Frankl (1946) serves the quest for meaning. So do cyborgs and cybernetic beings have unfair advantages to human beings' mortality? Does the augmented human have the desired upper hand physically, materially, spiritually, or cognitively? Does our desire for this *augmented other* way of life obscure raising the necessary ethical inquiries? Where does the homegrown human stop and the augmented digital cyber-being start?

SINGULARITY AND THE DIGITAL SELF

We begin with *The Island* (Bay, et al., 2005) to answer some of these queries. It offers a time and space where surrogates are created and maintained in peak physical health as a resource material for those who can afford the luxury of such services. The audience isn't entirely new to this idea; we currently donate blood and organs for the perpetuation and sustainability of human life, preserve cord blood (often referred to as cord blood banking) for one's newborn if in need later, and lest not forget the spiraling debate around the harvesting and usage of uncoded stem cell material. Director Michael Bay lays out a dual space of entertainment and reflection as we are introduced to Lincoln Six Echo (played by Ewan McGregor).

In a dream, early in the movie, he's informed of his specialness and purpose in life. These introductory lines of dialogue reverberate what families may tell their own children in preparing for life ahead. As the movie unfolds, we recognize the discontent that pervades the sterile environments enveloping characters. Our first hint into the true purpose of these healthy, but unhappy bodies is when Lincoln Six Echo witnesses a child being born to a young woman who has been selected by lottery to go to the island. He does not witness the fate of the just born child, yet sees the mother disposed of immediately after giving birth. His fate becomes clearer as he sees another surrogate wake up during a liver extraction surgery. After a true run for his life that surrogate is apprehended screaming, "I want to live. I don't want to die."

This is all fiction, right? So we are not immediately challenged with the realities of farming ourselves to sustain the original body. These clones are paid for and kept ready for whatever is wished (body parts, pregnancies, and experiments). These cloned surrogates are promised paradise for their compliance, although the island paradise is really their demise. The obscene control of the surrogate world is seen as critical to the preservation of this capital. Yet we are offered the promise of a glitch, of consciousness, of a slither of questioning by characters that resist this status quo. The heroic element of this SF action film is not built within the optimistic futures where we can live and give birth to strong healthy copies of ourselves for as long as we can afford such luxury.

Ironically, we cheer the threat to this dream of immortality. Lincoln Six Echo slips to an antagonist as he breaks the dream/ false consciousness of the island. Why do these characters question what appears utopic? Kincheloe (1999) and Alinsky (1989) are helpful here in understanding the bourgeoning resistance various characters display. Kincheloe notes "... workers with a vision do not passively accept hazardous workplaces ..." (p. 5); therefore, something shifts, is amiss, and ruptures in the highly controlled word of the surrogates. Strong emotions pervade as they recast their experiences. Alinsky (1989) contends:

> To the man of action the first criterion in determining which means to employ is to assess what means are available. Reviewing and selecting available means is done on a straight utilitarian basis—will it work? Moral questions may enter when one chooses among equally effective alternate means. But if one lacks the luxury of a choice and is possessed of only one means, then the

ethical question will never arise; automatically the lone means becomes endowed with a moral spirit. (p. 47)

Hence the one choice Lincoln Six Echo has or the surrogate running for his life becomes a highly personal/moral issue. The self is entwined and wrought through the decentering of the social sphere. Why is knowing his lot in life not enough to create the necessary state of compliance? Why is the reward of fulfilling his purpose not enough for Lincoln Six Echo (after all his name indicates multiple reverberations)? Doesn't he realize that upsetting this system could make it difficult for others? Why does he seem to be the only one with this distrust of the island? Our hero clearly is unable to be complicit because the personal cost has become too high.

In a similar film titled *Logan's Run* (David, 1976), the individual's freedom to *live* and *be* is subject to the social mechanisms and individual capacities; however, in this SF narrative, time is very limited. The goal is not to live forever, rather to live well for a short time. The optimism and worry free lifestyle is shared by most, except for the lead character, once again. Logan Five (played by Michael York), a sandman (officers who apprehend the runners) approaches the carousel, a social spectacle, death march, and assumed rebirth of citizens who have reached the age of thirty. This renewal is called one for one. In a conversation between Logan Five and Francis Seven, Logan openly questions the truth of the carousel, wondering if people who are assimilated into the carousel are actually reborn back into the nursery. Francis Seven, the content worker, answers:

Francis Seven: Well why not?! That's exactly how everything works. How else could the city stay in balance—You have a better idea?

Logan Five: No, but at least I wonder sometimes—instead of doing that 'one for one' song of yours. You sound like a sleepteacher with a stuck tape. (Goodman, 1975, n.p.)

Francis Seven intimates how simple, logical and fair the system is. He's convinced of its naturalness, which ultimately clouds any possibility of interrogation. Logan Five in contrast believes one must question regardless.

The social order in *Logan's Run* (David, 1976), as in many films that deal with mortality or scarcity as a SF theme, is split between a population that is indoctrinated with a truth of a failing outside world and group of awakened individuals who toil between work and survival. The latter group is primarily concerned with existing and can't contemplate their purpose and/or meaning. In *Logan's Run* (David, 1976) the ordered society provides a sanctuary. For the most part its citizens accept that their only way to maintain a healthy operational social system is to purge the aging non-productive burdens. Scarcity is used as a motivating conceptual framework in these films, creating specific guidelines for eugenic/social control practices and utopian aspirations, however these are not foolproof.

As we see in both *Logan's Run* (David, 1976) and *The Island* (Bay et al., 2005) the protagonists question the alleged utopia by deeply observing what they had previously taken for granted. As they begin to recognize what is happening, normativity looks strange and a counter narrative bubbles under the surface: "A social contract is in the collective interest of society as a whole, but individuals or social groups may well turn to criminal behaviour to achieve personal advantage, which erodes wider social benefits" (Turner & Rojek, 2001, p. 91). Their interrogations, resistance, and counter-activity are re-classified as criminal given the affront to this carefully controlled environment. The protagonists are made into rogue agents of the state. This film, in particular, presents a subtle platform to question truth, commerce, knowledge, productivity, control and order.

Logan (like Echo) is transformed into complex heroic figure through his questioning the status quo; the secret order of Sanctuary is the real hero. Sanctuary is supposedly a secret society that helps runners escape carousel. Later in the film, the computer that maintains order in the world asks Logan to find and destroy Sanctuary. What Logan later realizes is that sanctuary is a myth and something far better is true. The world outside of the computer-controlled city is fertile and rich with life. The machine-interposed reality is actually *the* myth and the sanctuary becomes reality, consequently there is a social rebirth for the entire community. Previous this discovery the authority structures confirmed the scarcity of a resource and its followers tended to accept the stated conditions and expectations without verification. Scarcity is based on quantity and if the actual quantity is not accessible we are caught in a cycle of speculation, presupposition, and faith. These cautionary tales of over-relying on technology and its agents too often provide us with a false sense of scarcity and a loss of humanity.

Because there are so few who understand the truths of technology, we find ourselves making significant life decisions about our health, our homes, and our futures in complicity with notions of scarcity. Technology also serves as a tool of scarcity in three more contemporary popular SF films. *Minority Report* (Molen et al., 2002), *Ghost in the Shell* (Mizuo et al., 1995), and *In Time* (Niccol et al., 2011) all utilize the mania of uncertainty to normalize extreme survival behaviors. In Steven Spielberg's *Minority Report* the goal is crime prevention through the use of Pre-Cogs. These are three scientifically created psychics who encompass the "hive mind" connected to a computer to predict crimes before they are executed. The element of scarcity in *Minority Report* (Molen et al., 2002) is humanity, free will, and trust in the non-linear unpredictable future. Here we run into another popular SF theme, fate. This inflexible future often runs opposite of all of the complexities embodied by human existence.

In *Ghost in the Shell* (Mizuo et al., 1995) we are allowed to fantasize about replacement bodies and enhanced cybernetics. Even in *Minority Report* (Molen et al., 2002), Anderton (played by Tom Cruise) must use transplanted eyes in order to access the visions of Agatha, one of the three Pre-Cogs. In *Logan's Run* (David, 1976), *Minority Report* (Molen et al., 2002), and *Ghost in the Shell* (Mizuo et al., 1995), there is an interconnected internet-like hub that no one appears to understand or service; yet everyone relies on it heavily to facilitate decision-making. The interconnected body of *Ghost in the Shell* (Mizuo et al., 1995) stands out because by preserving the brain and using a cybernetic body places fewer restriction in the face of danger. Our heroine, Major Motoko Kusanagi, often speaks of the philosophical nature of her humanity rather than the biological or physical. The Major's self perception is always in question because the criminals and sometimes her team will suggest that her humanity is somehow embodied in her sensual shell. She defies the projections of a sensual body by utilizing her shell strictly as a tool choosing not to get attached to her appearance. Although, this blatant disregard for her statue does nothing but draw more attention to her ultra-feminine physical structure. All of these films challenge us as viewers to feel empathy for the machine engineered-self and the physical form. Watching Anderton in *Minority Report* (Molen et al., 2002) give up his eyes for replacements in order to become undetectable by the machines and achieve his greater goal is a temporary shocking moment in the film; just as in *Ghost in the Shell* (Mizuo et al., 1995) when we witness an assault-tachikoma (robot) destroy Major Motoko Kusanagi's body, we feel the need to take a breath as a momentary pause.

In a slightly different vein, but central to this theme of voluntary scarcity of humanity is *In Time* (Niccol et al., 2011), which has the time limit of *Logan's Run* (David, 1976) and the bioengineering of *Ghost in the Shell* (Mizuo et al., 1995). The value of youth is illustrated by the limit placed on the 25-year lifespan. Given that the people of this version of our future have a limit of twenty-five years to live, the struggle of having to buy, beg, borrow, or steal more time to live becomes universal for all viewers. Will Salas (played by Justin Timberlake), the hero of *In Time* (Niccol et al., 2011), is given a seemly infinite amount of time by a stranger who voluntarily dies following the process of passing time forward to Will. The statement "time is money" becomes clear when you realize how much danger Will is in with his new bank of time. It is also obvious that you are a dead man with too much or too little time in this version of reality. The lack of life as an enforced limit on an uninformed populace and maintaining these constructs with wealth and power is what makes us celebrate the heroes and heroines that are trying to wrestle the control of their existence from the figures of authority.

Popular media has been preoccupied with a commercial-social concept of scarcity since the late 1940s. It appears as a motivational trigger, a mobilizer of sorts for the masses then and now. The anxiety and fear of shrinking resources works as stimulant for a commercially driven economy. Simmel (1900) explains, "Accordingly, we may say immediately that the scarcity of goods in proportion to the desires centering upon them objectively determines exchange; that, however, the exchange on its side brings scarcity into force as an element of value." Francis Seven, from *Logan's Run* (David, 1976), states that the relationship between the carousel and the nursery is logical, indicative of how accustomed they have become to this in their lives and how *natural* this all appears. The reality is these only appear natural to the ones who are benefiting in some way from the constrictions of these shrinking resources, even if the resource is life itself.

The Island (Bay et al., 2005), *Logan's Run* (David, 1976), *Minority Report* (Molen et al., 2002), *Ghost in the Shell* (Mizuo et al., 1995), and *In Time* (Niccol et al., 2011) offer metaphors for complexity, complicity, and awareness through the interface with technology. Are we failing to understand ourselves as already existing products of advanced bioengineering and careful care giving? Are we denying the future in the here and now? Our questions only scratch the surface of what these films might offer for an informed citizenry.

TEACHING TO UNDERSTAND THE SCIENCE IN "SCIENCE FICTION"

What interests us the most from these travels through various films and theories is the impact on pedagogy. Through SF we are afforded the opportunity to pilot a variety of futuristic concepts/ conditions, so we might ask why are we not maximizing this potential foresight about what occurs or is available to us. We also ponder why pedagogical dialogue might not engage the nuances within SF, the continuum of issues in transhumanism and posthumanism, which implicates the moral, ethical, technological, and physical. Often these are glossed over given the pace at which scientific decisions are made seemingly without much deliberation over ethical and cultural implications. In addition science and economy go hand in hand, many times positioning humans as expendable as we investigate the social tolerance of interactions or progress. Wilson (2007) believes if we qualify as humans then no matter the enhancement we will be moral equals. We'd argue that of course history tells us different. Even without scientific *enhancement* our moral worth has been questioned as a result of racism, sexism, classism, and ablebodiedness.

The fear of a transhuman is palpable not only through the various films we discuss, but throughout society. We hold suspect those that have by necessity or choice been scientifically modified. Yet within this range our rationalizations for human value vary tremendously. For example, a couple who may alter the physical composition of their reproductive system to conceive to the very same couple terminating the pregnancy because the unborn has developed some type of malformation or syndrome. Science and currently SF allowed for the conditions for conception and for the access to the type of information that allows for such decision towards termination. We tend to understand a pacemaker, but not a penis enlargement. We accept drinking something to stay awake longer to be more productive, but don't condone taking something to be more athletically competitive. How we determine the worth of a human being is already laden with specific Judeo-Christian values since this permeates the dominant perspective. Wilson (2007) critiques Fukuyama's concerns about the superiority afforded to scientifically enhanced humans and believes our real challenge is around "*justice* between those of equal moral status" (p. 425). Not sure if different groups in society could ever be completely transparent about what they privilege (human vs. augmented human) and where they ascribe power.

More specifically, we would be remiss not to discuss Asimov's (1950) Three Laws of Robotics in relation to our work here. These laws reinforce the hierarchy of human value over robots and positions robots in service of humans. The range of films analyzed above render this hierarchy suspect and so does the numerous examples from popular culture and everyday living. Like any theory, Asimov's has gone through a variety of modifications shifting from regarding robots only as "monstrous" entities to be reigned in to capable human-like beings sharing in our values and in relationship with us. Regardless of the robots' positonality, for Asimov they will always remain robots, second to humans. Given the trajectory of SF, transhumanism, and posthumanism the intersection of identity, technology, and progress provide a wealth of opportunity to carefully deconstruct ethical and pragmatic issues pertaining to our complicity, dependence, and desire on technology.

It will be required of us, more than ever, to be critically aware of our complicity within *progress*, especially when we need it. There are lots of venues/ conduits that may provide a more personal collision course with these issues. We'd emphatically advise to investigate these moments willingly as spaces of ethical conundrums referent to much broader social issues, which we must all wrestle with while we have the opportunity. A brief example is how intrusive 30 second commercials can be in subtly turning SF (like the Under Armour commercial we noted previously) into science fact and how this colludes in using mass media to shape mass culture, our culture, reality, and futures.

Many worry about the capacity now to digitally pursue deviancy and criminal behavior similar to *Minority Report* (Molen et al., 2002), yet this may not be the most worrisome issue in our digital lives, but rather the ways in which digital warfare can exercise far more detrimental physical effects than we have seen or contemplated before. This is where an informed critical SF pedagogy might offer a wide range of perspectives to deliberate and examine our role to SF's role in our lives and its presence in our culture, intellectual capital and well being.

REFERENCES

Alinsky, S. D. (1989). *Rules for the radicals*. New York, NY: Random House.
Asimov, I. (1950). Runaround. *I, Robot*. New York: Gnome Press.
Bay, M., Bates, K., & Parkes, W. F. (Producers), & Bay, M. (Director). (2005). *The island* [Motion Picture]. United States: DreamWorks.
Burrus, D. (2013). *Predicting the future*. Retrieved from
    http://www.youtube.com/watch?v=VV_v5HV9mtI
Burrus, D., & Mann, J. D. (2011). *Flash foresight: How to see the invisible and do the impossible*. New York, NY: Harper Collins Publishers.
Cork, J. (Producer), & Cork, J. (Director). (1995). The making of Thunderball: Thunderball ultimate edition, Region 2, Disc 2 (DVD). MGM/UA Home Entertainment.
David, S. (Producer), & Anderson, M. (Director). (1976). *Logan's Run* [Motion Picture]. United States: Metro-Goldwyn-Mayer.
Fekete, J. (2001). Doing the time warp again: Science fiction as adversarial culture critical theory and science fiction by Carl Freedman, review. *Science Fiction Studies, 28*(1), 77-96.
Frankl, V. (1946). *Man's search for meaning: An introduction to logotherapy*. New York, NY: Simon & Schuster.
Goodman, D. Z. (1975). *Logan's run* (1976) movie script. Retrieved from
    http://sfy.ru/?script=logans_run
Hefner, P. (2009). The animal that aspires to be an angel: The challenge of transhumanism. *Dialog: A Journal of Theology, 48*(2), 158-167.
Humanity+. (n.d.). Retrieved March 2013. http://humanityplus.org/
Kincheloe, J. L. (1999). *How do we tell the workers?: The socioeconomic foundations of work and vocational education*. Boulder, CO: Westview Press.

Mizuo, Y., Matsumoto, K., Iyadomi, K, Ishikawa, M. (Producers), & Oshil, M. (Director). (1995). *Ghost in the shell* [Motion Picture]. Japan: Shochiku.

Molen, G. R., Curtis, B., Parkes, W. F., deBont, J. (Producers). & Spielberg, S. (Director). (2002). *Minority report* [Motion Picture]. United States: 20th Century.

Niccol, A., Abraham, M., Israel, A., Laiblin, K., Newman, E. (Producers), & Niccol, A. (Director). (2011). *In time* [Motion Picture]. United Stats: 20th Century Fox.

Simmel, G. (1900). A chapter in the philosophy of value. *American Journal of Sociology, 5.* Retrieved from http://www.generation-online.org/c/fcvalue2.htm

Turner, B. S., & Rojek, C. (2001). *Society and culture: Principles of scarcity and solidarity.* Thousand Oaks, CA: Sage Publications.

Wilson, J. (2007). Transhumanism and moral equality. *Bioethics, 21*(8), 419-425. doi:10.1111/j.1467-8519.2007.00579.x

ERIN BROWNLEE DELL

7. TROUBLING NOTIONS OF REALITY IN *CAPRICA*

Examining "Paradoxical States" of Being

> To pass beyond the end—into the excess of reality, the excess of positivity, the excess of events, the excess of information—is to enter a paradoxical state, a state which can no longer be content with a rehabilitation of traditional values, and demands a thinking that is itself paradoxical: a thinking that no longer obeys a truth principle, and even accepts the impossibility of verification. (Baudrillard, as cited in Redhead, 2008, p. 146)

Science fiction (SF), particularly in television, has traditionally offered an escape from the confines of our seemingly boring and "normal" existence. Indeed, popular SF television shows, like *Star Trek* and the re-imagined *Battlestar Galactica* series gained cult-like followings from fans eager to tune in to weekly adventures of excitement and suspense involving compelling characters, spaceships and other technological advances. As viewers, we can identify with familiar characters in unfamiliar landscapes; such programs offer an alternative reality of sorts, a vision for the future. However, these visions may also offer reflections of current realities and struggles as exemplified by the Sy Fy network's short-lived series, *Caprica*.

A prequel to his wildly successful re-imagined *Battlestar Galactica* series, writer and creator Ron Moore's *Caprica* offers a historical framework for future *BSG* events, including the creation of the initial Cylons. Set 58 years prior to the beginning of the *Battlestar Galactica* series, the planet of Caprica exists as a society both replete and dependent on advanced technology. The arc of the series focuses on these advances as providing the foundation for alternate realties and identities, where fixed notions of what is real and what is human are disrupted. If we traditionally turn to SF to escape to more utopian worlds, *Caprica* remains eerily familiar: a world struggling with large corporate interests, terrorism, religious extremism and virtual realities. Indeed, *Caprica* complicates the very idea of what is considered real.

Central to this idea is the work of French philosopher and theorist Jean Baudrillard. His idea of a "paradoxical state" troubles conceptions of fixed realities and truths. Such a state of being allows for a simultaneous existence, one able to disrupt traditional boundaries between realities, virtual or otherwise. For Baudrillard (as cited in Lane, 2009), signs and symbols both simulate and permeate perceived realities, ultimately moving towards the "hyperreal" (p. 30). Simulation allows for multiple representations of reality so that any distinction is ultimately blurred and any one "true" reality questioned. This postmodern stance complicates perceptions of what is real, welcoming the chaos of uncertainty.

P. Thomas (ed.), Science Fiction and Speculative Fiction, 133–144.

ERIN BROWNLEE DELL

This "paradoxical state" of being frames much of *Caprica* and what follows in this chapter is a close examination of Baudrillard's concept of three levels or orders of simulation: an artificial representation of what is considered real, blurred boundaries between reality and representation and ultimately, the "hyperreal," a new reality based on its own symbols (as cited in Lane, 2009, p. 30). A close examination of *Caprica* through this Baudrillardian framework of simulation and, ultimately, the hyperreal, reveals identities, technologies and reality itself in flux, allowing a re-examination and re-imagination of what we consider "real," indeed problematizing notions of self and our existence both in the series itself and reflected in SF television.

HOLOBANDS, MEDIA AND CYLONS

The immense majority of present day photographic, cinematic and television images are thought to bear witness to the world with a naïve resemblance and a touching fidelity. We have spontaneous confidence in their realism. We are wrong. They only seem to resemble things, to resemble reality, events, faces. Or rather, they really do conform, but their conformity itself is diabolical. (Baudrillard, as cited in Redhead, 2008, p. 85)

Baudrillard's first order of simulation focuses on the artificial representation of what is considered real. For Daniel Graystone, *Caprica's* central protagonist, marketing a simulation of reality exists at the heart of his business empire, Graystone Industries. A leader in technology research and development, Graystone is recognized as a computer genius and inventor of both the holoband[i] and ultimately the robots known as Cybernetic Life-Form Node (Cylons). Holoband technology allows for participation in a virtual reality, one allowing the creation of and interaction with an alternate environment. While the wide-use of holobands is not immediately obvious, it is understood they are as present in Caprican culture as the iPod in contemporary America. Interaction with this technology allows for an escape to another space, following Baudrillard's observation that "[t]he aim of simulation is not to do away with reality, but on the contrary to realize it, make it real" (as cited in Butler, 1999, p. 23).

This notion of "doing away with reality" informs much of the interaction with this virtual or "V-world." Holobands offer new ways of seeing, both literally and figuratively, allowing for alternate spaces of existence. While these virtual worlds are modified copies of Caprican life, they represent an artificial reality, one where identities and experiences may be explored free from the confines of the real world. As Giroux and Simon (1989) observe, these are spaces where individuals may "...test the ways we produce meaning and represent ourselves, our relations to others and our relationship to our environment" (p. 244). This idea of meaning-making is particularly salient to Caprica's young adults. Holoband users are able to represent themselves in avatar form, a simulation of their bodies and thoughts. V-world allows them an alternative place to interact and experiment with their re-imagined identities.

Indeed, it is the alternate reality of their creation that offers this space, a place to collectively imagine and "... create [an] underground because now there's no more underground, no more avant-garde, no more marginality" (Baudrillard as cited in Redhead, 2008, p. 1). By creating and interacting with V-world, individuals as avatars are free to engage in behaviors perhaps not sanctioned by the social mores outside of this space. For example, the V-club is featured throughout the series as a space providing opportunities to experiment with alcohol, drugs and sex while at the same time serving as a central meeting place for characters. The sense of liberation here is dependent upon the simulation of reality. Baudrillard writes, "there is a kind of primal pleasure, of anthropological joy in images, a kind of brute fascination unencumbered by aesthetic, moral, social or political judgments" (as cited in Redhead, 2008, p. 94). V-world is a simulation, one that mirrors reality through images and symbols, encouraging an increased sense of abandon.

Similarly, this idea of "primal pleasure" offers a commentary on the genre of SF television itself. We are drawn in by the endless seduction of fascinating images and possibilities offered in these programs, though many elements of *Caprica* reflect our realities. Baudrillard (1991) writes that SF has traditionally offered a simulation, an alternative universe to examine; however, this simulation is no longer a reflection and "we can no longer move 'through the mirror to the other side" (p. 5). While images and symbols permeate V-world, a similar sense of simulation frames Caprica's real world through the media.

Serving as a meta-narrative of sorts, the influence of the media on Caprica, specifically television, is palpable. Clips of news stories and choice soundbytes maintain the tone and pace of the series, both informing and shaping viewers' perceptions of reality. Within the first episodes of *Caprica*, a terrorist bomb explodes on a crowded subway train, killing dozens of people. Although this tragedy serves as a catalyst for future events, it also becomes the center of a media frenzy. Daniel Graystone is forced to defend his reputation, not only because his daughter Zoe is the suspected terrorist, but also because the holoband (his creation) is considered dangerous, a bad influence on his daughter's impressionable mind. Graystone battles his public image, altered by television clips designed for ratings. For Baudrillard, such a practice of "cutting up events of the world into discontinuous successive and noncontradictory messages, into signs which can be juxtaposed and combined with other signs in the abstract realm of broadcasting..." represents a practice designed to influence perceptions of reality, ultimately observing, "What we consume then, is not a particular spectacle or image as such; it is the potential succession of all possible spectacles ..." (as cited in Redhead, 2009, p. 24).

These "possible spectacles" define the real world of Caprica, just as virtual images shape V-world. While the media do purport to reflect *truth* of events, the world created by slick images is not unlike the world created by holoband users. The constant montage of televised images reinforces the thought that "television is never critical of the hierarchy perpetuated by its own form or of the power rooted in its dynamic of vicarious (or virtual) participation" (Nichols, 2009, p. 569). The media, and more specifically, television influence the reality of Caprican life.

Indeed, media become the curricula of Caprica, one defining and setting expectations of a culture, becoming the "pedagogical machines," (Sholle, 1995, p. 145) the spaces of both creation and discovery.

Ironically, this is why we watch SF, to experience the "possible spectacles" and participate virtually in alternate worlds. Within *Caprica*, media, specifically televised media, craft an alternate reality, one not dissimilar to our own news and television programs. The idea of reflecting or reporting reality becomes complicated, particularly when "reality" television shows dominate ratings. SF television programs reflect this simulated reality for viewers as well, blurring the boundaries between what is considered real and what is fiction. According to Baudrillard, "there is no real and no imaginary except at a certain distance" (1991, p. 2). As television viewers, we are assimilated into the realities and simulations offered by writers and producers, infiltrating our world, creating a "collective marketplace not only for products but also for values, signs and models, thereby leaving no room any more for the imaginary" (Baudrillard, 1991, p. 3).

Although the holobands and the media offer constructed realities within Caprican society, it is the creation of the Cylon that offers the most significant example of Baudrillard's first order of simulation. Originally conceived as a futuristic soldier for the defense department, its creation troubles notions of existence. Visually, the prototype most resembles a machine, a giant robot. However, Graystone works tirelessly to infuse his creation with human instincts, to make it "more than a machine" ("There is Another Sky," 1.5). The Cylon's very existence is "a metaphor for the social as a process of boundary-drawing, of constructing subjects out of available material-semiotic resources ..." (Chouliaraki & Fairclough, 1999, p. 91). Although the Cylon prototype does simulate many actions of humans, as well as retain certain broad human physical traits (bipedal, head, hands, eyes), it troubles notions of existence, indeed what is considered alive. Daniel Graystone wants to define the boundary between human and Cylon, remarking, "Beyond artificial intelligence, this is artificial sentience .... This Cylon will become a tireless worker who won't need to be paid. It won't retire, or get sick. It won't have rights or objections or complaints. It will do anything and everything we ask of it, without question. We make them. We own them. They're real" ("There is Another Sky," 1.5).

Such a proclamation reveals Graystone's reliance on strict boundaries between real and virtual worlds. However, the creation of an artificial "other" disrupts fixed ideas of identity and existence. Indeed, "we gaze upon what we have created, and see something almost like ourselves, but not quite, gazing back at us" (Grumpert, 2008, p. 148). It is in this space of "not quite" where the boundaries between the real world and the virtual become blurred. The Cylons are similar to humans, but designed to engage in actions deemed harmful for us. This relationship between human and machine is further blurred upon Graystone's discovery of his daughter's avatar. Believing this avatar to be a representation of Zoe, he refuses to acknowledge her possible existence saying, "I don't know you. You're just a thing. You're an avatar, a virtual representation of Zoe" ("Pilot, Part 1," 1.1).

However, this positivist frame shatters upon realizing that Zoe's virtual avatar and the real Cylon could come together, reflecting Hinchey's (1999) observation, "post-formalist thinkers...have begun identifying borderless realms of shadowy territory where positivists assumed natural, sacrosanct boundaries" (p. 128). This synthesis of chrome and avatar signals a shift towards identities, even bodies in flux. Cylons and avatars were seemingly just representations or projections of "real" individuals, left to exist separately as Baudrillard states "... it is the very identically of the robot to the human which means there is no longer any relationship between the two" (as cited in Butler, 2009, p. 38). However, the discovery of these "borderless realms" forces a relationship between the virtual and real worlds, between representations of reality.

AVATARS AND BORDER CROSSINGS

This is a world in which one is condemned to wander across, within, and between multiple borders and spaces marked by excess otherness, difference and a dislocating notion of meaning and attention. (Giroux, 2000, p. 180)

I'm sort of her.

I am her.

I'm Zoe Graystone.

I'm not a person, but I feel like one.

—Zoe Graystone's avatar ("Pilot Part 1," 1.1)

Whereas Baudrillard's first order of simulation focuses on artificial representations of reality, the second order examines the blurring between reality and simulation. Perhaps nowhere is this more evident in Caprica than in the virtual or V-world, accessible by the holobands. Virtual worlds question elements of the real world offering spaces of both destruction and discovery. This idea of virtual reality offers freedom to interact as an avatar, a simulation of self, allowing individuals to "... leave behind our present world and migrate for the better domain. It is as if we could simply transcend the frustrating and disappointing imperfection of the here and now" (Robins, 2009, p. 797). SF offers this simulation, a copy of our world, but with better gadgets and technology. We watch SF for the possibilities, to see a glimpse of an imagined future. We want to escape the "disappointing imperfection" of our "real" worlds. For the characters on *Caprica*, V-world offers an escape. While V-world is initially portrayed as a distinct copy of reality, it becomes much more than a representation; it becomes the space of possibility, resistance and ultimately, rebellion.

Central to these possibilities is the avatar, as holoband-wearers explore V-world as copies of themselves. We only see the biological Zoe Graystone in the first episode of the series. Prior to her death in a terrorist bombing, she creates a separate avatar, a copy of herself. This creation is an amalgam of representations of her "real" identity. As Strayer (2010) observes, she is "... an assemblage of cannibalized records and nonhuman data…she is created from the detritus of everyday life" (p. 6). Initially, the Zoe-avatar appears only in V-world and her existence seems static. However, she possesses an awareness of self seemingly unthinkable for an illusion. Upon Zoe's death, the avatar appears in V-world, covered in blood, saying "So I'm dead? She's dead. I felt it. I felt her death" ("Pilot Part 1," 1.1). This feeling disrupts simple notions of what is real, bending the idea of existence itself. It is this fluidity of identity that mirrors Baudrillard's (1995) second order of simulation and reveals

> our consciousness is never the echo of our own reality, of existence set in 'real time.' But rather it is its echo in 'delayed time,' the screen of the dispersion of the subject and of its identity—only in our sleep, our unconscious, and our death are we identical to ourselves. (para. 2)

The Zoe-avatar exists without her anchor in the "delayed time" that is V-world. She has feelings and independent thoughts, an active participant in her reality.

Her existence continues to blur the boundaries between real and virtual when her father downloads the avatar program into the Cylon prototype. He explains to the Zoe-avatar that this robotic form is "just a temporary place" and that he will "find a way to make … a more human body" ("Ghosts in the Machine," 1.8). Such an act would name "… a reality that exists while at the same time negating (or even denying) other realities, but the fact that the participants (and creators) are self-conscious of its artificiality opens numerous possibilities for paradoxes" (Boskovic, 1997). Indeed, it is the fusion of the avatar and the Cylon chassis that creates such paradoxes. Zoe is at once real and virtual, realizing that "true hybridity is a fantasy of wholeness retrieved: the return to an Edenic world where there are not distinct identities at war with each other, but only undivided of Identity itself" (Grumpert, 2008, p. 151). Who we are and who we can become changes and offers possibility for the re-imagination of self. She exists in the real world through the Cylon body, but the essence of her identity is apart from this.

This re-imagination of identity challenges our notion of humanity in *Caprica*. The visual representation on screen of Zoe challenges our notions of personhood as the avatar-Cylon hybrid is portrayed on screen as both Zoe and then the Cylon, troubling the viewer's perception, knowing that

> … our eyes, too, are liminally enframed by the TV screen. Our eyes perhaps cynically, but certainly critically, are opened to the contrivance of image-making and of entitlement to what we see. (McNeilly, 2008, p. 188)

The images of Zoe in both human and Cylon form blur perceptions of what exists. While the human Zoe Graystone is dead, she continues to exist across realities with multiple identities: "It is so confusing. I am Zoe and the avatar and the robot" ("There is Another Sky," 1.5). Who she is cannot be strictly defined. In the Cylon's body, Zoe can interact with her father, dance with the lab tech and even drive a car. As Baudrillard observes, "It is in *form* that everything has changed: everywhere there is, in lieu and in place of the real, its substitution by a 'neo-real' entirely produced from a combination of coded elements (as cited in Redhead, 2009, p. 30).

Indeed, Zoe pioneers this frontier of the "neo-real," moving between V-world and the outside. This idea of "neo-real" resonates with the sub-cultures created from SF television. Viewers participate in the simulation not only by watching each week, but also by simulating what they see. Indeed, many SF television programs enjoy cult-like followings, with cultures of simulation. Comic Con, fan conventions and communities are built around this idea of crossing borders, between the real and simulated.

Another example of Baudrillard's notion of the "neo-real" is the creation of a separate avatar, Tamara Adama. Daniel Graystone befriends Tamara's father, Joseph, upon learning they have both lost children in the terrorist bombing. Graystone creates an avatar of Tamara and offers her father an opportunity to cross the boundary between real and virtual and reunite with his daughter, asking him "What if they could come back?" ("Pilot, Part 2," 1.1). Although skeptical, Joseph is initially thrilled to see and hold his daughter within this virtual space. However the avatar realizes her existence is troubling, saying, "I feel so strange. This is wrong. This isn't real. I don't feel real. My heart isn't beating" ("Pilot Part 2," 1.1). Tamara exists as a simulation of her former self, supporting Baudrillard's observation that "… images precede the real to the extent that they invert the casual and logical order of the real and its reproduction" (as cited in Redhead, 2009, p. 84). She is a representation, a simulation trapped within the confines of V-world.

While Zoe Graystone traverses the virtual and real world borders, Tamara is limited to a virtual existence. Upon discovering that she is unable to wake up and return to the "real" world, Tamara begins to explore and ultimately dominate New Cap City, a game within V-world. Within this game, if anyone gets killed, they de-resonate and are unable to return to "real" life. The irony of this space for Tamara is that while dead in the outside world, she is immortal on the inside. Her status as a "deathwalker" proves powerful, almost liberating. Indeed, "… breaking away from physical reality is understood as a kind of liberation—a liberation both of objects themselves and of the humans who use them" (Baudrillard, as cited in Butler, 1999, p. 31). While Tamara accepts her identity in the virtual space, it is her father who becomes obsessed with finding her, saying, "Tamara exists. I know she exists" ("Ghosts in the Machine," 1.8). Joseph spends more and more time with the holoband, searching for Tamara in New Cap City. This fluidity of movement between worlds allows an escape for Joseph; he is able to avoid the reality of loss by knowing "the technological realm offers precisely a form of psychic protection against the defeating stimulus of reality" (Robins, 2009, p. 802). Again, this is why we watch SF, to immerse ourselves in an alternate reality, a more improved version of a mundane existence.

Although both Tamara and Zoe are dead in the real world of Caprica, their existence within V-world disrupts constructed notions of reality. Zoe moves from one reality to the next, while Tamara comes to terms with her existence in V-world. In a flashback to the creation of her avatar, Zoe reminds her creation that, "A person with restricted movement is still a person" ("Things We Lock Away," 1.12). What, if anything determines existence? Perhaps we are, as Kincheloe and

Steinberg (1999) write, "... never independent of the social and historical forces that surround us—we are caught at a particular point in the web of reality" (p. 62). These surrounding forces blur the distinction between what is real or otherwise.

Ultimately, it is the continual border crossing between these worlds that begins to create Baudrillard's notion of the "hyperreal." For example, when Zoe encounters Tamara in V-world, they recognize each other, "I'm a copy, just like you" ("Things we Lock Away," 1.12). Tamara shows Zoe a copy of a newspaper containing not only the news of her death, but also the indictment of Zoe as the terrorist responsible for the bombing. Tamara offers the opportunity for individuals to fight Zoe in a gladiator-style match, to seek revenge for relatives and loved ones killed in the bombing. Though these avengers are avatars with "real" bodies on the outside, they succumb to the image of Zoe, following Baudrillard's observation that "Simulation attempts to resemble the real, to 'realize' it, to bring out what is only implicit in it and make it explicit" (as cited in Butler, 1999, p. 25). This distinction becomes explicit for viewers as well as we traverse these boundaries between "real" life and a televised fantasy.

HYPERREALITY

The real ... no longer has to be rational, since it is no longer measured against some ideal or negative instance. It is nothing more than operational. In fact, since it is no longer enveloped by an imaginary, it is no longer real at all. It is a hyperreal: the product of an irradiating synthesis of combinatory models in a hyperspace without atmosphere. (Baudrillard, as cited in Poster, 2001, p. 170)

A difference that makes no difference is no difference
—Daniel Graystone (Pilot Part 2, 1.1)

Baudrillard's third order of simulation moves from the blurring between the real and simulation to a world based solely on representation, a new reality. The simulated images (avatars) and artificial life forms (Cylons) form this newly created space. Indeed, technology's influence frames these images because "[f]or Baudrillard, this transference of power from the real to the hyperreal presents the fulfillment of the modern drive to master the world" (Nunes, 1995, p. 314). Daniel Graystone represents this drive as he attempts to market simulation, or hyperreality. Initially, the fusion of Zoe's avatar and the Cylon existed as a self-serving experiment, a way to be with his daughter again. However, he begins to see V-world as a space of transition, from image to a new reality.

In many ways, the representations in V-world have become this hyperreality. Zoe and Tamara decide to join forces and combat players in New Cap City. T-shirts and signs with images of them as Avenging Angels appear throughout the "real" world of Caprica. Zoe proclaims to Tamara, "We're Gods in here. We can build a place where no one will be able to touch us" and proceeds to create a new world within the virtual world ("Dirteaters," 1.15). At the same time, Daniel Graystone views his connections with V-world as attempts to perfect resurrection in the form of an avatar, a way to cheat death and then sell it. In a commercial spot for his company, he claims, "Imagine never having to say goodbye to loved ones again. Imagine a future without loss" ("False Labor," 1.13). In fact, Graystone sees the simulation as being very real, commenting, "Do you know what your brain is? It's a database and a processor. That's all. Information and a way to use it." ("Pilot, Part 2," 1.1). The simulation is the reality. Indeed, as Baudrillard (1991) writes, we "reinvent the real as fiction, precisely because the real has disappeared from our lives" (p. 4).

This exploration of identity ruptures any modernist notion of how we exist and who we are. Indeed, as Giroux (2000) writes, "Values no longer emerge from the modernist pedagogy of foundationalism and universal truths, nor from traditional narratives based on fixed identities and with their requisite structure of closure" (p. 181). Any notion of truth becomes troubled in this hyperreal state. For Zoe's parents, "...the system of simulation never actually collapses or comes to an end. For, if its increased perfection takes the system further away from the real, it also means that it is more real than ever" (Baudrillard as cited in Butler, 1999, p. 47). Their daughter exists for them. As Daniel Graystone says, "I know she is my daughter and I know the only place that matters, here (points to heart). The only difference between her and the Zoe that lived in this house is just that: she lived in this house rather than a virtual world" ("Pilot Part 2," 1.1).

Accepting this state of hyperreality, Amanda and Daniel Graystone search for Zoe in V-world. While they believed they mastered the technology to find her, they are drawn into, "... an endless enwrapping of images ... which leaves images no other destiny than images" (Baudrillard, as cited in Redhead, 1999, p. 95). Ultimately encountering Zoe's avatar, Amanda Graystone, Zoe's mother, confronts Zoe, asking her to come home. Zoe's avatar responds, "You don't want me, you want her. To you, I'm just spare parts" ("Here Be Dragons," 1.17). However, Amanda presses the avatar, asking if she remembers her, telling her, "Look at me Zoe, right here, right now and tell me you don't remember me" ("Here Be Dragons," 1.17). When the Zoe-avatar acknowledges memories, Amanda asks her how she feels, focusing on Zoe as her daughter, not a representation. Zoe's avatar represents, "... the new anthropomorphic technologies ... concerned with autonomous consciousness, abstracted power and identity" (Lane, 2009, p. 31). This creation possesses a distinct identity and feels emotions; although initially perceived as a technological construct, this Zoe is a product of hyperreality.

Indeed, the simulated becomes the real, mirroring Baudrillard's (1995) observation that "reality today is nothing more than the apocalypse of simulation." Existence is without strictly defined boundaries as Amanda and Daniel Graystone continue to interact with Zoe. Immediately following their encounter with Zoe, religious terrorists attack them. In this state of hyperreality, the model Cylon comes to life and saves her parents from certain death. The Cylon is Zoe, Zoe is the Cylon and the avatar, traversing the certainty of pre-defined borders and existing simultaneously, supporting Kincheloe's (1999) observation that "... the mind does exist beyond the skin" (p. 30). Offering Zoe an opportunity to interact between worlds, Daniel Graystone provides an exact replica of their home with a "real-time clone" of his entire computer network so they can "work in tandem, sharing data as we go" ("Here be Dragons," 1.17). Zoe's parents work on giving her a body, one with skin, allowing her to appear on Caprica, foreshadowing the proliferation of *Battlestar Galactica's* resurrection technology. Having lost their daughter once to death, they connect to the very real feelings of love and emotion. Amanda Graystone can hold her daughter again, talk with her. Therefore, "All that we believed over and done, left behind by the inexorable march of universal progress, is not dead at all; it seems to be returning to strike at the heart of our ultra-sophisticated ultravulnerable systems" (Baudrillard, as cited in Redhead, 2008, p. 157). The image or simulation disrupts modernist notions of reality and allows us to re-imagine existence.

As the series ends, the Cylons integrate into society. They are sentient beings and essential to everyday Caprican life. These new life forms are accepted in this hyperreality, whereas they were once distinctly different. In the final episode, *Apotheosis,* Daniel Graystone attempts to re-define Cylons under Baudrillard's first order of simulation by claiming, "Cylons are simply tools—nothing more. To forget that and blur the distinction between man and machine and attribute human traits is folly" ("Apotheosis," 1.18). Ironically, at the same time, both Daniel and Amada Graystone work to create a human body for Zoe's avatar. Perhaps Daniel cannot accept the sentience of his creation, understanding that "[s]imulation is infinitely more dangerous since it always suggests, over and above its object, that law and order themselves might really be nothing more than a simulation" (Baudrillard, as cited in Poster, 2001, p. 180). He works to re-draw the boundaries he disrupted. However, the hyperreal now frames Caprican society, and we are left with an image of Cylons in a house of worship listening to a liberation theology laced sermon defining their very existence:

> Are you alive? You are alive because you can ask that question. In the real world, you have bodies made of metal and plastic. Your brains are encoded on wafers of silicon. There is no limit on what you may become. No longer servants, but equals. ("Apotheosis," 1.18)

Indeed, with the final image of Zoe being "born" into in an eerily familiar resurrection tub and human form, there is no distinction between the real and the simulation; instead an infinite cycle of simulations, where "… nothing really comes to an end anymore, that is to say, when nothing ever really takes place, since everything is already calculated, audited, and realized in advance" (Baudrillard, in Redhead, 1999, pp. 156-157).

Examining *Caprica* through a Baudrillardian lens reveals a disruption of what is considered real. His concept of the three orders of simulation problematizes notions of existence and fixed boundaries, allowing for an alternative state, a re-imagined world. *Caprica* ultimately ends in a state of the hyperreal, dominated by representation and simulation. Avatar, Cylons and humans become border-crossers, altering our view of what is possible or real. Of course *Caprica* is fiction, but reflects much of our current reality. Offering us a glimpse of an unfamiliar worlds, but strangely familiar realities, SF television reflects Baudrillard's (1991) observation that "it is no longer possible to manufacture the unreal from the real, to create the imaginary from the data of reality" (p. 4). We exist in hyperreality.

The endless cycle of simulation troubles reality's construct and leaves us in Baudrillard's "paradoxical state," questioning our own perceptions of identity and self. Such a state is not without consequence:

> … we are going to have to pay the price for this artificial creation, and settle this new debt towards ourselves. How are we to be absolved of this technical world and this artificial omnipotence if not be destruction, which is the only possible decompensation for this new situation—the only future event which will leave us with nothing to answer for? (Baudrillard, as cited in Redhead, 1999, p. 142)

Indeed, Baudrillard's words seem to foreshadow future events and the consequences to Caprican society. Simulation is reality in *Caprica*, signifying the rupture of so-called societal truths of existence. Ultimately, Capricans, like us, must accept their existence as one replete with never-ending paradoxes, as "all of this has happened before and all of this will happen again" ("The Imperfections of Memory," 1.7).

NOTES

[i] Worn like a visor or glasses, the holoband interacts with the user to allow for full interaction with virtual reality.

REFERENCES

Baudrillard, J. (1991). Two essays. *Science Fiction Studies, 18*(55), 1-19.

Baudrillard, J. (1995, April 19). Radical thought. *Ctheory.net*. Retrieved from ctheory.net/articles.aspx?id=67

Baudrillard, J. (2001). Simulacra and simulations. In M. Poster (Ed.), *Baudrillard, selected writings* (pp. 169-187). Stanford: Stanford University Press.

Boskovic, A. (1997, October 29). Virtual places: Imagined boundaries and hyperreality in southeastern Europe. *Ctheory.net*. Retrieved from ctheory.net/articles.aspx?id=97.

Butler, R. (1999). *Jean Baudrillard: The defence of the real*. London: Sage Publications.

Chouliaraki, L. & Fairclough, N. (1999). *Discourse in late modernity*. Edinburgh: Edinburgh University Press.

Giroux, H. (2000). Postmodern education and disposable youth. In P. Trifonas (Ed.), *Revolutionary pedagogies: Cultural politics, instituting education, and the discourse of theory* (pp. 174-195). New York: Routledge Falmer.

Giroux, H., & Simon, R. (1989). Popular culture and critical pedagogy: Everyday life as a basis for curriculum knowledge. In H. Giroux & P. McLaren (Eds.), *Critical pedagogy, the state and cultural struggle* (pp. 236-257). Albany: State University of New York Press.

Gumpert, M. (2008). Hybridity's end. In T. Potter & C. W. Marshall (Eds.), *Cylons in America. Critical studies in Battlestar Galactica* (pp. 143-155). New York: Continuum.

Hinchey, P. (1999). Educational psychology's pound of flesh. In J. Kincheloe, S. Steinberg, & P. Hinchey (Eds.), *The post formal reader* (pp. 128-145). New York: Falmer Press.

Kincheloe, J. (1999). Trouble ahead, trouble behind: grounding the post-formal critique of educational psychology. In J. Kincheloe, S. Steinberg, & P. Hinchey (Eds.), *The post formal reader* (pp. 4-54). New York: Falmer Press.

Kincheloe, J., & Steinberg, S. (1999). A tentative description of post-formal thinking: the critical confrontation with cognitive theory. In J. Kincheloe, S. Steinberg, & P. Hinchey (Eds.), *The post formal reader* (pp. 55-90). New York: Falmer Press.

Lane, R. (2009). *Jean Baudrillard. Routledge critical thinkers*. London: Routledge.

McNeilly, K. (2008). "This might be hard for you to watch": Salvage humanity in "Final Cut." In T. Potter & C. W. Marshall (Eds.), *Cylons in America. critical studies in Battlestar Galactica* (pp. 185-197). New York: Continuum.

Nichols, B. (2009). Reality tv and social perversion. In S. Thornham, C. Bassett, & P. Marns (Eds.), *Media studies: A reader* (3rd edition) (pp. 393-403) New York: New York University Press.

Nunes, M. (1995). Baudrillard in cyberspace: Internet, virtuality, and postmodernity. *Style, 29*, 314-327.

Redhead, S. (2008). *The Jean Baudrillard reader*. New York: Columbia University Press.

Robins, K. (2009). Cyberspace and the world we live in. In S. Thornham, C. Bassett, & P. Marns (Eds.), *Media studies: A reader* (3rd edition) (pp. 796-811). New York, NY: New York University Press.

Sholle, D. (1995). Buy our news: The melding of news, entertainment and advertising in the totalized selling environment of the postmodern market. In P. McLaren, R. Hammer, D. Sholle, & S. Reilly (Eds.), *Re-thinking media literacy* (pp. 145-169). New York: Peter Lang.

Strayer, K. (2010). Reinventing the inhuman: Avatars, cylons and homo sapiens in contemporary science fiction television series. *Literature Film Quarterly, 38*(3), 194-204.

Caprica episodes referenced (in chronological order):

Pilot (Parts 1 and 2) , 1.0
There is Another Sky, 1.5
The Imperfections of Memory, 1.7
Ghosts in the Machine, 1.8
Things we Lock Away, 1. 12
False Labor, 1.13
The Dirteaters, 1.15
Here Be Dragons, 1.17
Apotheosis, 1.18

SEAN P. CONNORS

8. "I TRY TO REMEMBER WHO I AM AND
WHO I AM NOT"

The Subjugation of Nature and Women Represented in The Hunger Games

Several assumptions surround popular discourse about Suzanne Collins's
commercially successful Hunger Games series, including one that regards Katniss
Everdeen, its protagonist, as offering young female readers access to a newly
empowered subject position. In "Brave, Determined, and Strong: Books for Girls
(and Sometimes Boys)," Ward and Young (2009) state:

> When choosing a book for a girl, merely reaching for any old book with
> female characters isn't enough. Care should be taken to find books that
> feature strong female literary role models, allowing girls to explore their own
> identities, claim their own voices, and gain confidence, particularly during
> the adolescent years. (p. 257)

The authors identify *The Hunger Games,* the first novel in Collins's (2008) series,
as a literary text that educators can utilize to help female readers toward these ends.
In these terms, Collins is understood to present readers with a self-actualized
female character that breaks down gender inequalities.

Gonick (2006) identifies two competing discourses that offer opposing views on
femininity: what she calls "Reviving Ophelia," which portrays "girls as vulnerable,
voiceless, and fragile," and "Girl Power," which "represents a 'new girl': assertive,
dynamic, and unbound from the constraints of passive femininity" (p. 2). At first
glance, Collins's (2008) novel appears firmly ensconced in the latter category.
Katniss is athletic, adventurous, skilled with weapons and brave, characteristics
that are often drawn as masculine in popular culture texts. Moreover, she performs
tasks that are associated with men, and, in doing so, she subverts—sometimes
overtly, sometimes implicitly—traditional female gender roles. Following her
father's death, Katniss provides for her family by hunting, and throughout much of
the first novel she laments her inability to tend to the sick with the same degree of
care and aptitude her mother and younger sister exhibit. Seen in this light, Collins
(2008) does appear to open a greater number of subject positions to young women
by portraying a strong female protagonist. At the same time, however, this reading
overlooks the seemingly important fact that, at least in the first novel, Katniss *does*
struggle to define herself in the face of patriarchal institutions that *do*, in fact,
change her, even if only subtly. To survive in a society that is engineered by men
to benefit men, Collins (2008) demonstrates that even a strong female like Katniss
is forced to construct an alternative identity that enables her to create the

P. Thomas (ed.), Science Fiction and Speculative Fiction, 145–164.

impression of having conformed to gender expectations that her society imposes on her. In this sense, she assumes a sort of double consciousness.

In *The Dystopian Impulse in Modern Literature,* Booker (1994) argues, "The modern turn to dystopian fiction is largely attributable to perceived inadequacies in existing social and political systems" (p. 20). A critical examination of *The Hunger Games* reveals that, by engaging in the kind of social criticism that Booker (1994) suggests is characteristic of dystopian fiction, Collins (2008) accomplishes something considerably more complex in her novel, and potentially even subversive, than is commonly assumed. Specifically, she demonstrates how the same oppressive patriarchal conceptual framework that motivates governments and corporations to exploit nature and degrade the environment, both symbols of the feminine, leads them to enact policies that subjugate and exploit disenfranchised groups, including women, minorities, and people in poverty. In this way, *The Hunger Games* shares an assumption that is characteristic of ecofeminist philosophy—namely, that "the specifics that both environmentalism and feminism separately oppose stems from the same sources: the patriarchal construction of modern Western civilization" (Murphy, 1995, p. 48).

Critics occasionally deride speculative fiction—an umbrella term used to refer to a range of genres, including science fiction (SF), fantasy, utopian and dystopian fiction— as *genre fiction* with the result being that they dismiss it as a form of superficial entertainment. The cultural expectations that have historically accompanied young adult literature—namely, that it must perform a didactic function—coupled with its status as a commodity, subject it to additional stigmas and mischaracterizations. Indeed, as Daniels (2006) argues, there remain critics in both secondary and higher education who insist that young adult literature does not warrant serious "attention because it doesn't offer enough substance to be included within the traditional literary canon" (p. 78). One might assume, then, that young adult dystopian fiction represents the low-person on the literary totem pole.

In this chapter, I advocate reading speculative fiction for adolescents—specifically, young adult dystopian fiction—from the standpoint of critical theory to make visible the genre's potential complexity and to foreground the important political work it is capable of performing. To do so, I examine *The Hunger Games,* the first novel in Collins's (2008) series, from the perspective of ecofeminist philosophy to demonstrate how, in the fictional world that Collins constructs, the patriarchal mindset of the Capitol leads it to treat marginalized groups of people, specifically females, as fodder to be remade and consumed by the powerful.

This reading is evident in Collins's (2008) portrayal of Katniss, a teenage girl who, from the moment she volunteers to participate in the Hunger Games, a state-sponsored spectacle akin to reality television in which children of the poor murder one another for the entertainment of the elite, embarks on a journey that leads her to travel through a world dominated by powerful males. Ensnared in that world's ideology, Katniss struggles to demonstrate to those in power, and also to herself, that they don't control her in the same way that they do the material resources they extract from her community in District 12. At the same time, she discovers that her ability to survive in the Capitol, and later in the Hunger Games, is contingent on her performing gender in ways that parallel her society's expectations of her. As a result of her experiences, Katniss undergoes a metamorphosis that transforms a strong, independent female figure into a young woman who, at least at the conclusion of the first novel, is less sure of herself. Recognizing this, I advocate reading her character as a metaphor for the damage that patriarchal institutions inflict on young females by inundating them with a steady stream of messages that function to actively limit the subject positions they recognize as available to them.

SOCIAL CRITICISM AND YOUNG ADULT DYSTOPIAN FICTION

Arguments for the value of young adult literature abound, though it is perhaps most often celebrated for its ability to motivate reluctant readers, support struggling readers, and explore issues that adults, who, not coincidentally, author the majority of young adult novels, assume are of concern to adolescent readers. These ends are important, but, as others point out, young adult literature is also capable of complexity and literary sophistication, and it can challenge stronger readers as well (Connors, 2013; Miller & Slifkin, 2010; Soter & Connors, 2009). Reading young adult literature has the additional positive affect of preparing adolescents to participate in a democratic society by challenging them to reflect on a range of issues and problems that are endemic to the communities they inhabit (Wolk, 2009). This is especially true in the case of young adult dystopian fiction, a subgenre of young adult literature that, like dystopian fiction for adults, actively participates in social criticism.

In the past decade, a host of young adult dystopian novels have been written for (and marketed to) adolescents, including James Dashner's *The Maze Runner*, M. T. Anderson's *Feed*, Veronica Roth's *Divergent* series, Cory Doctorow's *Little Brother*, Jeff Hirsch's *The Eleventh Plague*, and Marie Lu's *Legend*, to name a few. Although these books are set in futuristic worlds, they invite readers to grapple with contemporary problems and social ills in much the same way that canonical literature does.

According to McDonald (2012), dystopian novels seize on "a negative cultural trend and imagine a future or an alternative world in which that trend dominates every aspect of life" (p. 9). In doing so, authors aim to construct a deeper understanding of the human condition by exaggerating its flaws and imagining the consequences of their being taken to an extreme. In this way, though the genre ostensibly presents stories that are set in the future, young adult dystopian fiction is best understood as inviting readers to wrestle with, and interrogate, contemporary problems and issues. In doing so, it challenges them to ask whether it is advisable for society to adhere to certain beliefs or persist in following a particular course of action. As Sambell (2004) argues:

> The dystopia foregrounds future suffering, then, to force readers to think carefully about where supposed 'ideals' may really lead, underlining the point that these hugely undesirable societies can and will come about, unless we learn to question the authority of those in power, however benign they may appear to be. In this way dystopian texts emphasize predominantly social concerns. (p. 248)

This concern with questioning authority motivates dystopian fiction to target social, religious, and political institutions for criticism with the intention of making visible impediments they erect in the path of human happiness. This penchant for questioning authority and exploring darker aspects of humanity can make some adults, especially those in positions of authority, uncomfortable. Nevertheless, reading dystopian fiction is a valuable exercise for readers of all ages if for no other reason than that it invites them to read the word and the world (Friere & Macedo, 1987). In this sense, like the larger umbrella category of young adult fiction, young adult dystopian fiction offers "a context for students to become conscious of their operative world view and to examine critically alternative ways of understanding the world and social relations" (Glasgow, 2001, p. 54). The potential for this to happen is heightened when one reads young adult dystopian fiction from the perspective of critical theory.

ECOFEMINIST LITERARY CRITICISM

Before offering an ecofeminist reading of *The Hunger Games,* I should first say a few words about this particular critical lens. Ecofeminist philosophy, which emerged in the 1970s, represents a fusion of concerns shared by ecologists and feminists. Like feminism, ecofeminism does not constitute a stable, unified theory. Rather, as Murphy (1995) argues, it is better understood as a conceptual home for theorists who define themselves in multiple ways—for example, as spiritual ecofeminists, traditional Marxist ecofeminists, cultural ecofeminists, and so on. Despite their philosophical differences, ecofeminists are united by a common concern—namely, a "masculinist linkage of women and nature that denigrates and threatens both" (Murphy, p. 49).

According to Bennett (2005), ecofeminism is concerned with a host of issues, including—but not limited to—women's rights, animal rights, water and air cleanliness, and the oppression of people in Third World countries by industrialized nations. Nevertheless, she argues that, at its core, ecofeminism is defined by its commitment to two concepts: its belief in the interrelatedness of all things and its commitment to supplanting hierarchically organized societies with egalitarian communities. In regard to the latter, she states:

> [Ecofeminists] assert that valuing one kind of life over another (white over black, male over female, human animals over other animals, industrialized living over agricultural life) will keep the hierarchy firmly entrenched, leaving traditionally defined "male" qualities—physical power, mechanistic ability, analytical and linear thinking—to be affirmed over "female" qualities—empathy, sensuality, emotion. (Bennett, p. 64)

Reading literature through the lens of ecofeminist theory, then, helps readers to disrupt these binaries and "become more aware of the interconnectedness in life, of cause and effect, and of the importance of taking personal responsibility for the consequences of our actions" (Bennett, p. 65).

In *The Hunger Games,* Collins (2008) presents readers with a futuristic society where the misapplication of science and technology blurs the boundary between public and private. Like Orwell's *Nineteen Eighty-Four*, she also depicts a world in which individual freedom is sacrificed to a surveillance society (Lyon, 1994) that demands compliance through the unceasing and omnipresent gaze of the state. Most importantly, Collins criticizes an oppressive patriarchal conceptual framework that treats marginalized groups of humans, including females, as raw materials it can remake for its own benefit. In the novel, those who occupy a position on the lower rungs of society, and who are subsequently regarded as disposable, struggle to define themselves in the face of definitions that other, more powerful figures impose on them. This includes hegemonic definitions of gender. As will be seen, Katniss struggles to maintain her identity as a strong female figure in a patriarchal system that demands compliance through a logic of domination (Warren, 2000). Read through the lens of ecofeminist literary theory, her involvement in the Hunger Games can be construed as a metaphor for the violence that society inflicts on young women by limiting the range of subject positions they recognize as available to them for performing gender.

"IF I CAN FORGET THEY'RE PEOPLE KILLING THEM WILL BE NO DIFFERENT AT ALL"

In *Ecofeminist Philosophy*, Warren (2000) identifies several features of a conceptual framework that patriarchal societies use to rationalize the oppression of humans by gender. This includes, but is not limited to, "conceptions of power and privilege that systematically advantage Ups over Downs, and a logic of domination" (p. 62). Significantly, Warren argues that this same conceptual framework "is used to justify the domination of humans by race/ethnicity, class, age, affectional orientation, ability, religion, marital status, geographic location, or nationality" (p. 62). She also regards it as offering a rationale for "the domination of nonhuman nature (and/or animals) by humans" (p. 62). Aspects of this conceptual framework are evident throughout Collins's (2008) novel, most notably in the relationship between the Capitol (Ups) and the citizens of Panem (Downs).

The economic structure of Panem, the setting of Collins's (2008) novel, is designed to privilege some groups (e.g., the wealthy, residents of the Capitol) at the expense of others (e.g., the poor, residents of the districts). Early in *The Hunger Games*, readers learn that a series of disasters—some man-made, others environmental—destabilized North America and brought about the collapse of society. From this devastation arose Panem, a country comprising twelve districts, all of which exist under the rule of a despotic government known as the Capitol. The relationship between the Capitol and those it governs resembles that of colonizer-to-colonized in so far as the state controls access to raw materials and industry that, by right, belong to the individual districts. Indeed, the association the Capitol forges between the districts and the goods and resources they produce for its benefit defines them. District 4, for example, is known for providing seafood; District 11 for generating grains and produce; District 12, which Katniss calls home, for mining coal used to power the Capitol, and so on.

149

In *The Death of Nature,* Merchant (1983/1980) argues that, in contrast to ancient civilizations that conceptualized the feminine earth as a nurturing mother figure humans were obliged to revere and protect, the modern world, organized as it is by a patriarchal mindset, is driven by a commitment to mechanization and a desire to control nature. The presence of this binary—nature/modernity—is felt throughout *The Hunger Games.* A large city replete with skyscrapers, the Capitol appears to exist apart from the natural world. Indeed, when Katniss encounters it for the first time she describes its colors as "artificial, the pinks too deep, the greens too bright, the yellows painful to the eyes" (Collins, 2008, p. 59). She is also struck by the Capitol's reliance on technology, including its sleek machines, its awe-inspiring aircraft, and its seemingly endless lines of cars parading down city streets.

McAndrew (1996) argues that ecofeminists oppose "science and technology as presently practiced, because science and technology view the natural world as something to be mastered or even conquered, the dominance theme of patriarchy" (p. 371). Significantly, the Capitol uses technology as a tool to control the natural world. This is evident in several ways, most notably in its decision to locate the Hunger Games in ecological environments it constructs. This includes forests, arctic landscapes, and deserts, all of which pose different challenges and obstacles for contestants to overcome. At the same time, the Capitol, through its various machinations, exerts complete control over these environments. Streams and riverbeds are drained overnight; conflagrations are ignited at the push of a button, sending panicked animals stampeding for their lives; temperatures rise during the day and unexpectedly plummet in the evening; the sun rises during what is ostensibly the middle of night, and more. The Gamemakers also blanket these environments with hidden cameras and microphones, literally imposing technology on the land to ensure that they have an omniscient view of the contestants. Despite their seeming authenticity, these landscapes are characterized by a sense of artificiality, as evidenced by Katniss's struggling to determine whether the moon she observes in the arena sky is "real or merely a projection of the Gamemakers" (Collins, 2008, p. 310). Unable to reach a definitive conclusion, she expresses her desire for it to be real, as it would give her "something to cling to in the surreal world of the arena where the authenticity of everything is to be doubted" (p. 310).

The Capitol uses science and technology to control nature in other ways, including engineering "muttations"—genetically altered animals—as weapons against its enemies. Jabberjays, a special kind of bird capable of repeating extended passages of human conversation, enable the Capitol to monitor the schemes of dissidents, while tracker jackers, a form of killer wasp "spawned in a lab and strategically placed, like land mines, around the districts during the war" (Collins, 2008, p. 185), provide a constant reminder to the districts of the power the Capitol wields over them. As Katniss explains, the synthetically altered venom of tracker jackers is sufficiently powerful to inspire hallucinations and, in some cases, death. By using science and technology to bastardize and remake nature in this way, the Capitol is able to preserve—and extend—its grip on power. In doing so, it signifies its commitment to a conceptual framework similar to the one that Warren (2000) associates with patriarchal cultures. Indeed, as McDonald (2012) persuasively argues, the Capitol, through its policies, effectively treats "the natural world as fodder to be set upon and remade into ever more grotesque and unnatural combinations" (p. 13).

In contrast to the Capitol, where people live in comfort, the residents of Panem's twelve districts exist under harsh conditions. Although people in District 12 are responsible for mining coal used to power the Capitol, an undertaking that is fraught with danger, they are poorly compensated for their labor and given minimal access to food and medicine. As a result, illness, starvation and death are rampant, a point that Katniss clarifies when she states:

> Who hasn't seen the victims? Older people who can't work. Children from a family with too many to feed. Those injured in the mines. Straggling through the streets. And one day you come upon them sitting motionless against a wall or lying in the Meadow .... Starvation is never the cause of death officially. It's always the flu, or exposure, or pneumonia. But that fools no one. (Collins, 2008, p. 28)

District 12 is not the only district to suffer in this way. The dark skinned residents of District 11 are responsible for generating crops and produce, yet they are not allowed to partake of the goods they harvest. Those who do are whipped mercilessly while others are made to watch, a punishment that calls to mind the institution of slavery as it was practiced in the American South, and which underscores the Capitol's commitment to governing through what Warren (2000) calls a logic of domination. By treating the residents of the districts harshly, and by conceptualizing power as "power over power" (p. 46), the Capitol enacts another feature of an oppressive conceptual framework. As Warren explains, "When power-over power serves to reinforce the power of Ups as Ups in ways that keep Downs unjustifiably subordinated ... such conceptions and practices of power are unjustified" (p. 47).

Under these harsh conditions, Katniss and her family turn to the natural world for sustenance. When, in the weeks following her father's death in a mining accident, she and her family face starvation, she gathers dandelion greens as a way to survive. In the months that follow, she recalls that, "The woods became our savior" (Collins, 2008, p. 51). In addition to fishing, stealing eggs from nests, and hunting squirrel, rabbit and other wild game, Katniss gathers plants for food, including one her parents named her for. Her mother, an apothecary, earns a living collecting herbs and plants she in turn uses to cure the sick and heal the injured in District 12. She later passes this knowledge on to Katniss's younger sister, Prim. In contrast to the Capitol, then, the Everdeen family values and appreciates nature for its restorative powers, as opposed to remaking and exploiting it for material gain.

According to Warren (2000), philosophers have long "argued that the language one uses mirrors and reflects one's concept of oneself and one's world. As such, language plays a crucial role in concept formation" (p. 27). In *The Hunger Games*, references to nature are interlaced throughout Katniss's speech, and they construct a binary between the world of District 12 (nature) and the Capitol (modernity). Her younger sister, Prim, is said to have "a face as fresh as a raindrop, as lovely as the primrose for which she was named" (Collins, 2008, p. 3). When the back of Prim's white shirt inadvertently comes undone, creating a tail of sorts, Katniss takes to calling her "little duck" (p. 15). In contrast, when she references nature to make sense of her experiences in the Capitol, her language often foregrounds the artificiality of the latter. City lights are said to "twinkle like a vast field of fireflies" (p. 80) while metallic cameras wielded by paparazzi are reminiscent of insects (p. 40). Even the residents of the Capitol, motivated by an aesthetic that leads them to dye their hair and paint their bodies, strike Katniss as alien, so much so that she regards the stylists assigned her as "unlike people" and more like "a trio of oddly colored birds…pecking around my feet" (p. 62). Significantly, when she undergoes a beautification process to remove excess hair from her body, she imagines herself as "a plucked bird, ready for roasting" (p. 61), an apt metaphor given what awaits her in the Hunger Games.

Derrida and other deconstructionists note that binary oppositions exist in a value-laden hierarchy in which one element is granted priority over another (Leggo, 1998). The dystopian world that Collins (2008) constructs in *The Hunger Games* is founded on binaries that privilege the wealthy over the poor, the strong over the weak, and modernity over nature. As will be seen in the section to follow, the same conceptual framework that sustains these binaries also gives the Capitol a rationale for controlling and remaking marginalized groups of people in the same way it does the natural world. In the end, it is the state's ability to dehumanize others that enables it to find entertainment in watching disadvantaged teenagers slaughter one another in an arena. Intuitively, Katniss seems to understand this, because when Gale, her hunting partner in District 12, compares killing tributes in the Hunger Games to hunting animals for food, she tells herself, "The awful thing is that if I can forget they're people, it will be no different at all" (p. 40).

"SOMEHOW IT ALWAYS COMES BACK TO COAL AT SCHOOL": A PROGRAM OF DEHUMANIZING OTHERS

Having foregrounded a series of binaries that structure the relationship between the Capitol and the residents of Panem, Collins (2008) examines the role an oppressive patriarchal conceptual framework plays in leading those in positions of power to enact policies that dehumanize marginalized groups of people. As explained, in Panem the twelve districts exist in a metonymic relationship with the goods they produce for the Capitol, so that District 4 is known for producing fish, District 11 for agricultural products, District 12 for coal, and so on. This conflation of people with goods is accomplished in several ways in the novel, both at a local and a global level.

In District 12, nearly every aspect of a person's existence is tied to the business of extracting coal from the earth. This includes one's experiences in school, where the bulk of "instruction is coal-related" (Collins, 2008, pp. 41-42). Additionally, Katniss and her family, along with their neighbors, inhabit a section of the district known as the Seam, a not so subtle allusion to a layer of coal sufficiently thick to be mined for profit. Perhaps because it permeates virtually every aspect of their daily lives, the residents of the Seam even begin to resemble coal, a fact that Katniss references when she observes that her neighbors "have long since stopped trying to scrub the coal dust off their broken nails, the lines of their sunken faces" (p. 4).

At a global level, the Capitol reinforces this association between people and resources by insisting that contestants who participate in the opening ceremony of the Hunger Games dress in a fashion that is indicative of their district's principal industry. As a consequence, contestants from District 12 traditionally wear miner's outfits, though Katniss is able to recall a year when the pair, a male and a female, "were stark naked and covered in black powder to represent coal dust" (Collins, 2008, p. 66). By forging this metaphorical association between coal and the people who mine it, the Capitol effectively dehumanizes the residents of District 12, relegating them to the realm of *things*. In doing so, it "mines" and exploits them for its own profit. This is most clearly evident in its sponsoring the Hunger Games, a bloody spectacle that pits 24 teenagers—two from each of Panem's twelve districts—against each other in mortal combat until one emerges victorious.

Having quashed a violent uprising, the Capitol created the Hunger Games to serve as a persistent reminder to the districts of their powerlessness. In addition to requiring parents to sacrifice their children in the Hunger Games, the Capitol forces them to watch the slaughter unfold on television in what is an extreme example of reality programming, thereby reinforcing its position of power over the districts by holding them complicit for participating in their own oppression. As Katniss explains:

> Taking the kids from our districts, forcing them to kill one another while we watch—this is the Capitol's way of reminding us how totally we are at their mercy. How little chance we would stand of surviving another rebellion. Whatever words they use, the real message is clear: "Look how we take your children and sacrifice them and there's nothing you can do. If you lift a finger, we will destroy every last one of you." (Collins, 2008, pp. 18-19)

The process wherein contestants are selected to participate in the Hunger Games, along with the discourse that surrounds the competition, can be read as additional evidence of the Capitol's dehumanizing the people of Panem. The names of two "tributes" from each district—one male, the other female—are selected from a glass container in what the Capitol calls a "reaping," an apt metaphor given that children of the poor are effectively harvested and consumed for entertainment by the powerful. Even if they manage to survive, their involvement in the Hunger Games functions to change them into something other than what they are. This is evident in the case of Katniss, who discovers early on that her ability to survive in the arena is contingent on her complying with expectations that males impose on her.

"IF YOU PUT ENOUGH PRESSURE ON COAL IT TURNS TO PEARLS": REGENDERING KATNISS

To this point I have argued that several popular assumptions surround *The Hunger Games*, one of which regards Katniss as offering young female readers access to a newly empowered subject position. This reading is not easily dismissed, as Katniss does exhibit qualities that are typically drawn as masculine in popular culture texts. She is a skilled hunter who is adept at using a bow and arrow, and after her father is killed in a mining accident she assumes his role by providing for her family. Likewise, Katniss is neither averse to killing nor prone to sentimentality, a fact that is evident when she recalls killing a lynx that took to following her in the woods. Though she regretted losing the animal's companionship, she nevertheless saw its death as an opportunity for her to profit by selling its pelt.

Miller (2012) argues that gender divisions are not as prevalent in the futuristic world that Collins (2008) envisions as they are in contemporary society. She rightly notes, for example, that men and women work alongside each other in the mines of District 12, and that males and females are selected to represent the districts in the Hunger Games where they compete against each other in a single competition as opposed to participating in separate contests according to gender. Furthermore, in the Capitol, men and women dye their hair, wear make-up, and sport tattoos, all of which seems to suggest that they are held to equivalent standards of beauty.

In much the same way that Katniss is thought to open up newly empowered subject positions to young female readers, Miller (2012) regards Peeta, a talented artist who is adept at decorating cakes, and who, with the exception of his physical strength, lacks either the ferocity or the athletic prowess other male contestants exhibit in the arena, as subverting hegemonic masculinity (Madill, 2008). Unlike Gale, Katniss's hunting companion in District 12, Peeta is not especially good with weapons. Indeed, with the exception of cutting short a mortally wounded girl's suffering, an act that could be interpreted as compassionate, and picking poisonous berries that inadvertently result in a death toward the end of the novel, he does not kill in the arena. He is actually wounded for most of the competition, and as a result is unable to care for himself. It consequently falls to Katniss to care for (and protect) him. For these reasons, Miller concludes that:

> Of the major characters in the Hunger Games trilogy, Peeta is the closest to being an androgynous blend of the most desirable masculine and feminine traits. He's confident and self-reliant like Katniss, but unlike his fellow District 12 tribute, he's also trusting and open. He's physically strong, but he avoids violence and aggression except in self-defense. His occupation of baking matches his warm and nurturing personality. He cleans up a drunk and disheveled Haymitch, offers a chilly Katniss his coat, and is generally kind and thoughtful. (p. 154)

At first glance, as Miller (2012) suggests, gender inequities do not appear to be as prevalent in Panem as they are in contemporary society, and, to a certain extent, Katniss and Peeta *do* disrupt hegemonic femininity and masculinity. Nevertheless, a closer reading of the novel reveals that Collins (2008) accomplishes something considerably more complex than simply engaging in a discourse of "Girl Power" which, as Gonick (2006) argues, detracts attention away from the very real inequalities that females face at the hands of patriarchal institutions. The novel is set in (and produced by) a patriarchal culture, after all, and as such Katniss's agency is circumscribed to some extent in both the world of the text and the world of readers. Peeta might be able to circumvent traditional gender norms without fear of retribution, but Katniss cannot, and this is precisely Collins's point—no matter how strong Katniss is, her ability to survive in the Capitol is ultimately contingent on her performing hegemonic femininity (Krane, 2001).

Shortly before the scheduled start of the Hunger Games, Katniss converses with Peeta atop the roof of the building in which they are staying. As they gaze out at the twinkling lights of the Capitol, Peeta confesses his desire to retain his identity in the Hunger Games. Specifically, he states, "I don't want them to change me in there. Turn me into some kind of monster that I'm not" (Collins, 2008, p. 141). Instead, he expresses his desire "to show the Capitol they don't own me. That I'm more than just a piece in their Games" (p. 142). Katniss, of course, is unable to grasp his meaning, which is symbolically important. Though he incurs a physical injury, Peeta *does* exit the arena with his identity largely in tact. As a male, his society neither demands nor expects him to reinvent himself. Katniss, on the other hand, has no choice but to do so. Ultimately, the odds of her surviving in the arena are contingent on her becoming something other than what she is at the start of the novel, suggesting that females are, in fact, held accountable to a different standard than males in Panem. An ecofeminist reading of the novel invites readers not only to contemplate that double standard, but also to consider the role that male characters play in regendering Katniss.

Though it presents readers with a strong female protagonist, the world of *The Hunger Games* is decidedly male. At home in District 12, Katniss enjoys the companionship of her sister, Prim, whom she loves deeply, and her mother, with whom she is less close, a result of the fact that she holds her accountable for abandoning her family emotionally following her husband's death. She is close to Gale, her male hunting companion, but her relationship with him is by her own account plutonic. In the world of the Capitol, on the other hand, Katniss is surrounded by males, the sole exception being Effie Trinket, a figure so hyper-feminine as to appear cartoonish. It is perhaps not surprising, then, that males play a central role in regendering Katniss. As a contestant in the Hunger Games, she is expected to perform gender in ways that Cinna (her stylist), Haymitch (her mentor), and Peeta (her fellow tribute from District 12) establish for her. This, coupled with the knowledge that she exists under the omnipresent gaze of television cameras, influences the way that she carries herself in both the Capitol and later in the Hunger Games.

Soon after arriving in the Capitol, Katniss is sent to a "Remake Center"—an obvious metaphor for the transformational nature of her journey—where she undergoes a series of cosmetic alternations designed to enhance her appearance. To begin, her prep team scrubs and waxes her, practices that are torturous for Katniss, who complains, "My legs, arms, torso, underarms, and parts of my eyebrows have been stripped of [hair], leaving me like a plucked bird, ready for roasting" (Collins, 2008, p. 61). At the conclusion of this process, however, she is taken by her transformation, suggesting that, at least on some level, she approves of it.

Confronted with an image of herself on a television screen, she states, "I am not pretty. I am not beautiful. I am as radiant as the sun" (p. 121).

As explained, the Capitol dehumanizes residents of the districts in a variety of ways, one of which involves its conflating them with raw materials and goods they produce for its benefit. Tributes are made to wear costumes that represent their district's principal source of industry in the opening ceremony of the Hunger Games. In Katniss's case, however, Cinna, her male stylist, elects to forego the coal miner outfit that contestants from District 12 traditionally wear. Although his motivation for doing so—to garner attention for Katniss and ensure that she comes across as memorable—is altruistic, he nevertheless replaces the costume with one that signifies the product her district produces—namely, coal. He and Peeta's stylist dress the couple in stylish black outfits that, when lit, emit real flames, the result of which earns them the approval of the viewing audience, and gains Katniss the moniker, "The girl who was on fire" (Collins, 2008, p. 70). In this way, Cinna's choice of wardrobe symbolically functions to reinforce the same dehumanizing association the Capitol constructed through its legislative policies. Whether he intended it or not, the metaphor can be read as suggesting that, much like flames consume coal, tributes are consumed by the hungry gaze of viewers in the Capitol.

When she goes on a television show following her sensational debut in the opening ceremony, Katniss is forced to submit to Cinna's aesthetic once again. Using a metaphor that reveals volumes about her feelings toward her style team's efforts to remake her, she states, "They erase my face with a layer of pale makeup and draw my features back out" (Collins, 2008, p. 120). The result is so impressive that Katniss again struggles to recognize herself, and, upon seeing her reflection, she is left with the impression that "[t]he creature standing before me in the full-length mirror has come from another world" (p. 120). Foregrounding a similar scene in *Catching Fire,* the second novel in the series, McDonald (2012) interprets the discomfort that Katniss feels when her prep team expresses their desire to transform her into "something special" as evidence of her understanding that "to 'make you something special' really means to unmake what you already are" (p. 14).

Like Cinna, Haymitch also plays a role in regendering Katniss. Though he is himself a resident of District 12, he treats her and Peeta as if they are something other than human when he meets them for the first time. Katniss recalls his circling them, "prodding us like animals at times, checking our muscles, examining our faces" (Collins, 2008, p. 58). Dissatisfied with her cold demeanor, Haymitch insists that Katniss experiment with alternative identities, one of which is that of a naïve girl who talks animatedly about the beautiful wardrobe her prep team assembled for her in the Capitol. This, of course, is completely out of character for Katniss, and at the conclusion of an exhausting afternoon spent playing vulnerable, arrogant, witty, mysterious, sexy and so on, she exasperatedly concedes that none of these identities suit her. She subsequently laments that, at the conclusion of her meeting with Haymitch, "I am no one at all" (p. 118).

Despite her concerns, Katniss does manage to endear herself to the television audience through a combination of humor and beauty. Prior to taking the stage, she reaches an agreement with Cinna to find him in the studio audience and respond to questions the show's host poses as if she were talking to him. Asked to model her dress at one point, Katniss observes Cinna making a subtle circular motion with his finger, as if to say *"Twirl for me"* (Collins, 2008, p. 128), which she does, much to the delight of the audience. Following her performance, however, she is disappointed by the image she cast, which she concedes amounted to little more than "[a] silly girl spinning in a sparkling dress" (p. 136).

Like Cinna and Haymitch, Peeta pressures Katniss to perform hegemonic femininity when, on the same television show, he unexpectedly confesses his unrequited love for her. Furious, she attacks him when they return to their complex. Yet when she expresses her frustration at being used, Haymitch angrily informs her:

> You are a fool .... *That boy gave you something you could never achieve on your own .... He made you look desirable.* [emphasis added] And let's face it, you can use all the help you can get in that department. You were as romantic as dirt until he said he wanted you. Now they all do. You're all they're talking about. (Collins, 2008, p. 135)

Katniss accepts his point, but is troubled by the knowledge that performing a role others prescribe for her means surrendering her autonomy. Angered by this injustice, which she attributes directly to the Hunger Games, she expresses her frustration at being made to "[hop] around like some trained dog trying to please people I hate" (p. 117).

Significantly, Collins (2008) represents Effie Trinket, the lone female character in a position to help Katniss during her stay in the Capitol, as completely ineffectual. With her make-up, stylish clothing, and her constant emphasis on proper manners, the character is a cartoonish equivalent of the "dutiful female" archetype. Throughout the novel, Effie's sole contribution of note includes teaching Katniss to walk in heels while wearing a dress, to maintain proper posture, and to smile when responding to an interviewer's questions, skills that call to mind those one might expect a beauty queen to possess. Despite her dissatisfaction with Katniss's performance in these areas, Effie persists in her mistaken belief that "if you put enough pressure on coal it turns to pearls" (p. 74). Collins likely intended this humorous slip as a sardonic comment on Effie's intellect. Nevertheless, the statement is symbolically important in that it comments directly on her prep team's efforts to transform Katniss, the daughter of a coal miner, into something other than what she is—namely, a desirable female figure.

Collectively, the influence (or *pressure*) that Cinna, Haymitch, Peeta, and, to a lesser extent, Effie, exert on Katniss suggests that she must be desired by males in order to gain the approval of her viewing audience. For this to happen, however, she has to submit to standards of beauty and behavior prescribed for her by males. In her own words, she is "made beautiful by Cinna's hands, desirable by Peeta's confession, tragic by circumstance, and by all accounts, unforgettable" (Collins, 2008, pp. 137-138). In contrast, the male characters in the novel earn followers as a result of their strength and physical prowess, not their ability to appear physically attractive to an audience. With this in mind, Miller's (2012) assertion that gender is not an issue in Panem is complicated by the knowledge that female competitors in the Hunger Games are, in fact, held to a different standard than males. Indeed, the odds of Katniss's surviving in the arena are contingent on her meeting that standard, a task that is complicated by the knowledge that she is forced to perform under the ever-present gaze of the Capitol.

"I CAN'T SHAKE THE FEELING THAT I'M BEING WATCHED CONSTANTLY": THE PERILS OF SCIENCE AND TECHNOLOGY IN A SURVEILLANCE SOCIETY

Sambell (2004) argues that "children's dystopias seek to violently explode blind confidence in the myth that science and technology will bring about human 'progress'" by illustrating how the two "can be used to bring about oppressive, inhuman and intolerable regimes, rather than 'civilized' ones" (pp. 247-248). As explained above, ecofeminists oppose science and technology when patriarchal societies use them to control and manipulate nature (McAndrew, 1996). Through its commitment to genetic engineering, for example, the Capitol treats "the natural world as fodder to be set upon and remade into ever more grotesque and unnatural combinations" (McDonald, 2012, p. 13). Its misapplication of science and technology leads it to treat people as "fodder to be set upon and remade" in much the same way.

In *The Hunger Games*, Collins (2008) imagines a world in which any sort of ethical code that might hold scientists accountable for their work has been stripped away, leaving them free to enact whatever monstrous visions their minds are capable of producing. Similar to the Capitol wresting nature out of its original form in the act of producing "muttations," it transmutes humans into animals in what is perhaps the most obvious, and extreme, example of its controlling and dehumanizing others. Toward the end of the novel, as Katniss and Peeta prepare to confront Cato, their last remaining opponent in the arena, they are unexpectedly set upon by a pack of wolves. Almost immediately, Katniss become cognizant of the fact that the wolves are unlike any animal she has encountered—they stand on two legs, for example, and gesture to one another with their paws. Upon closer examination, she is horrified to discover that the wolves—which she correctly identifies as a new breed of muttation—resemble her fellow tributes who were killed earlier in the competition, suggesting that the Gamemakers resurrected them for the express purpose of heightening the drama surrounding the climax of the games to further titillate the viewing audience. Likewise, the Gamemakers are able to control these muttations, so that, at the press of a button, they come and go from the battlefield.

This is, of course, an extreme example of how the Capitol uses technology to dehumanize those who come under its power. More insidious are the subtler ways it exploits science and technology to manipulate those it governs. Collins (2008) reserves her sharpest criticism for what Lyon (1994) calls a "surveillance society"—that is, a society that curtails individual freedoms by subjecting people to the omnipresent gaze of the state. She is especially critical of the media, which she holds complicit in blurring the boundary between public and private through its promotion of reality television, symbolized in the novel by the Hunger Games. In

158

Orwell's *Nineteen Eighty-Four*, the Party employs technology, represented in the form of telescreens and microphones, to monitor the public and private lives of its members. In Panem, however, surveillance has taken an even more insidious turn, as it has evolved into a popular form of entertainment. Throughout the novel, the knowledge that others watch her compels Katniss to perform gender in ways that enable her to win the favor of her viewing audience. To do so, however, she must compromise, even if temporarily, her identity as a strong, independent female.

Under the auspices of the Capitol, the citizens of Panem are denied freedom of speech, a result of the fact that the state uses cameras and other forms of surveillance technologies to monitor and control them. Hunting deep in the woods one day Gale tells Katniss, "It's to the Capitol's advantage to have us divided among ourselves" (Collins, 2008, p. 14). This is not a sentiment he would express openly in District 12 due to the ever-present threat of surveillance, suggesting that, though their lives are untenable, the residents of the districts have fallen so completely under the control of the state that they are no longer able to resist it. Instead, they self-monitor to ensure that they present themselves in a way that is consistent with what they assume the state expects of them. In this way, surveillance technologies promote discipline by conditioning people to behavioral codes established by those in positions of authority.

The same phenomenon is discernable in the Hunger Games, as the Gamemakers exploit many of the same surveillance technologies the Capitol uses to compel discipline. In the latter case, however, surveillance constitutes a form of entertainment as much as it does a form of discipline. From the time they are selected to participate in the Hunger Games, tributes are made subject to the prying eyes of television cameras that compete to capture and document their experiences for a viewing audience. Broadcasting the games is somewhat problematic, however, given that cameras must be able to track the movements of multiple contestants simultaneously in a sizeable space. To account for this, the Gamemakers construct an environment (literally, a forest, arctic plain, desert, etc.) they can manipulate. As explained above, they are able to turn night to day, cut off the flow of streams and rivers, ignite wildfires, and so on. They also blanket the arena with an elaborate web of surveillance cameras and microphones, ensuring that they are able to monitor and capture the movements of individual contestants. As a result, contestants act with the knowledge that they are watched, a situation that calls to mind Bentham's Panopticon, an architectural structure that Foucault (1977) theorized.

Bentham designed the Panopticon, which functioned as a prison, so that authorities could monitor the behavior of inmates without their knowing when (or whether) they were being watched. In this way, the knowledge that they were *potentially* watched was presumed to motivate the inmates to self-monitor and self-discipline. A surveillance society (Lyon, 1994) functions according to a similar precept in so far as it aims to monitor and control behavior through the application of technology. As Lavoie (2011) states, "With an observer or camera virtually everywhere, one cannot presume that one is in a private sphere at any time," the result of which gives rise to "a self-propelling machine of fear, paranoia, and *watchedness*" (p. 60, emphasis in original).

As Wise (2002) explains, "the Panopticon was not reserved for Big Brother only but was to be a public space," which suggests that we not only self-discipline but also "discipline each other" (p. 30). His observation is pertinent to my argument, as reality television programming constitutes a public space, albeit one in which an audience monitors the movements of those positioned on the opposite end of a camera. This complex situation is complicated still further in Panem, however, given that the viewing audience also exists under the gaze of the state. The resultant image is a highly wrought web of watchedness in which virtually everyone, oppressor as well as oppressed, is entangled.

From the time she volunteers to take her sister Prim's place as tribute for District 12, Katniss is acutely aware of the fact that she is surveilled by cameras, the result of which exposes her not only to the prying eyes of the Capitol, but also to viewers who could potentially sponsor her in the Hunger Games. Faced with the knowledge that a sponsor could mean the difference between life and death, she elects to present herself in a way that she assumes will position her as a formidable competitor. When she bids farewell to her mother and sister, for example, she makes a conscious decision not to cry out of concern that doing so will lead her opponents to construe her as weak. Likewise, when she is injured in the arena, she resolves not to show emotion. Faced with the need to help Peeta when he is mortally wounded, however, Katniss has no alternative but to perform a role that is decidedly more foreign to her—that of a love-struck girl. In this way, the knowledge that she is watched compels her to perform hegemonic femininity (Krane, 2001) in order to accommodate her audience's expectations of her.

In District 12, Katniss showed little interest in the opposite sex. Her relationship with Gale, her male hunting partner, was by her own account plutonic, and she characterized herself as lacking the knowledge that enabled other girls to attract attention from males. To gain the support of a sponsor wealthy enough to pay for Peeta's medicine, however, Katniss has no alternative but to adopt the role of star-crossed lover in a narrative that he and Haymitch scripted for her. When she kisses Peeta for the first time, an act that is designed to elicit teary-eyed sighs from her viewing audience, Haymitch rewards her efforts with nothing more than a bowl of soup. Cognizant that he is watching her, Katniss imagines him snarling, "You're supposed to be in love, sweetheart. The boy's dying. Give me something I can work with" (Collins, 2008, p. 261). She subsequently infers that he wants her to share something personal, which she does. Later, when she confesses her feelings for Peeta for the sake of the television cameras, she imagines Haymitch exclaiming, "Yes, *that's* what I'm looking for, sweetheart" (p. 302, emphasis in original). In this way, the knowledge that she is watched by a male compels Katniss to remake herself—or, more strongly, to regender herself—in a way that allows her to appease her audience.

Later, after Katniss and Peeta double-cross the Gamemakers, an event that I will address momentarily, she catches a reflection of herself in a plate of glass onboard the aircraft returning her to the Capitol. Taken by the image, she exclaims:

I startle when I catch someone staring at me from only a few inches away and then realize it's my own face reflecting back in the glass. Wild eyes, hollow cheeks, my hair in a tangled mat. Rabid. Feral. Mad. (Collins, 2008, p. 348)

Cleary, Katniss's experiences in the arena dehumanized her, reducing her to the status of an animal. This is not the final imposition that she incurs at the hands of the Capitol, however. In a galling example of hubris, doctors onboard the aircraft take it upon themselves to wipe her body of all signs of physical trauma it endured in the arena. In doing so, they also remove scars and imperfections she acquired while hunting in the woods with her father and Gayle at home in District 12. Were it not for the intervention of Haymitch, the doctors would have augmented her breasts as well. The end result of their labor, coupled with the work of her prep team upon her return to the Capitol, is a distinctly feminine image. Prior to appearing on television for the final interview of the Hunger Games, Katniss describes herself in the following way:

My hair's loose, held back by a simple hairband. The makeup rounds and fills out the sharp angles of my face. A clear polish coats my nails. The sleeveless dress is gathered at my ribs, not my waist, largely eliminating any help the padding would have given my figure. The hem falls just to my knees. Without heels, you can see my true stature. *I look, very simply, like a girl* [emphasis added]. A young one. Fourteen at the most. *Innocent. Harmless.* (Collins, p. 355)

The above image is made all the more striking by the knowledge that it stands in contrast to the image readers encountered of Katniss at the start of the novel when she appeared dressed in hunting boots, a pair of trousers, a shirt and a cap, a traditionally masculine attire.

By arguing that the presence of surveillance technology functions to regender Katniss, I am not proposing that she is completely under the control of those who watch her. Knowing that the Capitol must have a winner for their game, she and Peeta threaten to eat poisonous berries at the novel's climax, the result of which enables them to turn a surveilling eye back on their surveillors, thus ensuring their survival. Nor do Katniss's experience in the Hunger Games eradicate all semblance of her former self. As she washes away her makeup and returns her hair to its signature braid prior to returning to District 12, she gradually experiences the sensation of "transforming back into myself" (Collins, 2008, p. 371). Nevertheless, the pressure she faced to reinvent herself in the arena—to become something other than what she was—does appear to alter her, even if only subtly, a fact that is evidenced by her struggling "to remember who I am and who I am not" (p. 371). Likewise, her awareness of being watched is heightened at the novel's conclusion. Faced with the knowledge that her decision to challenge the Capitol's power placed her in harm's way, a wary Katniss notes that she is unable to "shake the feeling that *I'm being watched constantly*" (p. 366, emphasis added).

BEYOND "THE BASTARD STEPSON OF REAL LITERATURE"

Gonick (2006) identifies two competing discourses—"Girl Power" and "Reviving Ophelia"—that, upon first glance, appear to offer opposing views on femininity. Upon closer examination, however, Gonick argues that each of them is problematic, a result of the fact that they "direct attention from structural explanations for inequality toward explanations of personal circumstances and personality traits" (p. 2). Read through the critical lens of ecofeminist literary theory, it is possible to appreciate Collins's (2008) *The Hunger Games* as a novel that presents readers with a "new girl" character while at the same time directing attention to the role that patriarchal institutions play in limiting the empowered subject positions that young women recognize as available to them.

Left unquestioned, narratives that celebrate "girl power" can promote a post-feminist ideological assumption that society has successfully ameliorated gender inequities, ensuring that females have access to the same opportunities and privileges as males. This assumption is dangerous, especially at a time when women continue to earn less than men, when they are frequently subjected to male violence, and when they are held to standards of beauty and desirability that potentially place their health at risk. Furthermore, there is reason to believe that while young female readers are capable of identifying characters that challenge hegemonic masculinity and femininity, they may not necessarily approve of their doing so. Having conducted a case study that examined the experiences of four preadolescent girls who read and talked about *The Hunger Games* in the context of a book club, Taber, Woloshyn, and Lane (2013) found "that the girls appeared most comfortable when the characters enacted stereotypical gendered behaviors in the book." Quoting Younger (2003), the authors determined that "powerful cultural pressure still exists for young women to uphold an unrealistic standard of beauty" (Taber et al., 2013, p. 13).

In her novel, Collins (2008) captures the complexities of this problem by portraying the tensions that young women face in a culture that invites them to celebrate strong, independent female figures at the same time that it demands that they perform hegemonic femininity. In doing so, she demonstrates how an oppressive conceptual framework that leads governments and corporations to impose themselves on the environment also leads them to enact policies and legislation that actively work to oppress women. Moreover, in the spirit of ecofeminist philosophy, Collins invites readers to be less accepting of technology and, in doing so, to interrogate the role that it plays in reinforcing a patriarchal hierarchy. These are weighty issues for a young adult dystopian novel, indeed. Yet despite the fact that scholars in the field of children's literature acknowledge the literary merit of young adult fiction, it continues its quest to find legitimacy in academic settings where it remains, to quote Chris Crutcher, "the bastard stepson of real literature" (Manes, 2003, para. 2).

For the past several years I have taught an undergraduate course on young adult literature and literary theory. One of the assignments for the course requires students to interview secondary school librarians about young adult authors and titles that are popular with adolescent readers, as well as changing trends the librarians discern in the field of young adult literature. In recent years students have consistently returned to my class and reported that speculative fiction—specifically, young adult dystopian fiction, fantasy, and horror (e.g., werewolves, vampires, and zombies)—constitutes the most popular genre with students. This past year, however, as secondary schools near the university where I work implemented the Common Core State Standards, some librarians lamented that, in spite of speculative fiction's appeal to adolescents, teachers opted not to allow them to read it for independent reading assignments due to the fact that they didn't believe the genre was sufficiently challenging.

Young adult literature's status as popular culture, coupled with the knowledge that it is ostensibly written for adolescents, may lead some critics to dismiss the genre as low culture. Young adult dystopian fiction is at even greater disadvantage, given that it is branded pejoratively as *genre fiction*. As the ecofeminist reading of *The Hunger Games* that I offered in this chapter demonstrates, however, young adult dystopian fiction participates in social criticism with the intention of foregrounding obstacles that otherwise taken-for-granted institutions place in the path of human happiness. In doing so, it invites readers to imagine other ways of interacting with the world and other possible social relationships. In this way, it participates in the goals of literature with a capital "L." Indeed, as Booker (1994) argues, "If the main value of literature in general is its ability to make us see the world in new ways, to make us capable of entertaining new and different perspectives on reality, then dystopian fiction is not a marginal genre" (p. 176). Read through the lens of critical theory, it is possible to appreciate young adult dystopian fiction as a potentially complex, multilayered form of literature that, to borrow from Aristotle, is capable of instructing at the same time that it delights. In the end, the perceived value and complexity of young adult dystopian literature may depend as much on the questions that we, as readers, ask of individual novels as it does on the novels themselves.

REFERENCES

Bennett, B. (2005). Through ecofeminist eyes: Le Guin's "The ones who walk away from Omelas." *The English Journal, 94*(6), 63-68.

Booker, M. K. (1994). *The dystopian impulse in modern literature: Fiction as social criticism.* Westport, CT: Greenwood.

Collins, S. (2008). *The hunger games.* New York: Scholastic.

Connors, S. P. (2013). Challenging perspectives on young adult literature. *The English Journal, 102*(5), 69-73.

Daniels, C. L. (2006). Literary theory and young adult literature: The open frontier in critical studies. *The ALAN Review, 33*(2), 78-82.

Foucault, M. (1977). *Discipline and punish: The birth of the prison.* New York: Pantheon Books.

Friere, P., & Macedo, D. (1987). *Literacy: Reading the word & the world.* South Hadley, MA: Bergin & Garvey.

Glasgow, J. N. (2001). Teaching social justice through young adult literature. *The English Journal, 90*(6), 54-61.

Gonick, M. (2006). Between "girl power" and "reviving Ophelia": Constituting the neo-liberal girl subject. *NWSA Journal, 8*(2), 2-23.

Krane, V. (2001). We can be athletic and feminine, but do we want to? Challenging hegemonic femininity in women's sport. *Quest, 53*(1), 115-133.

Lavoie, D. (2011). Escaping the panopticon: Utopia, hegemony, and performance in Peter Weir's *The Truman Show. Utopian Studies, 22*(1), 52-73.

Leggo, C. (1998). Open(ing) texts: Deconstruction and responding to poetry. *Theory into Practice, 37*(3), 186-192.

Lyon, D. (1994). *The Electronic Eye: The Rise of Surveillance Society.* Minneapolis: University of Minnesota Press.

Madill, L. (2008). Gendered identities explored: The Lord of the Rings as a text of alternative ways of being. *ALAN Review, 35*(2), 43-49.

Manes, B. (2003). Writing it really real. *Orlando Weekly.* Retrieved from http://www2.orlandoweekly.com/news/story.asp?id=3056

McAndrew, D. A. (1996). Ecofeminism and the teaching of literacy. *College Composition and Communication, 47*(3), 367-382.

McDonald, B. (2012). The final word on entertainment: Mimetic and monstrous art in the hunger games. In G. A. Dunn & N. Michaud (Eds.), *The hunger games and philosophy: A critique of pure treason* (pp. 8-25). Hoboken, NJ: Wiley.

Merchant, C. (1983/1980). *The death of nature: Women, ecology, and the scientific revolution.* San Francisco: Harper & Row.

Miller, J. (2012). "She has no idea. The effect she can have." Katniss and the politics of gender. In G. A. Dunn & N. Michaud (Eds.), *The hunger games and philosophy: A critique of pure treason* (pp. 145-161). Hoboken, NJ: Wiley.

Miller, S. J., & Slifkin, J. M. (2010). "Similar literary quality": Demystifying the AP English literature and composition open question. *The ALAN Review, 37*(2), 6-16.

Murphy, P. D. (1995). *Literature, nature, and other: Ecofeminist critiques.* Albany: State University of New York Press.

Sambell, K. (2004). Carnivalizing the future: A new approach to theorizing childhood and adulthood in science fiction for young readers. *The Lion and the Unicorn, 28*(2), 247-267.

Soter, A. O., & Connors, S. P. (2009). Beyond relevance to literary merit: Young adult literature as 'Literature.' *The ALAN Review, 37*(1), 62-67.

Taber, N., Woloshyn, V., & Lane, L. (2013). 'She's more like a guy' and 'he's more like a teddy bear': Girls' perception of violence and gender in The Hunger Games. *Journal of Youth Studies*, 1-16.

Ward, B. A., & Young, T. A. (2009). Brave, determined, and strong: Books for girls (and sometimes boys). *Reading Horizons, 49*(3), 257-268.

Warren, K. J. (2000). *Ecofeminist philosophy: A western perspective on what it is and why it matters.* Lanham: Rowman & Littlefield.

Wise, J. M. (2002). Mapping the culture of control: Seeing through The Truman Show. *Television New Media, 3*(1), 29-47.

Wolk, S. (2009). Reading for a better world: Teaching for social responsibility with young adult literature. *Journal of Adolescent & Adult Literacy, 52*(8), 664-673.

Younger, B. (2003). Pleasure, pain, and the power of being thin: Female sexuality in young adult literature. *NWSA Journal, 15*(2), 45-56.

SEAN P. CONNORS

9. "IT'S A BIRD ... IT'S A PLANE ... IT'S ... A COMIC BOOK IN THE CLASSROOM?"

Truth: Red, White, and Black *as Test Case for Teaching Superhero Comics*

"All comics are political." – Alan Moore (quoted in McAllister et al., 2001, p. 1)

No study of speculative fiction would be complete without acknowledging the comic book, a staple of American popular culture since its inception in the twentieth century. Since Superman first appeared on the cover of *Action Comics #1* in 1938, the comic book, as a form of storytelling, has been virtually synonymous with speculative fiction, encompassing an array of genres, including (but not limited to) crime, horror, fantasy and—perhaps most famously—science fiction (SF). In the comic book's formative years, its relationship with speculative fiction elicited concerns on the part of anxious parents, educators, and civic leaders who worried that reading comic books would adversely impact the moral development of children and interfere with their growth as readers. Indeed, Frederic Wertham, a renowned psychologist whose book, *Seduction of the Innocent,* was integral in bringing about a congressional hearing on the comic book industry at the height of the great comic book scare (Hajdu, 2008), deemed comic books "death on reading" (Wertham, 1954, p. 121), a result of their blending pictures and words to tell a story. In subsequent years, an association between comics and genres such as fantasy, SF, and horror contributed to their being discounted as sub-literature. Today, thanks in part to the commercial and critical success the comic book's younger sibling, the graphic novel, enjoys, the medium of comics is afforded more respect than it was throughout most of the twentieth century.

As a barometer for gauging the extent to which popular conceptions of comics have changed, one need only examine contemporary educators' attitudes toward them. Institutions that historically criticized comic books for having a deleterious effect on developing readers, most notably schools and libraries, are just as likely to celebrate the pedagogical value of graphic novels today. Literacy educators, for example, advocate teaching graphic novels to motivate so-called reluctant readers (Crawford, 2004; Snowball, 2005); support struggling readers (Bitz, 2004; Frey & Fisher, 2004); scaffold English language learners (Chun, 2009); and promote the development of skills associated with visual literacy (Frey & Fisher, 2008; Gillenwater, 2009). Others regard graphic novels as a complex form of literature capable of withstanding close scrutiny and challenging readers of varying ability levels (Carter, 2007; Connors, 2010, 2013; Versaci, 2001, 2007). In higher education, it is not uncommon for English departments to offer courses of study

P. Thomas (ed.), Science Fiction and Speculative Fiction, 165–184.
© *2013 Sense Publishers. All rights reserved.*

designed to theorize comics and comics reading. Comics even appear in *Postmodern American Fiction: A Norton Anthology* (Chute, 2008). In short, all available evidence seems to suggest that contemporary educators accept comics (or, more precisely, graphic novels) as a potentially complex, multilayered form of literature. But is that really the case? The answer to this question depends in part on the genre of graphic novel one has in mind. With all due respect to George Orwell's *Animal Farm,* in the minds of many educators, some genres are more equal than others.

As marketers intended, the term "graphic novel" has proven useful in generating more respect for comics (they are, after all, graphic *novels* as opposed to lowly comic books), but its lack of specificity is sometimes problematic. Chute (2008), for example, observes that a substantial percentage of narratives marketed as graphic novels are, in fact, works of non-fiction. Likewise, Wolk (2007) conceptualizes graphic novels as falling into three categories: manga, the Japanese equivalent of American comics; mainstream comics, which he suggests are written and drawn by different people and published serially; and art comics, which he claims are generally—though not always—the work of a single artist, and which are conceived as a self-contained book. Although Wolk (2007) cautions against interpreting the term art comics as entailing any sort of value judgment, it is difficult to avoid that conclusion.

Having asked why comics continue their quest for cultural legitimacy, Groensteen (2009) argues that, in part, the form suffers from an association with what he calls "paraliterature, a badly defined set of popular genres that includes adventure stories, historical novels, fantasy and science-fiction, detective novels, erotica, and so on" (p. 9). One cannot help noting a resemblance between paraliterature and speculative fiction, which has also been dismissed by critics as genre fiction. Perhaps it is not surprising, then, that many of the graphic novels that educators celebrate, and which have made their way into classrooms—including *Maus* by Art Spiegleman*, Persepolis* by Marjane Satrapi*, American Born Chinese* by Gene Luen Yang, and *Essex* County by Jeff Lemire—belong to the category of art comics. At the opposite end of the spectrum, mainstream comics—and superhero comics in particular—continue to languish in the ghetto of comic art much as they have for the past 75 years.

When it comes to teaching graphic novels, ignoring some genres (for example, those associated with speculative fiction) in favor of others reinforces a binary between high and low art. It also marginalizes, and devalues, reading material that students embrace outside of school. In a study that asked how six high school students read and talked about graphic novels in the context of an after school reading group, for example, I found that two students who expressed a preference for reading superhero comics, and who did so voraciously, lamented what they felt was an inability (if not a refusal) on the part of their teachers to recognize any value in them. Instead, they thought teachers privileged what they (the students) called "academic graphic novels." While they conceded that most superhero comics are action-oriented, they insisted that the genre is capable of addressing socially and culturally relevant issues, a point they maintained throughout the study.

In this chapter, I advocate reading superhero comics, a genre that is anchored in the tradition of speculative fiction, critically to understand how individual works function to reinforce or challenge aspects of the dominant ideology. As others argue (Groensteen, 2009), the term "comics" is a misnomer given that, for most people, it calls to mind funny, light-hearted stories associated with childhood reading. As a slew of recent publications demonstrate, however, graphic novels and comic books also tackle mature storylines and dark subject matter intended for consumption by an adult audience. Moreover, as the quotation from Alan Moore at the beginning of this chapter suggests, "comics are political" (McAllister et al., 2001, p. 1). By imagining a world in which science and technology imbue the common person with superhuman powers at the same time that they threaten the fate of the planet, superhero comics manifest society's aspirations and fears. In doing so, they also document social and political issues that concern the larger culture and lend themselves to being examined critically.

Attention has rightfully been given the role superhero comics play in reinforcing aspects of the dominant ideology. The overwhelming majority of superheroes, for example, are white, and they have historically championed white, middle-class values. They are also predominantly male, and all too often creators of superhero comics depict female characters as hypersexualized figures at the same time that they reinforce hegemonic masculinity (Brown, 1999; Taylor, 2007). In this way, superhero comics constitute a site for transmitting ideology. Indeed, as Dittmer (2005) argues, "the seemingly innocent nature of the comic book medium contributes to its significance in the battle over American identity because it usually operates beneath the gaze of most cultural critics" (p. 628).

That said, in the pantheon of superhero comics, there are graphic novels that set out to challenge and disrupt the dominant ideology. In *Watchmen*, for example, author Allen Moore and cartoonist Dave Gibbons deconstruct the idea of the superhero and interrogate the concept of power. *The Dark Knight Returns*, a graphic novel by Frank Miller, pits competing ideologies against one another using the characters of Batman and Superman. Though she has intermittently been used to reinforce traditional female gender norms, writers and artists have also used the character of Wonder Woman to disrupt hegemonic femininity. Against this backdrop, *Truth: Red, White, and Black*, written by Robert Morales and drawn by Kyle Baker (2003/2009), can be read as a graphic novel that aims to disrupt aspects of the dominant ideology. As such, it constitutes an ideal test case for gauging the value involved in teaching superhero comics in classrooms.

By presenting the story of Isaiah Bradley, a fictional character known to the African American community as the black Captain America, Morales and Baker (2003/2009) examine paradoxes in a nation that embraces democracy and egalitarianism at the same time its institutions marginalize large segments of its population. In doing so, they deconstruct the idea of Captain America, challenging readers to ask who and what the symbol represents. In this way, *Truth* is a graphic novel that educators can profitably examine with students with the goal of engaging them in critical conversations that challenge them to read the word and the world (Friere & Macedo, 1987). Prior to examining some of the complex questions and issues that *Truth* invites readers to explore, I first situate the graphic novel in the larger tradition of superhero comics.

A SHORT HISTORY OF SUPERHERO COMIC BOOKS

In 1938, National Comics, the predecessor of what is today known as DC Comics, published the first comic book in what was slated to be a new series. Titled *Action Comics,* the series was conceived as an anthology of short stories, and the first issue featured a story written and drawn by two young men from Cleveland, Ohio, Jerry Siegel and Joe Shuster respectively. An active member of the SF fan community, Siegel had self-published a series of fanzines, one of which, *Science Fiction,* included a story about a villain with telepathic powers. The story was titled "The Reign of the Superman." Siegel later reimagined the character as one who used his powers for good, and some time later National Comics, searching for new material to publish, included a story in which the character appeared in the inaugural issue of *Action Comics.* As seen on the cover, Siegel and Shuster's creation wore blue tights, red boots, and a red cape. Panic-stricken figures (whether they are innocent bystanders or villains is not clear) ran for cover as he smashed the frontend of a car, which he held effortlessly above his head, against a boulder. On his chest was what readers today recognize as the eponymous "S" of Superman.

For a generation of adolescents who came of age in the 1930s, Siegel and Shuster's creation likely provided a welcome distraction from the hardships of the Great Depression. In just a few issues the character proved commercially viable, so much so that National gave him his own comic book, *Superman,* just one year later: "By 1940, *Superman* comics were selling 1,250,000 copies per month" (Hajdu, 2008, p. 31). The dawn of the superhero had arrived, and profit-driven publishers scrambled to usher it in by introducing their own legions of brightly colored caped crusaders. According to Hajdu (2008), imitators of Superman "flourished in superabundance: Amazing Man, Wonder Man, Sandman, Doll Man, the Flash, Master Man, Hawkman, the Whip, Hourman, Roy the Superboy (no relation), Captain America, Captain Marvel, Bulletman, Johnny Quick, Aquaman, and Wonder Woman, all published by the end of 1941" (p. 31). This competition came at a cost though. As Duncan and Smith (2009) argue, while the gallery of imitators Superman spawned proved lucrative for publishers, it also ensured "that the comic book medium would be forever … associated with adolescent power fantasies of muscular men in tights" (p. 32).

While the narratives presented in early superhero comic books were often frivolous, there were stories that touched on social issues from the beginning. Today, Superman is a symbol of "truth, justice, and the American way," but in his early years he battled capitalists, gangsters and others who prayed on the weak. Indeed, according to Jones (2004), almost two years passed before the stories the character appeared in took an explicit turn toward SF and fantasy. At a time when the United States stood on the brink of entering World War II, some creators actively encouraged its doing so. In 1940, for example, a character known as the Sub-Mariner fought Nazis, and a year later Captain America punched Hitler on the cover of his first comic book (Hajdu, 2008). After the Japanese bombed Pearl

Harbor, most superheroes abandoned fighting crime to pursue "saboteurs, spies, scientists working for the Axis, and other domestic threats" (Hajdu, 2008, p. 55). By the end of World War II, however, the genre had largely fallen out of favor with readers who, having grown older, craved more mature stories, something they found in the form of crime, and later horror, comics.

Superhero comics are woven into the fabric of American popular culture today, but they had their fair share of detractors in their early years. Children's author and literary critic Sterling North (1940), for example, challenged the aesthetic value of superhero and other comic books, arguing that they interfered with young people's ability to appreciate quality literature. Teachers and librarians also questioned the influence superhero comics had on developing readers. Others, like psychologist Frederic Wertham, argued that superhero comics promoted fascism of the sort the United States had recently fought to defeat in World War II. These concerns did not come close to approximating the fear that gripped adults when adolescent readers turned to crime and horror comics in the late 1940s and early 1950s though. Suddenly, criticism of comic books had less to do with their perceived impact on readers (though that remained a concern for years to come) and more to do with what authority figures saw as a link between comic books and an escalation in juvenile delinquency. Faced with graphic images and violent stories whose aesthetic appeal was lost on them, many adults, including teachers, librarians, parents, and civic leaders, embarked on a nationwide campaign to sanitize comic books and reign in an industry they felt had run roughshod over good taste. At its most extreme, these campaigns culminated in organized comic book burnings. In other communities, children who turned in their comic books were rewarded with works of canonical literature (Hajdu, 2008).

Faced with the threat of external regulation in the wake of a congressional hearing on the comic book industry in 1954, a group of publishers came together and formed the Comics Magazine Association of America (CMAA). In doing so they adopted a self-regulating code similar to one the motion picture industry had adopted some years earlier. This newly established Comics Code relegated writers and artists to addressing non-threatening subject matter, the result of which effectively sanitized comic books. It should be noted that the Comics Code was ideological insofar as it treated comic books as a vehicle to indoctrinate young readers into the dominant culture's values and beliefs. Summarizing some of the provisions made in the Code, Nyberg (1998) explains:

> There was never to be any disrespect for established authority and social institutions. Good always triumphed over evil, and if evil had to be shown, it was only in order to deliver a moral message. Content would foster respect for parents and for honorable behavior. With these provisions, the publishers were plying to the conservative critics who were just as concerned about morality as they were about violence, or perhaps more so. (p. 113)

As publishers hoped would be the case, their decision to implement the Comics Code effectively silenced their critics.

SEAN P. CONNORS

In subsequent years, mainstream comic book publishers were desperate to find a genre they could market to the baby-boom generation (Nyberg, 1998). This led them to return to the site of their previous glory and they once again put their weight behind the superhero genre. This new generation of superheroes was different, however, in that it reflected the social upheaval of the 1960s. Some characters, like Captain America, questioned the integrity of social institutions they once defended. Others tackled timely social issues such as drug abuse, racism, and poverty (Harvey, 1996), leading writers and artists to engage in social commentary. In *Green Arrow/Green Lantern*, for example, writer Dennis O'Neil and artist Neil Adams examined a host of social and political issues. Years later, O'Neil recalled some of the questions he and his colleague faced:

> Could we dramatize the real-life issues that tormented the country in the context of superheroics? Could we fashion stories about drug addiction, environmental destruction, corporate rapacity, cults, racism, poverty, bigotry—the whole catalogue of national discontent that energized the era— and still deliver the heroic fantasy that people bought comic books for? (quoted in Harvey, p. 223)

Around the same time, the comic book industry experienced a change in how it distributed comic books to readers, the result of which made it easier for creators to tell stories the Comics Code would have deemed impermissible. In the heady days of underground comics, for example, creators often sold their work directly to readers in spaces associated with the counterculture movement. Their success doing so established an unofficial retail network that led mainstream publishers to recognize the potential for direct market comics sales (Harvey, 1996). Although they continued to sell comic books on newsstands for years to come, DC and Marvel also began to distribute them to independent dealers who ran comic book stores.

Freed from the restraints of the Comics Code, creators and publishers were able to produce stories that addressed mature themes and subject matter (Nyberg, 1998). By the 1980s, superhero comics like *Watchmen*, written by Alan Moore and drawn by Dave Gibbons, and *Batman: The Dark Knight Returns,* by Frank Miller, began to challenge the dominant ideology by deconstructing the concept of the superhero. In doing so, they challenged the idea that superhero comics amounted to little more than a childish form of entertainment. Later, after *Maus*, a Holocaust narrative published serially in *RAW* magazine before being collected as a two-volume book, won the Pulitzer Prize, institutions that had previously discounted the value of comics gradually began to embrace graphic novels, the result being that "books-of-comics became the province of bookstores and libraries—'respectable' places—as much as comic shops" (Wolk, 2007, p. 43). Today, graphic novels are written for children, adolescents, and adults, and they are reviewed in mainstream publications such as *The New York Times*.

Literacy educators have also embraced graphic novels. Indeed, contemporary practitioner journals abound with articles celebrating the educational merit of works such as Art Spiegleman's *Maus,* Marjane Satrapi's *Persepolis,* Josh Neufeld's *A.D.: New Orleans After the Deluge,* David Small's *Stitches,* and Gene

170

Luen Yang's *American Born Chinese,* a text that was named a finalist for the National Book Award for Young People's Literature in 2006. These are all exemplary graphic novels, but it is worth noting that they all fall under the category of what Wolk (2007) calls art comics. Superhero comics, meanwhile, remain conspicuously absent in schools.

The likelihood of teachers asking students to examine superhero comics (or art comics for that matter) is further diminished by the implementation of the Common Core State Standards (CCSS) in the United States. These standards, which purport to prepare students for the challenges of college and the workplace, narrow-mindedly emphasize the value of exposing students to rigorous reading assignments. In recent years, the creators of the CCSS have disseminated lists of so-called "exemplar texts" that are said to reflect the level of textual complexity students ought to encounter in the different grades to ensure that they are prepared to take the standardized assessments that will inevitably be tied to the CCSS. Needless to say, the overwhelming majority of the titles on these lists are canonical. Yet the measure of a text's complexity depends as much on the questions that readers ask of it as it does on the text itself (see, for example, Connors 2013). Read through the lens of critical theory, it is possible to appreciate superhero graphic novels as complex texts capable of fostering and sustaining discussions that promote deep critical thinking.

As explained, many superhero comic books and graphic novels reinscribe mainstream values and behavioral norms, but there are examples of texts that aim to disrupt aspects of the dominant ideology, one of which is *Truth: Red, White, and Black,* a graphic novel written by Robert Morales and drawn by Kyle Baker. In *Truth,* Morales and Baker (2003/2009) tackle the complex problem of race relations in the United States and foreground the role that institutional racism has historically played in marginalizing members of the African American community. A brief summary of the graphic novel follows.

TRUTH: RED, WHITE, AND BLACK

Originally published by Marvel Comics as a seven-issue comic book series, *Truth: Red, White, and Black* was collected and released as a graphic novel in 2009.[1] The story revolves around the experiences of three African American men from disparate backgrounds who enlist in the Army following the Japanese attack on Pearl Harbor only to have their all-black battalion commandeered as part of a top-secret military intelligence program known as Project Super Solider. Three hundred soldiers are randomly selected to participate in the experiment, and the rest are murdered to preserve the military's secret. Tragically, all of the men's families are told that their loved ones died in action.

To ensure the safety of a volatile serum the military eventually administers to a frail white solider, Steve Rogers, to transform him into the iconic figure of Captain America, scientists working for Project Super Soldier first test it on black soldiers, only five of whom survive the experiment. Bestowed with tremendous strength and athleticism, yet suffering from severe side effects associated with the Super Soldier

SEAN P. CONNORS

serum, the soldiers are dropped behind enemy lines with the objective of disrupting a German convoy that is transporting an equivalent serum that Nazi scientists are working to develop. In the ensuing battle, two of the black soldiers are killed. Later, in a fit of rage brought on by a racist soldier's taunts, one of the remaining soldiers murders a peer who intervenes to restrain him, and he is in turn shot by the white soldier. Isaiah Bradley, the lone survivor, is subsequently sent on a suicide mission to destroy a German concentration camp. Before leaving, however, Bradley takes a uniform and shield set aside for Captain America, whose arrival is delayed by weather and who is ignorant of both Bradley's existence and the fate of the black soldiers who died to ensure the safety of the serum that imbued him with exceptional strength and speed.

Having infiltrated the concentration camp, Bradley stumbles upon a medical facility housing the remains of Jewish prisoners who died participating in Nazi experiments. Weeping as he sets out charges to destroy the building, Bradley, in a moment of introspection, reflects on his own mistreatment at the hands of American scientists, who, like their German counterparts, exploited an oppressed group of people. In this way, the graphic novel's creators foreground a bond, forged in suffering, between Jews and African Americans (for an excellent discussion of this point, see Wanzo, 2009). Later, after he is trapped in a gas chamber while attempting to free the camp's prisoners, Bradley is captured and taken before Hitler and his Minister of Propaganda, Josef Goebbels, both of whom cite the oppression of African Americans at the hands of the United States government as reason for him to defect to their side. When Bradley declines their invitation, Hitler orders him killed, dismembered, and returned to the military to embarrass the United States. Before this can happen, however, a small group of African German freedom fighters rescue Bradley and return him to the Americans. Upon his return to the United States, he is promptly court-marshaled and sentenced to 17 years in solitary confinement for having stolen, and worn, Captain America's uniform.

In the seventh, and final, issue of *Truth*, Steve Rogers, having learned about his African American predecessor, and dressed in the iconic blue uniform of Captain America, visits Bradley's wife, Faith, with the intention of returning the uniform her husband once wore. He is consequently surprised to discover that Isaiah is still alive, though a combination of the Super Soldier serum and the years he spent in isolation have caused his mental faculties to deteriorate. On the walls of the family's apartment, Rogers observes a series of photographs of Isaiah posing alongside famous members of the black community, including Muhammad Ali, Colin Powell, Richard Pryor, Nelson Mandela, and Alex Haley. In the story's closing panel, which comprises an entire page, a smiling Steve Rogers is photographed standing alongside the black Captain America, who, also smiling, wears the torn and tattered remnants of a red, white, and blue uniform over his clothing.

Readers unfamiliar with the history of Captain America comics may be surprised to learn that the character appears in a story that is so openly critical of esteemed American institutions. Yet the tension the character navigates between his desire to serve his country and his distrust of its institutions is representative of the kind of stories he appeared in after he returned to print in the 1960s. From the time he punched Hitler on the cover of his first comic book through the end of World War II, Captain America served a propagandistic function insofar as he was designed to rally readers around the war effort. In subsequent years, with the war over, the character was no longer needed, and he only occasionally appeared in comic books. In the 1960s, however, after Marvel resuscitated him, Captain America grappled with feelings of cynicism not unlike those readers faced in the wake of Kennedy's assassination, the Vietnam War, and the assassination of Martin Luther King, Jr. According to Wanzo (2009), "[the character] eased away from military service in the 1970s, his disillusionment in the Watergate era reflecting the country's disillusionment. The black Captain America is thus one of the more recent manifestations of the hero expressing ambivalence about US politics" (p. 344).

Read critically, *Truth* is a graphic novel that educators can profitably examine with students to promote close reading and to inspire conversations that encourage critical thinking and engagement with relevant social and political issues. Because it relies in part on pictures to tell a story, the graphic novel also affords teachers and students an opportunity to practice visual analysis and to consider the role that visual rhetoric plays in shaping their interpretations of multimodal narratives—that is, stories told through two or more semiotic channels. When reading a graphic novel, it is not enough to pay attention to a text's verbal design. Instead, one has to devote equal attention to the role pictures play in conveying meaning. In the section to follow, I demonstrate how Morales and Baker (2003/2009) use *Truth* as a vehicle to problematize the symbol of Captain America. In doing so, I treat the graphic novel as a test case for assessing the potential value involved in asking students to read superhero comics critically and in the context of wider issues of genre.

WHO DOES CAPTAIN AMERICA REPRESENT?

The cover art for the second issue of *Truth*, titled "The Basics," depicts a hyper-muscular black soldier, veins bulging in his arms and neck, standing alone in front of an American flag (see Figure 1). Viewed in profile from the waist up, the soldier wears a blue shirt with a white star at its center, an outfit that readers in the know recognize as the iconic uniform of Captain America. In place of Captain America's mask, however, the soldier wears an Army helmet and a do-rag, an item of clothing associated with the African American community. On the soldier's right arm is a tattoo symbolizing the Double Victory Campaign, a movement that some African Americans initiated during World War II, an era of Jim Crow laws, and which advocated fighting for democracy at home and abroad. In his right hand, which hangs at his side, the soldier holds a battle-scarred shield. His left hand, balled-up in a fist, clutches a portion of the flag that he has pulled taut, and which he appears to contemplate meditatively. Although he appears to be snarling, the soldier's face is hidden in shadows, making it difficult to gauge his expression, and thus to interpret his motivations and feelings. The time of day, whether sunrise or sunset, is also unclear, an ambiguity that is potentially important.

Figure 1. Cover Issue 2, Truth *(© 2013 MARVEL. Used with permission)*

At least two competing interpretations of the above image are available to readers. On one hand, the soldier appears ready to drape himself in the American flag, which he presumably fought to defend, thus signifying patriotism and allegiance to state. In this reading, the use of orange and yellow hues in the background may be thought to represent dawn, and hence the start of a new era for a community that has historically served its country in spite of the oppression it has faced. At the same time, however, it is also possible to read the soldier as contemplating his betrayal at the hands of a nation that promised him equality, but which limited his access to the American Dream through a combination of segregationist legislation and institutional racism. Seen in this light, the soldier may appear poised to tear the flag, a portion of which he holds taut, from its mast in a moment of disgust and anger. Collectively, these competing interpretations point to a question that Morales and Baker (2003/2009) raise and explore in the graphic novel—namely, who (and what) does the symbol of Captain America represent?

The first issue of *Truth* introduces readers to three African American men, each of whom enlists in the military following the bombing of Pearl Harbor, albeit for different reasons. The first, Luke Evans, a life-long serviceman recently demoted to the rank of sergeant for confronting a racist superior, is on the verge of committing suicide when he receives word of Pearl Harbor. He subsequently regards service in the war as offering him a purpose in life. Maurice Canfield, the socialist son of a wealthy capitalist who made his fortune on the backs of "Negros that are compelled to lighten their skins and straighten their hair" (TF), enlists after a judge gives him the choice of joining the military or serving 20 years in prison for demonstrating against the war. The motivations of Isaiah Bradley, a newly married father-to-be and the story's protagonist, are less obvious, though it is suggested that he enlisted to protect his wife and unborn child. As Wanzo (2009) observes, none of the characters enlist in the war out of a sense of duty to country, a fact that sets them apart from Steve Rogers, the white Captain America, who is eager to defend the nation, and who is coopted by the military as a symbol for the war effort.

This is not to say that African American soldiers are depicted as unpatriotic in *Truth*. Rather, in contrast to Rogers, whose whiteness assures him a certain measure of power in society, their familiarity with discrimination and oppression complicates their motives for defending a country that extends a promise of equality at the same time its institutions limit their access to the American Dream. For Wanzo (2009), Bradley exemplifies what she calls "melancholic patriotism" – that is, a form of patriotism that she associates with an "African American patriotic identity that must be understood as strongly tied to both an investment in democracy and the affect resulting from its phantasmagoric nature for many citizens" (p. 341).

The idea that African Americans occupy a place in limbo, caught between the promise of equality and the reality of segregation, is established early in the narrative when Bradley and his wife, Faith, whom readers later discover is the story's narrator, visit the World Fair during what organizers set aside as "Negro Week." At the fair, the couple strolls through the entertainment section where they come across a white carnival barker selling tickets to view exotic international women. When Isaiah attempts to purchase two tickets, however, the obviously nervous worker dissuades him from doing so, explaining that the performers "don't like being looked at like they're animals" (TF). For Bradley and his wife, this exchange is emblematic of the illusory promise of equality extended to African Americans in the United States. Indeed, as Faith explains, the cost of admission to the fair could buy a person the promise of equality right up until the moment that "somebody decided it didn't" (TF).

In the second issue of *Truth*, Morales and Baker (2003/2009) turn their attention to the problem of institutional racism, specifically, the marginalization of African Americans in the military. Despite being called on to defend their country, black soldiers are segregated and subjected to racist slurs by their white counterparts. They fare little better in the eyes of ranking officers, who regard them as cannon fodder. When Dr. Reinstein, the physician in charge of Project Super Solider, and

Mr. Tully, a government operative, requisition two battalions of black soldiers to participate in a highly classified experiment, the commanding officer, lacking the clearance needed to contextualize their request, casually asks whether they intend to use the men to "mop up a battlefield" (TB). Later, after three hundred black soldiers are chosen to receive an experimental serum designed to transform them into super-humans, the remainder are slaughtered by white soldiers to preserve the military's secret.

Of the soldiers selected to participate in Project Super Soldier, a total of five survive. The others suffer gruesome deaths. Strapped to metal gurneys in a laboratory, they are injected with a serum that causes their bodies to grow and swell to the point that they finally explode, coating the walls, ceiling, and floor with their blood. White doctors and nurses appear untroubled by this, however, a result of their objectifying the soldiers, who they refer to by number much as the Germans did Jewish prisoners in concentration camps. Following a particularly horrific death, a scientist, talking coolly into a microphone, summarizes the result of the experiment, stating, "Subject A-23 expired at 1718 hours. Now it is certain that 5 cc's of the serum is too much" (TP). In the background, two scientists are seen recording notes on clipboards, while what appears to be an African American custodian stands between them, mop and dustpan in hand, ready to clean the room.

In the afterward found in the graphic novel, Morales explains that his idea for re-envisioning Project Super Solider grew out of a long tradition of exposing disadvantaged groups to unethical research practices in the United States. This includes the infamous Tuskegee experiment, a longitudinal study that took place between 1932 and 1972 in which scientists knowingly withheld treatment for syphilis from approximately 400 African American men who entered the study having contracted the disease. As a result of the researchers' negligence, several of the men died in the study, as did wives who were exposed to the disease and children who were born with abnormalities due to their being exposed in utero.

Despite facing injustices of the sort described above, Isaiah Bradley does step forward to serve his country, and in the process of doing so he inadvertently becomes a highly charged political symbol. Throughout the graphic novel, Morales and Baker (2003/2009) play with the concept of symbols, asking who reserves the right to control them, and how their meanings change according to what different audiences project on them. When Maurice Canfield produces an issue of a newspaper, *The Negro American*, that contains a headline referencing the Double Victory Campaign, he asks his sergeant, Luke Evans, to share his thoughts about it. Although Evans appreciates the importance of the campaign's slogan, "Democracy at home and abroad," he rejects its usefulness to the average foot soldier. "Symbols are well and good for noncombatants," he explains, "but they're just foolishness if you want to win on the battlefield" (TB). In this way, symbols are constructed in the story as a tool the powerful use to rally the masses around a cause. This idea is reinforced soon after when another solider in the platoon encourages Canfield to place the Victory Campaign symbol in a drawer with the Nazi swastika and allow the two to fight to determine which is superior.

This isn't to say that symbols aren't powerful. To the contrary, those in positions of power employ them precisely because they appreciate their ability to move people emotionally, an idea that Evans and Bradley touch on when they discuss incongruities in the timeline surrounding the release of a Captain America comic book that Bradley reads in the context of the story. In the course of their conversation, Bradley observes that the comic book, whose historically accurate cover depicts Captain America punching Hitler, anticipated the men's experiences in Project Super Soldier by a full year. Moreover, though the narrative touches on specific events and details surrounding their story, the black soldiers themselves are conspicuously absent from it. Instead, the story focuses on Steve Rogers, a white soldier "the brass is so high on" (TC). Evans responds by informing Bradley that, in a time of war, the military reserves the right to commandeer anything it deems necessary to its cause, including symbols. "If the Army determines they need a Steve Rogers," he argues, "they're going to move heaven and hell to get one, the poor bastard" (TC). Readers, of course, appreciate that this is precisely what the Army has done, albeit on the backs of black soldiers it keeps hidden from view.

In asking who reserves the right to wear the uniform of Captain America, Morales and Baker (2003/2009) simultaneously ask who (and what) the symbol represents, an important question given the country's long history of failed race relations. As explained, Captain America emerged in the early 1940s as a symbol designed to rally the American public around the nation's war effort. Like the vast majority of superheroes, the character is white, and in this way the comic book functions to transmit ideology. Nama (2009), for example, references the work of scholars who emphasize the importance of race in superhero comics, and who argue that black children warrant access to superheroes that resemble them. In *Truth*, Morales and Baker (2003/2009) take a slightly different approach, disrupting the dominant ideology by considering how a white audience would respond to the idea of a black Captain America.

Isaiah Bradley's decision to appropriate Steve Rogers' iconic uniform and shield, which he subsequently wears into battle, begs the question, "Who reserves the right to wear the uniform of Captain America?" In the context of the story, white characters construe Bradley's act as treasonous, and they punish him for it by sentencing him to prison. Yet his actions highlight the challenges the military faces in its efforts to control the symbolic meanings Captain America conveys. Toward the end of the fourth issue, "The Cut," Morales and Baker (2003/2009) present a single full-page panel that depicts Bradley parachuting behind enemy lines while wearing the uniform of Captain America (see Figure 2).

It is the first time readers see the character in uniform, and the perspective of the image situates the audience in a position to view him from a low vertical angle, thus establishing a power relationship. According to Kress and van Leeuwen (1996/2006), vertical angles are effective in establishing power relationships between readers and subjects in an image. They argue, for example, that readers experience the sensation of occupying a position of power when they encounter a figure from a high vertical angle, the result of which places them in a position to gaze down on it. Conversely, when viewed from a low angle, a represented figure appears to tower over readers so that it seems more intimidating. As seen in the image below, the artist's use of a low vertical angle creates the impression that Bradley, a determined look on his face, looms over the audience, establishing him as a force to be reckoned with. Though he wears the red, white, and blue uniform, the shield he carries depicts the symbol for the Double Victory Campaign. It is not surprising, then, that in an accompanying line of dialogue a ranking officer in the military, having learned of the theft, and cognizant of the political ramifications it poses, informs his colleagues that the mission has "escalated to a new level of deniability" (TC).

Figure 2. Panel from Issue 4, Truth *(© 2013 MARVEL. Used with permission)*

Later, after Nazis capture Bradley and bring him before Hitler, he awakens to a newsreel recounting the exploits of Captain America, "the U. S. of A.'s new secret weapon" (TW). Upon opening his eyes, however, he, along with the audience, encounters the image of his white counterpart, Steve Rogers, battling Nazis, suggesting that the government has successfully re-appropriated the symbol. Recognizing an opportunity to lure him to his side, Hitler instructs Bradley that Germany is not at war with his people. When Bradley mistakenly construes Hitler as referring to Americans, Josef Goebbels corrects him, stating, "Not America, Private Bradley, your people" (TW).

Recognizing that the symbol of Captain America is meant to stand in proxy for the United States, the question arises whether the white character represents all segments of the American population. The possibility that he may not surfaces again in the story when, in issue six, titled "The Whitewash," Steve Rogers interviews a racist veteran involved in covering up both Bradley's participation in Project Super Soldier and his subsequent imprisonment. Having shared his dream to participate in the program as a younger man, the character exclaims, "Imagine my disgust that no one running the project cared what it meant to real Americans" (TW). He punctuates his remarks by insisting that the country would find the idea of a black Captain America anathema. Sadly, these loathsome remarks proved somewhat prescient. In an interview, Axel Alonso, the editor of *Truth*, talked about the criticism Marvel faced from fans who objected to Morales's reimagining of Captain America's origin story. According to Alonso, critics objected to the series on several grounds, including "outright racists who just don't like the idea of a black man in the Cap uniform" (Sinclair, para 5).[ii]

The title of the seventh, and final, issue of *Truth*, "The Blackvine," refers to a chain of communication that African Americans used to exchange sensitive information while ensuring that it remained in the community. Having unearthed Bradley's story, Steve Rogers, the white Captain America, visits his wife, Faith, with the intention of returning the uniform her husband bravely wore, but which is now tattered and torn. For years, the individual who helped the military cover up Bradley's role in Project Super Soldier had kept the uniform hidden away in a locked room, ensuring that Bradley's story went unrecognized by history. Confronted with a series of photographs in Faith's apartment of Bradley posing alongside famous black figures, however, Rogers discovers that the African American community had known about the legacy of the black Captain America all along.

When Rogers first encounters Faith on the street outside her apartment building she is wearing a burqa, the result of which masks her face. Later, as the pair converses in the kitchen, Faith explains that she chose to wear the garment to challenge anti-Islamic sentiments that arose following 9/11. She adds, however, that she also appreciates the burqa's ability to direct attention away from femininity, placing it instead "on what I say, or on what people choose to project onto me" (TBV). She consequently asks Rogers whether his experiences wearing the uniform of Captain America led him to experience something similar. Unsure how to answer her question, he replies, "Faith, I'll have to think that over, but I probably do" (TBV).

The final image in *Truth*, a full page panel, depicts Steve Rogers, dressed as Captain America, posing for a photograph alongside a smiling Isaiah Bradley, who is seen wearing the tattered remnants of a red, white, and blue uniform over his dress shirt (see Figure 3). With this final image, Morales and Baker (2003/2009) challenge readers to ask a question similar to the one Faith asked Rogers—that is, what meanings do *you* project on the image of Captain America?

Figure 3. Panel from Issue 7, Truth *(© 2013 MARVEL. Used with permission)*

Consistent with the idea that symbols are fluid, it is possible to interpret the image of two Captain Americas—one black, the other white—in multiple ways. On one hand, the image can be interpreted as commenting on the progress that African Americans have made in their fight for equality. The battle has come at a cost, as evidenced by Bradley's tattered uniform, but the artist's decision to position the two figures alongside each other seems to suggest that American society is at long last willing to acknowledge the many sacrifices that African Americans have historically made for their country. On the other hand, it is possible to interpret the image of Bradley, dressed in a shabby red, white, and blue uniform and standing alongside a pristinely groomed white Captain America, as commenting on the United States' failure to live up to its ideals of democracy and egalitarianism. Seen in this light, the image can be read as suggesting that African Americans have been, and continue to be, treated as second-class citizens in a country that has fallen well short of its ideals.

Wanzo (2009) offers an even more interesting interpretation of the panel. She begins by observing that, in the photographs that depict Bradley alongside famous members of the black community, the character, mentally addled as a result of both the Project Super Soldier serum and the years he spent in solitary confinement, consistently mimics their expressions and gestures. She consequently asks how readers ought to interpret the fact that Bradley appears smiling alongside Rogers, who is also seen smiling. Querying the possible meanings this seemingly minor detail in the text's visual design makes available, she asks:

> In what is left of Isaiah Bradley's shattered consciousness, what is the source of the smile? Is it mere mimicry of the smile of the man by his side, the kind of man he was told he has no right to be? Is it a trickster-like pleasure informed by his possession of an identity and property denied him by the state? Or is it pleasure in draping himself in a symbol of his accomplishments in the name of the abstract principles in which he believed? (p. 358)

These questions, as Wanzo (2009) concedes, are not easily answered, nor do the graphic novel's creators presume to answer them. In a classroom setting, however, the questions do provide teachers and students with an opportunity to engage in meaningful conversations that inspire analytic thinking, and which require them to evaluate their answers with the intention of understanding how their situatedness as readers relative to the issues the graphic novel raises influences the meanings they project on it.

FINAL THOUGHTS

In the early years of the 21st century, popular attitudes toward comic books and graphic novels are evolving. As argued in this chapter, a growing number of educators are willing to acknowledge the literary potential of graphic novels, and, to judge from the number of articles published in practitioner journals, graphic novels are making their way into the literature curriculum. In many instances, however, these titles belong to the category of what Wolk (2007) calls art comics, suggesting that educators are reinforcing a binary between high and low culture even as they embrace a form of popular culture that has historically been stigmatized. Seventy-five years after the character of Superman appeared on the cover of *Action Comics #1*, schools continue to ghettoize the genre of superhero comics.

That educators should struggle to take superhero comics seriously is not surprising. In its formative years, children embraced the genre, establishing a link that persists today, and which leads many adults to construct the genre as a puerile form of literature. Superhero comic books and graphic novels are also a commodity, which may lead critics to question the motives of profit-driven publishers. Helford (2000) argues that film producers, driven to earn a profit, are required to determine how to "negotiate the particular cultural mood of the era" with the intention of "[alienating] as few viewers as possible and [targeting] specific audiences without pushing the boundaries too far" (p. 7). The same can be said about comic book publishers and distributors, which may explain why mainstream graphic novels often do reinforce aspects of the dominant ideology.

Still more, there is a sense that superhero comics lack literary ambitions. In fairness, the narrative and artistic complexity evident in *Truth* is greater than one would expect to find in most superhero comics. That said, the same thing can be said of most traditional novels relative to the classics.

To some extent, the superhero genre's affiliation with speculative fiction may also account for the lack of respect extended it. While it is possible to find graphic novels in institutions that historically frowned on them—for example, bookstores and libraries—it is interesting to consider the space they occupy, as it can be read as a sign of the larger culture's inability to determine what to make of the form. In one nationally recognizable chain of bookstores, for example, the space that graphic novels and manga occupy is contiguous with the SF and fantasy section, the result of which reinforces a link between comics and speculative fiction. Adjacent to both sections is an assortment of toys, connoting a link to childhood, and immediately beyond that are shelves of popular magazines. Moreover, the graphic novels shelved in this particular section of the bookstore represent a haphazard mix of art and mainstream comics, with superhero comics predominating. Of particular interest is the fact that critically acclaimed graphic novels such as *Persepolis* and *Maus* are not present in this section. Instead, they are shelved in the Literature section.

This chapter is not offered as an apology for superhero comics. As explained, most superhero comics lack the narrative complexity evident in *Truth: Red, White, and Black*. Moreover, as Duncan and Smith (2009) argue, examples of graphic novels such as *Truth* should not be construed as evidence "that comics are fully integrated, or that problems with representation for women, people of color, or any other minority have been fully addressed" (p. 262). On a final note, it goes without saying that an exclusive diet of superhero comics (or any single genre for that matter) is inadvisable. That said, if one is willing to take time to become acquainted with superhero comics, and to elicit recommendations from others, it is possible to find works that lend themselves to being read critically, and which invite students to understand that even seemingly innocuous forms of text are capable of challenging or reinforcing aspects of the dominant ideology. In the end, as is true of other forms of speculative fiction, it is up to readers to determine whether they want to embrace the ideologies that a text imparts, or whether they wish to set them aside in favor of other, more compassionate beliefs and values.

NOTES

[i] Given that page numbers are not used in the graphic novel, subsequent references direct readers to the issue in which a particular panel or line of dialogue appears. In chronological order, these include: "The Future" (TF); "The Basics" (TB); "The Passage" (TP); "The Cut" (TC); "The Math" (TM); The Whitewash" (TW); and "The Blackvine" (TBV).

[ii] In some ways, *Truth: Red, White, and Black*, which was published serially as a comic book in 2003, anticipated the vitriolic response that greeted the election, and subsequent re-election, of Barack Obama, the first African American to occupy the office of President. Indeed, the Southern Poverty Law Center documented a series of hate crimes that occurred following his first election.

REFERENCES

Bitz, M. (2004). The comic book project: Forging alternative pathways to literacy. *Journal of Adolescent & Adult Literacy, 47*(7), 574-586.

Brown, J. A. (1999). Comic book masculinity and the new black superhero. *African American Review, 33*(1), 25-42.

Carter, J. B. (Ed.). (2007). *Building literacy connections with graphic novels: Page by page, panel by panel.* Urbana, IL: National Council of Teachers of English.

Chun, C. W. (2009). Critical literacies and graphic novels for English-language learners: Teaching *Maus. Journal of Adolescent and Adult Literacy, 53*(2), 144-153.

Chute, H. (2008). Comics as literature? Reading graphic narrative. *Publications of the Modern Language Association of America, 123*(2), 452-465.

Connors, S. P. (2010). The best of both worlds: Rethinking the literary merit of graphic novels. *The ALAN Review, 37*(3), 65-70.

Connors, S. P. (2013). Weaving multimodal meaning in an after-school reading group. *Visual Communication, 12*(1), 27-53.

Crawford, P. (2004). A novel approach: Using graphic novels to attract reluctant readers and promote literacy. *Library Media Connection, 22*(5), 26-28.

Dittmer, J. (2005). Captain America's empire: Reflections on identity, popular culture, and post-9/11 geopolitics. *Annals of the Association of American Geographers, 95*(3), 626-643.

Duncan, R., & Smith, M. J. (2009). *The power of comics: History, form & culture.* New York: Continuum.

Frey, N., & Fisher, D. (2004). Using graphic novels, anime, and the internet in an urban high school. *English Journal, 93*(3), 19-25.

Frey, N, & Fisher, D. (Eds.). (2008). *Teaching visual literacy: Using comic books, graphic novels, anime, cartoons, and more to develop comprehension and thinking skills.* Thousand Oaks, CA: Corwin Press.

Friere, P., & Macedo, D. (1987). *Literacy: Reading the word & the world.* South Hadley, MA: Bergin & Garvey.

Gillenwater, C. (2009). Lost literacy: How graphic novels can recover visual literacy in the literacy classroom. *Afterimage, 37*(2), 33-36.

Groensteen, T. (2009). Why are comics still in search of cultural legitimization? In J. Heer & K. Worcester (Eds.), *A comics studies reader* (pp. 3-11). Jackson, MS: University of Mississippi Press.

Hajdu, D. (2008). *The ten-cent plague: The great comic-book scare and how it changed America.* New York: Picador.

Harvey, R. C. (1996). *The art of the comic book: An aesthetic history.* Jackson: University Press of Mississippi.

Helford, E. (2000). *Fantasy girls.* Maryland: Rowman and Littlefield.

Jones, G. (2004). *Men of tomorrow: Geeks, gangsters, and the birth of the comic book.* New York: Basic Books.

Kress, G., & van Leeuwen, T. (1996/2006). *Reading images: The grammar of visual design* (2nd ed.). London: Routledge.

McAllister, M. P., Sewell, E. H., & Gordon, I. (Eds.). (2001). *Comics & ideology.* New York: Peter Lang.

Morales, R., & Baker, K. (2003/2009). *Truth: Red, white, and black.* New York: Marvel Comics.

Nama, A. (2009). Brave black worlds: black superheroes as science fiction ciphers. *African Identities, 7*(2), 133-134.

North, S. (1940). A national disgrace. *Childhood Education, 17*(2), 56.

Nyberg, A. K. (1998). *Seal of approval: The history of the comics code.* Jackson: University Press of Mississippi.

Sinclair, T. (2002, Nov.). Back in action. *EW.com.* [Online]. April 2013. Retrieved from http://www.ew.com/ew/article/0,,390672,00.html

Snowball, C. (2005). Teenage reluctant readers and graphic novels. *Young Adult Library Services, 3*(4), 43-45.

Taylor, A. (2007). "He's gotta be strong, and he's gotta be fast, and he's gotta be larger than life": Investigating the engendered superhero body. *The Journal of Popular Culture, 40*(2), 344-360.

Versaci, R. (2001). How comic books can change the way our students see literature: One teacher's perspective. *English Journal, 91*(2), 61-71.

Versaci, R. (2007). *This book contains graphic language: Comics as literature.* New York: Continuum.

Wanzo, R. (2009). Wearing hero-face: Black citizens and melancholic patriotism in *Truth: Red, white, and black. The Journal of Popular Culture, 42*(2), 339-362.

Wertham, F. (1954). *Seduction of the innocent.* New York: Rinehart.

Wolk, D. (2007). *Reading comics: How graphic novels work and what they mean.* Cambridge, MA: Da Capo Press.

P. L. THOMAS

10. THE ENDURING POWER OF SF, SPECULATIVE AND DYSTOPIAN FICTION

Final Thoughts

This volume is part of a series about *challenging* authors, genre, text, reading, and medium. In its essence, this series intends to raise the critical context of what we examine, how we examine, and why we examine a wide range of authors, genres, media, and texts in formal and informal learning and teaching environments. In the chapters preceding this conclusion, I have been placing SF and the many extensions radiating from that focus within the realm of critical pedagogy and critical literacy because I have simultaneously been making the case that SF by its nature is critical in its patterns of creating other worlds, of raising satirical and serious questions about the Big Questions surrounding being human, of placing the individual human in a social context, of viewing the role of science through a skeptical microscope, and of narrating the essential political nature of being human.

I have come to recognize that my affinity for and nearly lifelong connection with SF in various media and genre overlaps (novels, comic books, film, TV) has both fueled and nested my eventual self-identification as a radical scholar (Thomas, accepted). And that leads to my including as a conclusion to this volume a collection of commentaries that I have written that frame discussions of politics, education, and related topics through the use of SF works. The following are those commentaries with slight edits and some context offered for each. This conclusion, then, becomes an argument that SF is a type of radical scholarship, a sort of activism.

* * *

Captain America is a Marvel Comics superhero that blends many of the characteristics found in SF as well as the tensions some of those characteristics create. As I discuss in Chapter One, SF has an interesting habit of including the military in many works. I detail in that chapter specifically The Hulk and Iron Man as SF genre comic book characters and narratives deeply tied to the military.

Captain America as a character and narrative has presented a complex history of America's caustic nationalism and idealized patriotism. The Captain America comic book has reflected the current times in which it has been nested for many decades (see Wright, 2001), and that reality has also exposed the failures of comics to raise a critical voice as much as highlighting the power of comics to challenge social and cultural norms (see Chabon, 2000).

P. Thomas (ed.), Science Fiction and Speculative Fiction, 185–216.

The following commentary was posted at OpEdNews.com *(October 16, 2010) as a challenge to the government's treatment of Pat Tilman and his family after the former professional football player died while serving his country, a decision he chose voluntarily while abandoning his lucrative athletic career. Part of the discussion examines the concept of masking and unmasking inherent in superhero comics, specifically the character of Captain America.*

"DON'T ASK, DON'T TELL":
THERE'S A REASON CAPTAIN AMERICA WEARS A MASK[i]

With the release of *The Tillman Story*, Pat Tillman's brother, Richard, appeared on Bill Maher's *Real Time* (Maher, 2010) and offered yet another narrative of Pat's life and death, one the Tillman Family is willing to tell, but one the American public and ruling elite are unwilling to ask about or retell. Richard was frank and struggling on Maher's HBO show, which included a clip from Pat's memorial where Richard made a blunt and impassioned effort to tell the truth about his brother in the face of the political need to maintain American Mythology—even when those myths are deceptive, even when those myths are at the expense of people.

Pat Tillman was a stellar athlete who succeeded in college and rose to unique status in the NFL, where he did a very *un-American* thing, stepped away from a multi-million dollar contract, to do a very *American* thing, enlist in the military after 9/11 in order to serve his country. The news and political stories of Tillman's decision played down the apparent rejection of materialism in Tillman's volunteering to serve in the military, but the official stories began to craft a narrative starring Pat Tillman as Captain America.

Apparently, we could mask a not-so-subtle challenge to our materialistic existence and consumer culture as long as that masked hero would justify our wars.

Then Tillman died in the line of duty.

Then the U.S. government was exposed for building a story around Tillman's death that was untrue: Pat was killed by "friendly fire" (a disarming term for an incomprehensible and gruesome fact of wars) and not at the hands of the enemy as officials initially claimed—to Pat's brother who was also serving and nearby, to Pat's family, and to the entire country (White, 2005).

Then Richard Tillman, still boiling with anger, said on Maher's show that Pat should have retaliated in order to save himself against the "friendly fire" (Maher, 2010).

Beyond the continuing chasm between the real life and death of Pat Tillman and the narratives created around him, the release of the documentary presents the American public with a story that isn't very flattering. *The Tillman Story* depends on the ambiguous meaning of "story," as a synonym for "narrative" and "lie," to offer another layer to the growing truths and distortions connected with why Pat Tillman joined the military, how he died, and the complex human being who he was.

Now, if we place the Tillman *stories* against the ongoing debate in the military over "don't ask, don't tell," we notice that in this culture we endorse masking reality as a good and even honorable thing. We confront the Great American Myth that never allows us to ask, much less tell.

This military policy based on deception is ironically our central cultural narrative, one the ruling elite perpetuates as political success depends upon speaking to our cultural myths instead of to reality. We are a country committed to don't ask, don't tell.

Pat Tillman's life story and the corrupted narrative invented by politicians and the military to hide the truth and propagandize at the expense of a man and his life are tragic and personal myths that we are ignoring still. If the ruling elite will fabricate preferred stories at the expense of a single person, we can expect the same about the institutions central to our democracy, such as our public education system and teachers.

Such is a disturbing confirmation of the "myths that deform" that Paulo Freire (2005) cautioned about in his examination of the failures of "banking" concepts of education (Freire, 1993).

In this new era of hope and change, the Obama administration, we must be diligent to ask and tell, especially when it comes to our public schools. The false dichotomy of Republican and Democrat, conservative and liberal, is a distraction from the reality of the political elites expressing corporatist narratives to ensure the balance of power favoring the status quo. Leaders are often compelled to maintain cultural myths because black and white messages are politically effective.

President Obama and Secretary of Education Duncan are now leading a renewed assault on public education, and indirectly teachers, under the banner of civil rights--just as Pat Tillman's life and death were buried beneath claims of *patriotism* raised like Captain America's shield so no one could see behind it.

The reality that Obama and Duncan cannot ask or tell about is poverty—and its impact on the lives and learning of children. Acknowledging poverty is an affront to the American Dream; confronting poverty is political dynamite. Blaming teachers and schools instead without offering the evidence works because this is a message we are willing to acknowledge and hear (Giroux, 2010, October 5).

Recently, a group from the ruling elite of schools, self-described as "educators, superintendents, chief executives and chancellors responsible for educating nearly 2 1/2 million students in America," placed themselves squarely in the context of President Obama's and Secretary Duncan's charge against teachers and the status quo; their manifesto states: "As President Obama has emphasized, the single most important factor determining whether students succeed in school is not the color of their skin or their ZIP code or even their parents' income—it is the quality of their teacher" (How to fix our schools, 2010).

The names of the leaders—Klein, Rhee, Vallas—are impressive, and their sweeping claims are compelling—except that the substance of their message is false (Krashen, 2010).

Narratives are powerful, and telling those narratives requires diligence, a willingness to say something often enough to make the created story sound more credible than reality—until the truth is masked beneath a web of narratives that makes truth harder to accept than the lies that seem to conform to all the myths that deform us (rugged individualism, pulling oneself up by the bootstrap, a rising tide lifts all boats).

"Let's stop ignoring basic economic principles of supply and demand" speaks to our faith in the market. "[U]ntil we fix our schools, we will never fix the nation's broader economic problems" triggers our blind willingness to compete and our enduring faith in schools as tools of social reform (How to fix our schools, 2010). They are compelling because we have been saying them for a century.

Just as the fabricated story of Pat Tillman and his sacrifice justified war.

"I don't believe that even the best teachers can completely overcome the huge deficits in socialization, motivation and intellectual development that poor students bring to class through no fault of their own" sounds weak, fatalistic, in the face of our myths, the words of soft people eager to shift the blame (Gardner, 2010). It is something we dare not tell.

Just as the smoldering facts of Pat Tillman's death remain too hard to ask about and too hard to tell.

But only the latter are supported by evidence. But only the latter contradict the Great American Myths about which we dare not ask, we dare not tell.

Captain America wears a mask for a reason: The myth is easier to look at, easier to tell about than the truth hidden underneath—whether we are asking about and looking hard at the death of a complex man, Pat Tillman, or the complex influences of poverty on the lives and learning of children across our country.

* * *

One aspect of the U.S. that has been exposed by SF is the inherent danger of both government and corporate overreach. With Big Brother in Orwell's Nineteen Eighty-Four, *we also have* Robocop *(1987) exposing the corporatization of inner-city Detroit, specifically the corruption of justice when a private entity controls the police force.*

Kurt Vonnegut speaks to the dangers of corporate America and particularly how corporate America feeds off and perpetuates quantifying the humanity out of people in his Player Piano *(1952). During the high-accountability era in education, since the Ronald Reagan administration, corporate-style education reform has accelerated, reinforced by No Child Left Behind under George W. Bush. The next commentary was posted at OpEdNew.com (January 3, 2011) as an examination of how Vonnegut's* Player Piano *informs the flaws in the corporate takeover of public education, grounded as that movement is in standardized testing and narrow quantitative measures of both student achievement and teacher quality.*

CALCULATING THE CORPORATE STATES OF AMERICA: REVISITING VONNEGUT'S *PLAYER PIANO*[ii]

Few people could have imagined the acceleration of corporate influence that has occurred in the last two years despite the economic downturn associated with those corporations and the election of Barak Obama, who was repeatedly demonized as a socialist.

More shocking, possibly, has been the corporate influence on the public discourse about universal public education, driven by Secretary of Education Arne Duncan and promoted through celebrity tours by billionaire Bill Gates and ex-chancellor Michelle Rhee.

Recently, Bessie (2010, December 29) has speculated about the logical progression of the current accountability era built on tests and destined to hold teachers accountable for their students' test scores (despite the evidence that teachers account for only about 10-20% of achievement [Rothstein, 2010])—hologram teachers. And Krashen (2011) believes that the corporate takeover of schools is at the center of the new reformers' misinformation tour.

While Bessie's and Krashen's comments may sound like alarmist stances—possibly even the stuff of fiction—I believe we all should have been seeing this coming for decades.

The science fiction genre has always been one of my favorites, and within that genre, I am particularly fond of dystopian fiction, such as Margaret Atwood's brilliant *The Handmaid's Tale*, *Oryx and Crake*, and *The Year of the Flood*. Like Atwood (2011), Kurt Vonnegut (1965) spoke and wrote often about rejecting the SF label for his work—but Vonnegut's genius includes his gift for delivering social commentary and satire wrapped in narratives that *seemed* to be set in the future, *seemed* to be a distorted world that we could never possibly experience.

In 1952, Kurt Vonnegut published *Player Piano*, offering what most believed was a biting satire of corporate American from his own experience working at GE (Reed, 1995). A review of the novel in 1963 describes Vonnegut's vision of our brave new world:

> The important difference lies in the fact that Mr. Vonnegut's oligarchs are not capitalists but engineers. In the future as he envisages it, the machines have completed their triumph, dispossessing not only the manual laborers but the white collar workers as well. Consequently the carefully selected, highly trained individuals who design and control the machines are the only people who have anything to do. Other people, the great majority, can either go into the Reconstruction and Reclamation Corps, which is devoted to boondoggling, or join the army, which has no real function in a machine-dominated world-society. (Hicks, 1963)

Yes, in Vonnegut's dystopia, computers are at the center of a society run itself like a machine, with everyone labeled with his or her IQ and designated for what career he or she can pursue (although we should note that women's roles were even more constrained than men's, reflecting the mid-twentieth century sexism in the U.S.). Where corporations end and the government begins is difficult in this society that is simply a slightly exaggerated of the life Vonnegut had witnessed while working at GE before abandoning corporate America to be a full-time writer.

For me, however, Vonnegut's *Player Piano* is as much a warning about the role of testing and labeling people in our education system as it is a red flag about the dangers of the oligarchy that we have become.

Today, with billionaire Bill Gates speaking for not only corporate America but also for reforming public education, how far off was Vonnegut's vision?

In the first decade of the twenty-first century, how different is Vonnegut's world to what we have today, as income inequity and the pooling of wealth accelerates (Noah, 2010)?

We have witnessed where political loyalty lies during the bailouts as corporate America collapsed at the end of George W. Bush's presidency. With corporate American saved, and most Americans ignored, the next logical step is to transform public education by increasing the corporate model that has been crippling the system since the misinformation out of Ronald Reagan's presidency grabbed headlines with the release of A Nation at Risk (Holton, 2003; Bracey, 2003).

If Vonnegut had written this storyline, at least we could have been guaranteed some laughter. But this brave new world of public education is more grim—like George Orwell's *Nineteen Eighty-Four*.

Our artists can see and understand when many of the rest of us are simply overwhelmed by our lives. In *Player Piano*, we see how successful corporate life disorients and overwhelms workers in order to keep those workers under control. And in the relationship between the main character Paul and his wife Anita, we watch the power of corporate life—and the weight of testing and reducing humans to numbers—being magnified by the rise of computers when Paul makes a plea to his wife:

> "No, no. You've got something the tests and machines will never be able to measure: you're artistic. That's one of the tragedies of our times, that no machine has ever been built that can recognize that quality, appreciate it, foster it, sympathize with it." (Vonnegut, 1952, p. 178)

In the novel, Paul's quest and the momentary rise of some rebels appear to be no match for corporate control. Today, I have to say I am no more optimistic than Vonnegut.

When Secretary Duncan (2010, December 7) offers misleading claims about international test scores and bemoans the state of public schools for failing to provide us with a world-class workforce, and almost no one raises a voice in protest (except those of within the field of education, only to be demonized for protesting [Michie, 2011]), I am tempted to think that we are simply getting what we deserve—like Paul at the end of *Player Piano*: "And that left Paul. 'To a better world,' he started to say, but he cut the toast short, thinking of the people of Ilium, already eager to recreate the same old nightmare" (Vonnegut, 1952, p. 340).

* * *

Kurt Vonnegut's Cat's Cradle *(1963) has been one of Vonnegut's greatest popular and critical successes, notably ranking highly in Vonnegut's own self-assessment. While the work is a powerful SF work confronting religion, it also serves as a perceptive unmasking of militaristic and corporate paradigms corrupting democracy.*

The commentary below posted at Daily Kos *(October 11, 2011) uses Vonnegut's* Cat's Cradle *as an entry point to examining and confronting the failure of both major political parties in the U.S. to support public education's democratic purposes to feed the corporate needs driving Republicans and Democrats.*

EDUCATION IN THE CORPORATE STATES OF AMERICA[iii]

In *Cat's Cradle*, Kurt Vonnegut (1963) introduces into his fictional world Bokononism, a religion in which its messiah through the sacred text, *The Books of Bokonon*, confesses: "All of the true things I am about to tell you are shameless lies" (p. 5).

The country of San Lorenzo finds it stability built on a fabricated conflict between General McCabe and the founder of Bokononism, Bokonon:

"Well, when it became evident that no governmental or economic reform was going to make the people much less miserable, the religion became the one real instrument of hope. Truth was the enemy of the people, because the truth was so terrible, so Bokonon made it his business to provide the people with better and better lies." (p. 172)

The charade driven by McCabe outlawing Bokononism and declaring Bokonon a fugitive continues at the expense of McCabe and Bokonon as men until their faux war between the righteous McCabe and renegade holy man Bokonon becomes essential itself: "McCabe was always sane enough to realize that without the holy man to war against, he himself would become meaningless" (p. 175).

While science fiction, or better described as speculative fiction (Atwood, 2011), tends to be more a commentary on its time rather than an attempt to predict some certain future, Vonnegut offers here a stark insight into the current false political dichotomy of Democrats and Republicans in the U.S.

Democrats and Republicans: Two Sides of the Same Corporate Coin

Anyone who believes that the U.S. has a two-party system is living in a delusion similar to the people of San Lorenzo; at best, we have Corporate Democrats and Corporate Republicans. And these two enemies, like McCabe and Bokonon, put on a simplistic passion play with both sides pretending to be the great messiahs and the ultimate sacrificial lambs seeking to preserve or save the U.S. of A.

Except their claims are nothing more than veneer for their corporate interests that lie only millimeters apart while the Democrats accuse the Republicans of being Fat Cats who care nothing for the regular person (failing to acknowledge that the Democrats themselves tend to be Fat Cats as well, pockets lined with corporate affiliations and allegiances) and the Republicans call the Democrats socialists (failing to acknowledge that the Republicans want government to bail out Wall Street and big banks when capitalism fails and that the slandered Democrats are too deep in the market even to see a socialist). Yes, this is all drama, designed to distract and mask that Democrats and Republicans embrace the worst that corporate paradigms have to offer—dehumanizing practices built on hierarchies, authoritarianism, and mechanistic views of humans as interchangeable parts in the great machine of the economy.

The reality that Americans are trapped in a one-party Corporate States of America can be seen directly in the debate over public education stretching back to the early 1980s when President Ronald Reagan simultaneously called for abolishing the U.S. Department of Education and initiated the Republican (and even Democrat) plan to use that same department to impose corporate federalism on the states through public education.

Education in the Corporate States of America

Florida has served as one of the most aggressive states embracing the accountability movement and represents the role of school policy as a lever for rebuilding a state in the image of the governor's political party and corporate commitments.

Former Governor Jeb Bush provided President George W. Bush the state model, along with Texas after George W. Bush was governor, for merging federal and state government in a corporate allegiance. Now, we have Governor Rick Scott taking Florida to new heights:

> Florida's unpopular tea party governor, Rick Scott, wants more of the state's youths to pick up college degrees … but only if the degrees are useful to corporations and don't teach students to question social norms. "You know what? They need to get education in areas where they can get jobs," Scott told a right-wing radio host Monday morning. He continued: "You know, we don't need a lot more anthropologists in the state. It's a great degree if people want to get it, but we don't need them here. I want to spend our dollars giving people science, technology, engineering, math degrees. That's what our kids need to focus all their time and attention on. Those type of degrees. So when they get out of school, they can get a job." (Weinstein, 2011)

Education reform—starting with Reagan and including George H. W. Bush, Clinton, George W. Bush, and now Obama—represents the unmasking of the false battle that Democrats and Republicans often wage over health care, abortion, capital punishment, war, and a whole host of hot button issues that generally change very little in the lives of Americas but serve as pedestals upon which both parties can cry, "Crisis!"

The people of San Lorenzo are drawn to one powerful aspect of Bokononism, foma, defined as harmless lies. But even in this fictional world, Vonnegut shows that the greatest threat to the lies and the fabrications is knowledge—learning, specifically the writing down of history:

I record that fact for whatever it may be worth. "Write it all down," Bokonon tells us. He is really telling us, of course, how futile it is to write or read histories. "Without accurate records of the past, how can men and women be expected to avoid making serious mistakes in the future?" he asks ironically. (p. 237)

So in 2011, well into the presidency of a Democrat, we were faced with the harsh evidence that both political parties claim to be seeking public education reform by creating a school system that is privatized, teachers who are de-professionalized as members of the service industry, and students who are trained to be compliant—even after attending college where they shouldn't be thinking but learning how to fit into the Corporate States of America.

And here it seems appropriate to switch to another classic work from Vonnegut: So it goes.

* * *

*In Atwood's (2011) distinction between SF and speculative fiction, she considers the aspect of fiction considering "what if?"—which I would suggest is at the heart of Atwood's works often associated with SF (*The Handmaid's Tale, Oryx and Crake, *and* The Year of the Flood*). In the "what if?" tradition of SF or speculative fiction, I'd also place Tom Perrotta's* The Leftovers, *a satirical look at the world once the Rapture comes to fruition (much to the surprise of the characters).*

A central quality of SF and speculative fiction (fantasy and historical fiction as well) that is significant is that the creation of some form of an other world helps frame for the readers this *world. Whether the other world is conjured by a shift in time or reality, the other world becomes both a commentary on this world and a possibility of other ways of being (again, a powerful and critical element in SF). The following commentary was posted at* Daily Kos *(October 20, 2011), and it suggests that Perrotta's speculative novel serves as a foundation for embracing our existence more fully and deeply now.*

WHENCE COME "THE LEFTOVERS"?:
SPECULATIVE FICTION AND THE HUMAN CONDITION[iv]

Nora Durst finds herself at the intersection of something routinely normal for middle-class Americans living in the comfort of suburbia and distinctly otherworldly at the same time in Tom Perrotta's (2011) *The Leftovers*, his newest novel venturing into speculative/ dystopian fiction.

Visiting the mall with her sister during the Christmas season, Nora confronts the sudden disappearance of her entire family several years before on October 14, when millions of people also vanished in the Sudden Departure that prompts many to believe the world has finally experienced The Rapture:

Her heart was still racing when she stepped inside, her face hot with pride and embarrassment. She'd just forced herself to make a solo circuit of the big Christmas tree on the main level, where all the parents and kids were waiting to meet Santa Claus. It was another holiday challenge, an attempt to face her fear head-on, to break her shameful habit of avoiding the sight of small children whenever possible. That wasn't the kind of person she wanted to be—shut down, defensive, giving a wide berth to anything that might remind her of what she'd lost. A similar logic had inspired her to apply for the day-care job last year, but that had been too much, too soon. This was more controlled, a one-time-only, bite-the-bullet sort of thing. (p. 193)

This moment for a fictional woman who has lost her family, has lost *everything*, is the essence of Perrotta's mix of dark satire and moving authenticity about the human condition. But it also leads me to move beyond the book and consider what dystopian fiction, what speculative fiction offers readers that proves time and again to be so compelling.

Our Speculative World, "Off-to-the-Side"

Margaret Atwood has provided her readers three brilliant dystopian/speculative works of fiction—which she often uses to argue against simplistic labels such as "science fiction": *The Handmaid's Tale, Oryx and Crake*, and *The Year of the Flood*. In "Writing Utopia" (from *Writing with Intent*), Atwood (2005) clarifies her distinction about genre, specifically about science fiction:

> I define science fiction as fiction in which things happen that are not possible today—that depend, for instance, on advanced space travel, time travel, the discovery of green monsters on other planets or galaxies, or that contain various technologies we have not yet developed. But in *The Handmaid's Tale*, nothing happens that the human race has not already done at some time in the past, or that it is not doing now, perhaps in other countries, or for which it has not yet developed the technology. We've done it, we're doing it, or we could start doing it tomorrow .... So I think of *The Handmaid's Tale* not as science fiction but as speculative fiction; and, more particularly, as that negative form of Utopian fiction that has come to be known as the Dystopia. (pp. 92-93)

Atwood (2011) has more recently turned to considering science fiction, speculative fiction, and dystopian fiction more fully in her *In Other Worlds*, where she writes about Kazuo Ishiguro's (2006) *Never Let Me Go*:

> Ishiguro likes to experiment with literary hybrids, and to hijack popular forms for his own ends, and to set his novels against tenebrous historical backdrops .... An Ishiguro novel is never about what it pretends to pretend to be about, and *Never Let Me Go* is true to form. (p. 168)

And Perrotta's dystopia can be described in much the same way; it isn't "about what it pretends to pretend to be about"—which may be just that *thing* that makes the hard-to-explain genres of science fiction, speculative fiction, and dystopian fiction so hard to explain.

"I Can't Look at Everything Hard Enough"

I found reading the passage about Nora quoted above nearly as overwhelming as the experience appears to be for Nora herself. I began to think about my own daughter, Jessica.

Jessica, the three-year-old, is gone, disappeared, seemingly instantaneously, lost forever.

Jessica, the twelve-year-old, gone.

Jessica, the nineteen-year-old, gone.

My daughter is alive, now twenty-two, but the scene with Nora in Perrotta's world "off-to-the-side," as Atwood describes Ishiguro's dystopia in *Never Let Me Go*, is not about what *might* happen, not a speculative work about the possibility of The Rapture.

Perrotta is offering his readers a timeless message, one found in Thornton Wilder's (1938/2003) *Our Town*. In Wilder's play, Emily grows from childhood to falling in love to marriage and to her own too-early death.

In the final act, Emily views her life in replay from beyond and exclaims: "I can't look at everything hard enough."

She then turns to the Stage Manager and asks, distraught: "Do any human beings ever realize life while they live it—every, every minute?" And the Stage Manager replies, "No—Saints and poets maybe—they do some."

And this is the very real and starkly True center of Perrotta's pervasive dark satire and insightful authenticity as a novelist staring at and then breathing life into the human condition, masked as fantastic events that are unimaginable, except for those who look at everything hard enough and pause to realize life every, every minute.

* * *

In the late 1960s and early 1970s, comic book writer Dennis O'Neil and artist Neal Adams switched the superhero comics series Green Lantern *into a social commentary including the Green Lantern as a voice of the establishment and the Green Arrow as a radical. SF often matches this powerful undressing of social ills, but we must be careful about always honoring a text, genre, or medium simply because it reaches some ends beyond itself. SF is credible for its own sake.*

However, like the Green Lantern/Green Arrow issues from DC during the turbulent 1960s and 1970s, Ursular Le Guin's works often shake readers with her perceptive social commentary. One of her most ominous and cutting stories is "The Ones Who Walk Away from Omelas." This sparsely narrated tale creates tension and builds a truly eerie mood around a society that gains its privilege from the oppression of one oppressed child.

In a commentary published at Daily Kos *(October 30, 2011), I incorporate Le Guin's story to question the status of privilege at the expense of other's oppression.*

LE GUIN'S "THE ONES WHO WALK AWAY FROM OMELAS":
ALLEGORY OF PRIVILEGE[v]

"With a clamor of bells that set the swallows soaring, the Festival of Summer came to the city Omelas, bright-towered by the sea," opens Ursula Le Guin's (1975) "The Ones Who Walk Away from Omelas."

The reader soon learns about a people and a land that leave the narrator filled with both a passion for telling a story and tension over the weight of that task:

> How can I tell you about the people of Omelas? They were not naive and happy children—though their children were, in fact, happy. They were mature, intelligent, passionate adults whose lives were not wretched. O miracle! but I wish I could describe it better. I wish I could convince you. (Le Guin, 1975, p. 278)

The narrator offers an assortment of glimpses into these joyous people and their Festival of Summer, and then adds: "Do you believe? Do you accept the festival, the city, the joy? No? Then let me describe one more thing" (Le Guin, 1975, p. 280).

The "one more thing" is a child, imprisoned in a closet and its own filth—a fact of the people of Omelas "explained to children when they are between eight and twelve, whenever they seem capable of understanding":

> They all know it is there, all the people of Omelas. Some of them have come to see it, others are content merely to know it is there. They all know that it has to be there. Some of them understand why, and some do not, but they all understand that their happiness, the beauty of their city, the tenderness of their friendships, the health of their children, the wisdom of their scholars, the skill of their makers, even the abundance of their harvest and the kindly weathers of their skies, depend wholly on this child's abominable misery. (Le Guin, 1975, p. 282)

And how do the people of Omelas respond to this fact of their privilege? Most come to live with it: "Their tears at the bitter injustice dry when they begin to perceive the terrible justice of reality, and to accept it" (Le Guin, 1975, p. 283)

But a few, a few:

> They leave Omelas, they walk ahead into the darkness, and they do not come back. The place they go towards is a place even less imaginable to most of us than the city of happiness. I cannot describe it at all. It is possible that it does not exist. But they seem to know where they are going, the ones who walk away from Omelas. (Le Guin, 1975, p. 284)

Le Guin's sparse and disturbing allegory has everything that SF/speculative/dystopian fiction can offer in such a short space—a shocking other-world, a promise of happiness, the stab of brutality and callousness, and ultimately the penetrating mirror turned on all of us, now.

196

At its core, Le Guin's story is about the narcotic privilege as well as the reality that privilege always exists at someone else's expense. The horror of this allegory is that the sacrifice is a child, highlighting for the reader that privilege comes to some at the expense of others through no fault of the closeted lamb.

In the U.S., we cloak the reality of privilege with a meritocracy myth (Fielding, 2008), and unlike the people of Omelas, we embrace both the myth and the cloaking—never even taking that painful step of opening the closet door to face ourselves.

What's behind our door in the U.S.? Over 21% of our children living lives in poverty through no fault of their own.

While Le Guin's story ends with some hope that a few have a soul and mind strong enough to walk away from happiness built on the oppression of the innocent, I feel compelled to long for a different ending, one where a few, a few rise up against the monstrosity of oppression, to speak and act against, not merely walk away.

* * *

In Atwood's The Handmaid's Tale, *she confronts the reader with logical progressions of her "what if" scenarios, notably the racial make-up of the U.S. The end of this dystopian novel reveals a world where minority status by race has shifted, leaving people of color in the majority in the U.S. and Caucasians in the minority. The following commentary was posted at* Daily Kos *(November 15, 2011) and connects Atwood's dystopia with data showing that majority-minority schools are on the rise in the U.S.*

DIVERSITY AND THE RISE OF MAJORITY-MINORITY SCHOOLS[vi]

In the "Historical Notes" conclusion of Margaret Atwood's (1985) *The Handmaid's Tale*, the reader discovers through a darkly biting satire of academia that the world of the novel's main character, June/Offred, developed in part through the shifting proportion of races in the U.S. and throughout the world. The shift in majority and minority status among races resulted in cataclysmic events, including the creation of a bible-based nation, Gilead, that also sought to preserve the Caucasian race through the subjugation of fertile women as handmaids.

Atwood (2005) explains in "Writing Utopia" that every event in her dystopian novel has already happened in human history—explaining that speculative fiction serves as warnings about *what is* as much as *what may come to be.*

Race and power have a long and complex history in the U.S., from the institution of slavery clouding the first century of the nation to Reconstruction segregation to the Civil Rights movement of the mid-twentieth century. And that social history has often been reflected as well in the history of U.S. education.

With the release of *Teaching Diversity Matters: A State-by-State Analysis of Teachers of Color*, by Ulrich Boser (2011), the U.S. and our education system appear poised to enter into the next phase of race and power dynamics that will once again challenge our resolve as free people dedicated to democracy, human agency, and social justice.

197

Confronting Diversity, Equity, and Cultural Assumptions

Boser (2011) opens *Teaching Diversity Matters* with the new reality of public schools:

> At some point over the next 10 to 12 years, the nation's public school student body will have no one clear racial or ethnic majority. In other words, students of color—students who are not classified as non-Hispanic whites, for purposes of this analysis—will constitute more than half of our primary and secondary students. This demographic trend is already manifest in some of the nation's most populous states, including California and Texas, where the majority of students are students of color.

This report forces us to confront two stark realities: (1) the student population is shifting (and has already shifted in some states) toward majority-minority racial characteristics that require a reconsideration of both the terms "diversity" and "minority," and (2) the racial status of teachers exposes a serious gap between that student population and the teachers in our schools:

> At the national level, students of color make up more than 40 percent of the public school population. In contrast, teachers of color—teachers who are not non-Hispanic white—are only 17 percent of the teaching force. (Boser, 2011)

Beyond sounding an alarm about the racial shift among students and the failure to attract and support an equal proportion of teachers of color in our schools, the report presents two more key policy problems for educators and leaders concerned with policy and reform:

- Alternative certification avenues to teaching have attracted a greater percentage of teachers of color than traditional certification. If colleges of education and state departments of education charged with certifying teachers genuinely embrace a commitment to diversity, then this report suggests both need to reconsider why traditional certification appears to fail in recruiting and supporting teachers of color.
- Teachers of color are less satisfied with their pay, and

> [t]eachers of color also are far less satisfied than white teachers with the way in which their school is run. Only 70 percent of African-American teachers are satisfied with the way that their school is run, 8 percentage points lower than white teachers. Hispanic teachers as well as Asian and Pacific Islander teachers are also less likely than white teachers to say that they liked how their school was run. (Boser, 2011)

This finding is a powerful message about the intersection of power and race. In the HBO documentary *Little Rock Central: 50 Years Later*, the high school at the center of the desegregation of schools in the U.S. exposes that a change in laws has failed both the ideals of desegregation and the children and teachers of color now walking the halls of a school-within-a-school; teachers of color express a vividly different Little Rock Central High than the white teachers included in the film.

This report from the Center for American Progress and documentaries such as *Little Rock Central: 50 Years Later* must serve as hard evidence that current education policy, social programs, and political and public education reform discourse (such as "poverty is not destiny") are all misguided and hollow.

Boser (2011) ends the report with this call:

> Our nation's student body is rapidly diversifying, but our teaching workforce has not kept up with the trend. This must change. Students of all backgrounds deserve teachers of all backgrounds. Some initiatives are working to tackle this issue. But it's not enough to match our demographic future. Policymakers at the national, state, and local level must show the necessary leadership and answer the call for an effective and diverse teacher workforce.

To this, I believe we need to add a call for the U.S. public and its political leaders to confront the masked cultural assumptions driving our social and education policies that refuse to acknowledge inequity in society and schools as well as corrosive systemic forces at the center of our commitment to capitalism and consumerism driving that inequity.

With the statistical facts of gaps between the outcomes of students disaggregated by race and affluence and with the statistical facts of disproportionate numbers of teachers among races and with social realities such as the disproportionate numbers of males of color sitting in our prisons, we must expose those cloaked policies and discourse that blame individuals as well as painting entire races as somehow inferior or simply not willing to work hard enough (policies and discourse coming from those in power, those from privilege who want us to believe that privilege is actually merit) and confront the economic, corporate, and social forces that are in fact at the root of the measurable inequities.

Martin Luther King Jr. (1967), in his "Final Words of Advice," confronted the failure of social programs in the U.S.: "In addition to the absence of coordination and sufficiency, the programs of the past all have another common failing—they are indirect. Each seeks to solve poverty by first solving something else."

Our social and education policy remains "indirect"—along with the indirect ways in which the discourse and policies of our leaders reinforce stereotypes and racism as cultural norms. After calling for a guaranteed income for all people in the U.S., King (1967) confronts the systemic failure of the American Way:

> We have come a long way in our understanding of human motivation and of the blind operation of our economic system. Now we realize that dislocations in the market operation of our economy and the prevalence of discrimination thrust people into idleness and bind them in constant or frequent unemployment against their will. The poor are less often dismissed from our conscience today by being branded as inferior and incompetent. We also know that no matter how dynamically the economy develops and expands it does not eliminate all poverty.

And here is where King (1967) presents our need to shift our views of diversity as well as our discourse and policy regarding education:

We are likely to find that the problems of housing and education, instead of preceding the elimination of poverty, will themselves be affected if poverty is first abolished. The poor transformed into purchasers will do a great deal on their own to alter housing decay. Negroes, who have a double disability, will have a greater effect on discrimination when they have the additional weapon of cash to use in their struggle.

Those in power, those at the top due to their privilege use discourse such as "poverty is not destiny" and "reclaim America" to keep all eyes on those trapped in poverty, thus away from the exact people with the power, money, and opportunity to create a path toward equity within our society and our schools.

We are entering yet another phase of race and power in the U.S. It seems time now for addressing these realities directly.

* * *

*Suzanne Collins not only lit a fire in young adult readers but also crossed over into mainstream popularity, including spawning a movie from her young adult SF trilogy—*The Hunger Games *(2008),* Catching Fire *(2009), and* Mockingjay *(2010). In two commentaries at* Daily Kos *(February 27 and March 6, 2012), I drew from* The Hunger Games *and* Catching Fire *to examine the doublespeak inherent in 21st century calls for education reform and to highlight the racial, socioeconomic, and gender inequity that maintains the status quo of the power-elite in the U.S.*

THE EDUCATION GAMES: REFORM AS DOUBLESPEAK[vii]

Although we currently live in a world informed by George Orwell's (1983) dystopian unmasking-as-novel, *Nineteen Eighty-Four*, we seem unable to acknowledge that the Ministry of Peace is actually waging war. In our current education reform debate, educators must come to terms with Orwell's (2003) recognition of the essential nature of political speech:

> I have not here been considering the literary use of language, but merely language as an instrument for expressing and not for concealing or preventing thought. Stuart Chase and others have come near to claiming that all abstract words are meaningless, and have used this as a pretext for advocating a kind of political quietism. Since you don't know what Fascism is, how can you struggle against Fascism? One need not swallow such absurdities as this, but one ought to recognize that the present political chaos is connected with the decay of language, and that one can probably bring about some improvement by starting at the verbal end. If you simplify your English, you are freed from the worst follies of orthodoxy. You cannot speak any of the necessary dialects, and when you make a stupid remark its stupidity will be obvious, even to yourself. *Political language—and with variations this is true of all political parties, from Conservatives to Anarchists—is designed to make lies sound truthful and murder respectable and to give an appearance of solidity to pure wind* [emphasis added]. One cannot change this all in a moment, but one can at least change one's own habits, and from time to time one can even,

if one jeers loudly enough, send some worn-out and useless phrase ... into the dustbin where it belongs.

In 2012, The U.S. Department of Education is the Ministry of Peace, and from the USDOE, we are facing doublespeak that thinly masks the de-professionalizing of teachers and the dismantling of public education—all in the name of reform under the banner of "hope and change."

"One Need Not Swallow Such Absurdities as This"

One consequence of calling for educators to be apolitical (Thomas, 2012, February 24) is that the education reform debate remains in the hands of the inexpert and that reform is allowed to maintain and perpetuate the status quo. Here, however, I want to call for educators to expose and reject the doublespeak driving the education agenda under President Obama and personified by Secretary of Education Arne Duncan (Thomas, 2011) by addressing four key areas of that debate: (1) high-stakes standardized testing, (2) Common Core State Standards (CCSS), (3) expertise in education, and (4) claims based on ends-justify-means logic.

High-stakes Standardized Tests
The doublespeak around high-stakes standardized testing is one of the most powerful weapons used today by Duncan. The Obama administration has produced mountains of evidence that claiming to reject and decrease testing is a cloak for the inevitability of more testing and more corrosive accountability for teachers. But that debate is masking a deeper problem with confronting high-stakes standardized tests: Many educators are quick to reject the high-stakes element while adding that standardized testing is being misused. And here is where educators are failing the debate.

The high-stakes problem is the secondary problem with standardized testing. Yes, high-stakes create inexcusable outcomes related to testing: teaching to the test, reducing all course content to what-is-tested-is-what-is-taught, reducing teacher quality to test scores, reducing student learning to test scores, and cheating. But rejecting or even calling for removing the high-stakes ignores that standardized tests are flawed themselves. *Standardized tests remain primarily linked to the race, social class, and gender of students; standardized tests label and sort children overwhelmingly based on the coincidence of those children's homes.*

The standardized testing debate is the cigarette debate, not the alcohol debate. Alcohol can be consumed safely and even with health benefits; thus, the alcohol debate is about the use of alcohol, not alcohol itself. Cigarettes are another story; there is no healthy consumption of cigarettes so that debate is about the inherent danger of tobacco.

Educators must expose the double-speak calling for less testing while increasing the testing and the stakes for students and teachers, but we must not allow that charge to trump the need to identify standardized testing as cancerous, to state clearly there is no safe level of standardized testing.

Common Core State Standards

Few moments of double-speak can top Duncan's recent comment about the CCSS: "The idea that the Common Core standards are nationally-imposed is a conspiracy theory in search of a conspiracy. The Common Core academic standards were both developed and adopted by the states, and they have widespread bipartisan support" (Statement by U.S. Secretary of Education Arne Duncan, 2012).

Among a few others (Krashen, 2012), Susan Ohanian and Stephen Krashen have spoken against the CCSS movement. But as with the high-stakes standardized tests debate, many educators have rushed to seek how best to implement CCSS without considering the first-level question: Why do we need national standards when the evidence shows that *multiple* standards movements have failed repeatedly in the past? (Thomas, 2012, February 13).

The current dytopian-novel-de-jure is *The Hunger Games*. Like Orwell's *Nineteen Eighty-Four*, this young adult sc-fi novel offers insight into defiance against compliance to power. Before they are plunged into the Hunger Games (a horrifying reality TV show), the two main characters, Katniss and Peeta, confront their ethical dilemma:

> "No, when the time comes, I'm sure I'll kill just like everybody else. I can't go down without a fight. Only I keep wishing I could think of a way to … to show the Capitol they don't own me. That I'm more than just a piece in their Games," says Peeta.

> "But you're not," I [Katniss] say[s]. "None of us are. That's how the Games work." (Collins, 2008, p. 142)

One of the most relevant messages of Collins's novel is that Katniss comes to understand Peeta's critical nature, embracing that her agency is about rising above the Hunger Games, not simply winning the Games as they are dictated for her.

For educators and professional organizations to justify supporting CCSS by demanding a place at the table, they are relinquishing the essential question about whether or not that table should exist.

And this is where educators sit with the CCSS: To implement the CCSS is for the Capitol to own us, to reject CCSS for our own professional autonomy is to be more than just a piece in their Games.

Expertise in Education

The Los Angeles Times has now been followed by *The New York Times* as pawns in the USDOE's games designed to label, rank, and dehumanize teachers the way our education system has treated children for decades. Again, the pattern is disturbing since publishing VAM-related data on teachers creates a debate about the publishing of the data and ignores first-level issues. But in this case, another problem concerns *who* has the expertise to frame these debates.

As the backlash mounted against the NYT's publishing teacher rankings, Bill Gates inexplicably rejected publishing VAM-data, and quickly all over Twitter and in blogs, educators began citing Gates's criticism. And here is the problem.

Gates is inexpert about education (Thomas, 2011, March 3); he has no credibility whether his claims are flawed (most of the time) or accurate (although only on the surface since we must ask why he makes these claims). Thus, if educators wish to claim our rightful place as the experts on education, we must not embrace the inexpert, ever. (And this overlaps with the testing dilemma; we must also stop referring to test data when it serves our purposes just as we reject test data when they are harmful.)

Doublespeak as a weapon of the political and cultural elite depends on masking the value of expertise. To expose that to sunshine requires that the expert remain steadfast in honoring who determines our discourse and where we acknowledge credibility and judiciousness.

The Ends-Justify-the-Means Logic

The ugliest and seemingly most enduring double-speak surrounds the rise of support for Teach for America (TFA) and Knowledge Is Power Program (KIPP) charters schools (Thomas, 2011, October 23)—both of which promote themselves as addressing social justice and the plight of poverty. These claims often go unchallenged because both TFA and KIPP keep the debate on the metrics (the ends) and not the "no excuses" ideology (the means).

As long as TFA and KIPP keep the argument about whether or not their approaches raise test scores or graduation rates, we fail to examine the essential flaws in each: TFA creating leaders at the expense of children and schools trapped in poverty, and KIPP (and many charters) implementing "no excuses" practices that are re-segregating schools and perpetuating classist and racist stereotypes.

And this may capture the overarching issue with all of the four points I have addressed here: The ends do not justify the means.

As Orwell has warned, however, politicians craft their words regardless of political party to mask the means with the ends—"to make lies sound truthful and murder respectable and to give an appearance of solidity to pure wind."

It is now ours as educators to expose the double-speak of the education reform movement while also taking great care not to fall prey to the allure of that strategy ourselves.

About two-thirds into the narrative of *The Hunger Games*, Katniss is forced to confront the earlier discussion between her and Peeta because she has come to love one of her competitors, Rue:

> "It's the Capitol I hate, for doing this to all of us ...." Then I remember Peeta's words on the roof ... And for the first time, I understand what he means.

> "I want to do something, right here, right now, to shame them, to make them accountable, to show the Capitol that whatever they do or force us to do there is a part of every tribute they can't own. That Rue was more than a piece in their Games. And so am I." (Collins, 2008, pp. 235-236)

Universal public education and the autonomy and professionalism of teachers in America are worth this same sentiment, and it is past time for our voices to be heard and our actions to matter.

* * *

SEPARATE, UNEQUAL ... AND DISTRACTED[viii]

When research, history, and allegory all converge to tell us the same story, we must pause to ask why we have ignored the message for so long and why are we likely to continue missing the essential thing before us.

The New York Times and *Education Week* reveal two important lessons in both the message they present and the distinct difference in their framing of that message:

"Black Students Face More Discipline, Data Suggests [sic]" headlines the NYT's article with the lead: "Black students, especially boys, face much harsher discipline in public schools than other students, according to new data from the Department of Education" (Lewin, 2012).

And *EdWeek* announces "Civil Rights Data Show Retention Disparities," opening with:

New nationwide data collected by the U.S. Department of Education's civil rights office reveal stark racial and ethnic disparities in student retentions, with black and Hispanic students far more likely than white students to repeat a grade, especially in elementary and middle school. (Adams, Robelen, & Shah, 2012)

One has to wonder if this is truly news in the sense that this research is revealing something we don't already know—because we should already know this fact: America's public schools and prisons are stark images of the fact of racial, gender, and socioeconomic inequity in our society (Thomas, 2011, December 22)—inequity that is both perpetuated by and necessary for the ruling elite to maintain their artificial status as that elite.

The research, coming from the U.S. Department of Education, and the media coverage are not evidence we are confronting that reality or that we will address it any time soon. The research and the media coverage are proof we'll spend energy on the research and the coverage in order to mask the racism lingering corrosively in our free state while continuing to blame the students who fail for their failure and the prisoners for their transgressions.

X-Men and The Hunger Games: Allegory as Unmasking

Science fiction allows an artist to pose worlds that appears to be "other worlds" (Atwood, 2011) in order for the readers to come to see our own existence more clearly.

In the most recent film version of Marvel Comics superhero team, *X-Men: First Class*, the powerful allegory of this comic book universe portrays the isolation felt by the mutants—one by one they begin to discover each other and share a common sentiment: "I thought I was the only one."

These mutants feel not only isolation, but also shame—shame for their looks, those things that are not their choices, not within their direct power to control. While this newest film installment reveals the coming together of the mutants, this narrative ends with the inevitable division of the mutants into factions: Professor X's assimilationists and Magneto's radicals.

It takes only a little imagination to see this allegory in the historical factionalism that rose along with the Civil Rights movement between Martin Luther King Jr. and Malcolm X.

In whose interest is this in-fighting?

Although written as young adult literature, *The Hunger Games* trilogy is beginning to spread into mainstream popular consciousness. The savage reality show that pits children against children to the death gives the first book in the series its title, but as with the research on racial inequity in our schools, I fear we fail to look at either the purpose of these Hunger Games in that other world of the novel or how it speaks to us now.

In *Catching Fire*, Katniss Everdeen, the narrator, confronts directly that her country, Panem, has created stability by factionalizing the people into Districts, ruled by the Capitol.

Panem exists because of the competition among the Districts, daily for resources and once a year personified by two lottery losers, children form each district.

In this second book, Katniss learns something horrifying but true when the winners of the most recent Games, Katniss and Peeta, visit District 11—home of Katniss's friend killed in the Games, Rue: During the celebration, the people of District 11 repeat Katniss's act of rebellion:

> What happens next is not an accident. It is too well executed to be spontaneous, because it happens in complete unison. Every person in the crowd presses the three middle fingers of their left hand against their lips and extends them to me. It's our sign from District 12, the last good-bye I gave Rue in the arena. (Collins, 2009, p. 61)

Then as Katniss and Peeta are rushed from the stage, they witness Peacekeepers executing people in the District 11 crowd. As President Snow has warned Katniss about the possibility of uprisings:

> "But they'll follow if the course of things doesn't change. And uprisings have been known to lead to revolution .... Do you have any idea what that would mean? How many people would die? What conditions those left would have to face? Whatever problems anyone may have with the Capitol, believe me when I say that if it released its grip on the districts for even a short time, the entire system would collapse." (Colllins, 2009, p. 21)

What maintains the stability of Panem? Competition, division, and *fear*.

What threatens the stability of Panem and the inequity it maintains? Solidarity, compassion, cooperation, and rebellion.

Separate, Unequal ... and Distracted

U.S. public education has always been and remains, again like our prisons, a map of who Americans are and what we are willing to tolerate.

Children of color and children speaking home languages other than English are disproportionately likely to be punished and expelled (especially the boys), disproportionately likely to be retained to suffer the same grade again, disproportionately likely to be in the lowest level classes with the highest student-teacher ratios (while affluent and white children sit in advanced classes with low student-teacher ratios) in order to prepare them for state testing, and disproportionately likely to be taught by un- and under-certified teachers with the least experience.

And many of these patterns are distinct in pre-kindergarten (Thomas, 2012, February 11).

We don't really need any more research, or history lessons, or SF allegory, or comic books brought to the silver screen.

We need to see the world that our children live in and recognize themselves (just ask an African American young man), and then look in the mirror ourselves.

Why do those in power remain committed to testing children in order to label, sort, and punish them?

Who does the labeling, sorting, and punishing benefit? And what are the reasons behind these facts, the disproportionate inequity in our schools and in our prisons?

We only need each minute of every day to confront what the recent data from the USDOE reveal, but it is always worth noting that this sentiment is often ignored despite its value:

> ... I recognized my kinship with all living beings, and I made up my mind that I was not one bit better than the meanest on earth. I said then, and I say now, that while there is a lower class, I am in it, and while there is a criminal element I am of it, and while there is a soul in prison, I am not free. (Debs, 1918)

How and why?

Eugene V. Debs is marginalized as a socialist, a communist so no one listens to the solidarity of his words. Because this sentiment is dangerous for the Capitol.

If we persist in being shocked by the research or enamored by the exciting story of Katniss, we will remain divided and conquered.

Katniss in *Catching Fire* responds to the president with: "It [Panem] must be very fragile, if a handful of berries can bring it down." To which the president replies, "It is fragile, but not in the way that you suppose" (Collins, 2009, p. 22).

The fragility is masked by the 99% as separate, unequal, and distracted—fighting among ourselves in fear of what we might lose otherwise.

It is time to suppose otherwise.

* * *

An enduring power of SF is its allegorical lens, the ability to move one step away from reality in order to make reality even more clear. The film In Time *(2011) accomplishes that maneuver by reframing time as capital.*

The commentary below from Daily Kos *(July 15, 2012) builds on the film's examination of capital as it relates to creating a frantic class that benefits corporate interests. Further, the discussion connects the need for frantic students in corporate America as preparation for frantic workers.*

TIME AS CAPITAL: THE RISE OF THE FRANTIC CLASS[ix]

Imagine a world where time is capital.

This is the dystopian future of 2161 brought to film by Andrew Niccol's (2011) *In Time*—triggering some powerful parallels to *Logan's Run* (both the original novel from 1967 and the film adaptation in 1976).

Both *Logan's Run* and *In Time* expose the human condition in terms of age and mortality—in the first, life ends at 30, and in the latter, people stop aging at 25, but at a price, which involves time.

Science fiction (SF) as a genre presents us with allegory in the form of other worlds, as Margaret Atwood (2011) argues, and speculations, but the most engaging aspect of SF for me as a fan and teacher is when SF unmasks universal and contemporary realities by presenting those other worlds.

One of the recurring messages of SF is the crippling inequity that continues to plague human societies, such as the haunting and sparse Ursula Le Guin's "The Ones Who Walk Away from Omelas" that forces reader to admit privilege exists on the backs of the innocent and oppressed.

The world of *In Time* presents an apparent meritocracy in which all people are given life until 25, when they stop aging but an embedded clock starts ticking forcing everyone to earn time in order to live. This deal with the devil positions all labor as literally necessary to live and puts banks at the center of who survives.

The Frantic Distraction of Surviving

Americans' faith in a meritocracy is often expressed in claims of the U.S. being a post-racial society as well as a classless society. Like the *Hunger Games* trilogy (Collins, 2008, 2009, 2010), *In Time* highlights class distinctions as people are segregated in Time Zones. Eventually, the narrative brings together the two main characters, Will Salas from the ghetto and Sylvia Weis from the affluent zone, New Greenwich.

Due to both personal tragedy and a huge gift of time from a stranger, Will confronts the norms of this dystopia while being hunted by a Timekeeper, Raymond Leon. One scene, I think, deserves closer consideration.

When Will travels from the ghetto through several Time Zones (incrementally costing him more and more time) to New Greenwich, he steps out of the cab and immediately begins jogging, a habit common in the ghettos since almost everyone is living, literally, from paycheck to paycheck (or under the weight of time loans, loan sharks, or pawn shops) until he notices that in New Greenwich people are eerily casual. This distinction comes up again when he is eating breakfast and the waitress notices that he isn't from New Greenwich because he does everything fast.

People in the ghettos, what can reasonably be called the working class and the working poor, lead lives that are so frantic that no one has the time to confront the inequity of the society, and because of the segregated society, these frantic workers have little insight into the lives of privilege, casual lives, that Will witnesses for himself and the viewer.

Also worth closer consideration is the role of the Timekeeper, Leon, who presents a truly complex character who functions under a code of ethics that is perfectly ethical within the norms of the culture, but ultimately self-defeating and dehumanizing. Timekeepers enforce the laws, primarily couched in time as capital, but because of their close proximity to crime, they carry with them only small quantities of time, thus leading frantic lives very similar to the working class/poor they help keep both in line and frantic.

Ultimately, Will exposes truths that challenge the norms of this society, truths that are in fact just as relevant to the world we now inhabit:
- Will discovers that time is not a limited commodity; there is plenty of capital, but the privileged create scarcity to keep the masses frantic, and distracted.
- Timekeepers as a police force are unmasked as not seekers of justice (Leon admits this directly), but as agents of the privileged.
- The moving target of the free market is exposed as not so much "free" but an arbitrary mechanism that puts most people in a life like caged gerbils on running wheels. Interest rates and prices incrementally increase daily as the workers accumulate time. The system is designed to keep workers trapped in their roles as workers.
- And privilege, as Le Guin's story shows, is always at the expense of others, captured by this exchange from *In Time*:

Sylvia Weis: Will, if you get a lot of time, are you really gonna give it away?

Will Salas: I've only ever had a day. How much do you need? How can you live with yourself watching people die right next to you?

Sylvia Weis: You don't watch. You close your eyes. I can help you get all the time you want.

In effect, while the details may be exaggerated, the lessons learned by Will are disturbingly relevant to contemporary Americans, as much as how it informs us as workers as it highlights that education reform is more concerned with producing workers than proving all children with equity, liberation, and autonomy.

Frantic Students, Frantic Workers: The Rise of the Frantic Class

The frantic state of being among the working class and working poor of *In Time* is a perceptive dramatization of the American worker, increasingly stripped of rights as unions are dismantled and the essentials of human dignity (income, health care, retirement) are further tied to being employed (Parramore, 2012).

But the allegorical messages of *In Time* also speak to how and why current education reform claims and policies are designed to appease corporate needs for frantic workers. One characterization of U.S. public education today is well represented in this dystopian world—frantic.

Current corporate education reform is built on implementing national standards designed to continue the historical call to incrementally increase both expectations and outcomes (the target for success in education has always been a moving target) so that students, teachers, and schools are always under duress, always falling short, always so frantic that no one can pause to question, challenge, or do anything other than comply.

Imagine a world where time is capital, where all of any person's time is spent compiling time, a fruitless cycle of acquisition, of seeking to comply with the mandates none of the masses have chosen for herself/himself.

But you don't have to imagine this.

This frantic world of *In Time* is the frantic existence of the American worker, and this frantic world is being fed by the corporate takeover of public schools (Thomas, 2012) where accountability, standards, and testing have reduced teachers and students to gerbils on running wheels.

In 2012, workers, students, and teachers are the frantic class; like Will, we don't have time:

> **Will Salas**: I don't have time. I don't have time to worry about how it happened. It is what it is. We're genetically engineered to stop aging at 25. The trouble is, we live only one more year, unless we can get more time. Time is now the currency. We earn it and spend it. The rich can live forever. And the rest of us? I just want to wake up with more time on my hand than hours in the day.

The rising frantic class is necessary for the privileged few, the 1% controlling both manufactured austerity and the perpetually moving targets of success.

While universal public education was created to feed the promise of the American Dream, the current corporate takeover of public schools is driving the American Nightmare of the frantic class.

We don't need a movie to see that.

* * *

David Mitchell's Cloud Atlas *(2004) takes readers on a multi-genre narratives that includes at least two SF storylines. By the novel's end, one of the central themes reveals itself—the need for equity among humans.*

In Daily Kos *(December 10, 2012), I examined further the connection between students and workers trapped in cultural norms or working, which I identify as wage slavery. This piece confronts the corrosive power of capitalism that enslaves workers with the promise of freedom and wealth.*

CLONES, ASSEMBLY-LINE CAPITALISM, AND WAGE-SLAVES[x]

Beyond its flair for the fantastic, science fiction (SF) almost always offers the allegorical. In SF, humankind literally masters cloning and produces not quite human slaves, facilitating some sort of truce between the long history of human conquering human to enslave and the contemporary illusion that eradicating institutional slavery absolves us of culpability in the de facto wage-slavery of assembly-line capitalism.

David Mitchell's (2004) often tedious but always masterful *Cloud Atlas* builds through a menagerie of genres and modes of discourse to a powerful ending that highlights a motif central to the novel, of human (and clone) bondage:

> Belief is both prize & battlefield, within the mind & in the mind's mirror, the world. If we *believe* humanity is a ladder of tribes, a colosseum of confrontation, exploitation & bestiality, such a humanity is surely brought into being, & history's Horroxes, Boerhaaves & Gooses shall prevail. You & I, the moneyed, the privileged, the fortunate, shall not fare so badly in this world, provided our luck holds. What of it if our consciences itch? Why undermine the dominance of our race, our gunship, our heritage & our legacy? Why fight the "natural" (oh, weaselly word!) order of things?

> Why? Because of this:—one fine day, a purely predatory world *shall* consume itself ....

> If we *believe* that humanity may transcend tooth & claw, if we *believe* divers races & creeds can share this world as peaceably as the orphans share their candlenut tree, if we *believe* leaders must be just, violences muzzled, power accountable & the riches of the Earth & its Oceans shared equitably, such a world will come to pass. (p. 508)

One of the most satisfying and compelling narratives in Mitchell's novel revolves around the clone Somni-451, who the reader encounters as she nears her execution in "An Orison of Somni-451." What counts as "human" and what constitutes the ethical limits of slavery are complex questions raised in this narrative, along with the possibility of clone revolt and a clone messiah.

But the allegorical value in the story of Somni-451 must not be ignored, must not be mere fictional soma that clouds our recognition of universal public education not liberating children into a free society, but feeding wage-slaves into assembly-line capitalism's grind.

"Such a World Will Come to Pass"

During my nearly two decades of teaching high school English I encountered a recurring situation.

A bright young person who had tended to be a diligent student would gradually do less and less work in my classes. When I would approach the student about my

210

concern, the student would invariably offer an interesting explanation and our conversation would go something like this:

Me: Why are you missing so many assignments?
Student: I'm sorry. I gotta work til 2 or 3 in the morning and I just can't keep up.
Me: Do you have to work?
Student: Yea, I gotta make my car payments.
Me: Why do you have to make car payments?
Student: I gotta have a car to get to work.

This cycle of "gotta" (gotta work, gotta have a car, gotta make money) was powerfully engrained in my students; in fact, the need to work, earn money, and own things were all clearly essential for them to feel adult, and ultimately as essential for them to feel fully human—ironically pushing them into the dehumanizing work cycle identified above.

Writing from her experiences as an adjunct instructor in a college, Professor Beth (2012) personifies the cycle of "gotta" within which she found herself as a part-time worker coaxed into compliance by the allure of a full-time status:

Quickly the demands of the classroom and of the school grew. I was asked to sit on textbook selection committees, to organize guest lecturers to come to campus, and to test out new books. I was told that doing these things would build my CV and provide me with an edge when applying for a full time teaching position. Every demand was couched under the advice that this would position me better for a full time position. I was teaching three courses —sometimes four—and said, 'yes' to every demand …

I applied for a permanent full-time position four separate times and never once was even invited to interview.

The twenty-first century American worker sits many decades past institutional slavery in the U.S., but the contemporary worker finds her-/himself trapped in assembly-line capitalism as a wage-slave. And increasingly, public schools are being reformed to guarantee corporate America will see compliant workers sprout from compliant students (who are being trained by compliant teachers): The endless cycle of accountability built on standards and tests is an act of surveillance and control, not education and liberation.

More and more American workers are having their professions reduced to interchangeable functions, creating for any worker the very real fear that she/he can and will be replaced, easily. In public education, the corporate allure of Teach for America is not that the recruits are bright or special, but that they are inherently interchangeable and cheaper than a full-time labor force of professionals.

Manufactured fear insures compliant workers, benefitting the corporate elite.

As well, American workers must work, not just for wages but for basic human necessities such as healthcare and retirement, tightening the grip that corporations have on workers even beyond wage-slavery.

The systematic dismantling of unions and tenure, specifically teachers unions and tenure, is not something to be ignored, like a SF clone war. The de-professionalization of educators at the K-12 and high education levels is not just an assault on academia.

The belittling of the status of "worker," the dehumanizing of the American worker, the rise in the working poor and children living in poverty, and the growing chasm between the privileged and all the rest of us are conditions that we create and sustain—they are all what we *believe* to be the "natural order of things" within assembly-line capitalism, the Social Darwinism of our self-inflicted rat race, the dog-eat-dog of being a frantic worker.

Most of us will always be workers, and to be a worker is an honorable thing; it doesn't need to be a condition tolerated on the way to something better, and it shouldn't be twenty-first wage slavery.

"one fine day, a purely predatory world shall *consume itself"* …

As the last paragraphs of *Cloud Atlas* express, however, the wage-slavery of workers in the U.S. is a condition we have chosen, but it is also a condition we can change—if we *believe* it is wrong, "such a world will come to pass."

NOTES

[i] Thomas, P. L. (2010, October 16). "Don't ask, don't tell": There's a reason Captain America wears a mask. *OpEdNews.com*. http://www.opednews.com/articles/Don-t-Ask-Don-t-Tell--T-by-Paul-Thomas-101014-950.html

[ii] Thomas, P. L. (2011, January 3). Calculating the Corporate States of America: Revisiting Vonnegut's *Player Piano. OpEdNews*. http://www.opednews.com/articles/Calculating-the-Corporate-by-Paul-Thomas-110103-130.html

[iii] Thomas, P. L. (2011, October 11). Education in the Corporate States of America. *Daily Kos*. Retrieved from http://www.dailykos.com/story/2011/10/11/1025307/-Education-in-the-Corporate-States-of-America

[iv] Thomas, P. L. (2011, October 20). Whence come *The Leftovers*?: Speculative fiction and the human condition. *Daily Kos*. Retrieved from http://www.dailykos.com/story/2011/10/20/1028381/-Whence-Come-The-Leftovers-Speculative-Fiction-and-the-Human-Condition

[v] Thomas, P. L. (2011, October 30). Le Guin's "The ones who walk away from Omelas": Allegory of privilege. *Daily Kos*. Retrieved from http://www.dailykos.com/story/2011/10/30/1031651/-Le-Guin-s-The-Ones-Who-Walk-Away-from-Omelas-Allegory-of-Privilege

[vi] Thomas, P. L. (2011, November 15). Diversity and the rise of majority-minority schools. *Daily Kos*. Retrieved from http://www.dailykos.com/story/2011/11/15/1036589/-Diversity-and-the-Rise-of-Majority-Minority-Schools

[vii] Thomas, P. L. (2012, February 27). The education games: Reform as double-speak. *Daily Kos*. http://www.dailykos.com/story/2012/02/27/1068659/-The-Education-Games-Reform-as-Double-Speak

[viii] Thomas, P. L. (2012, March 6). Separate, unequal … and distracted. *Daily Kos*. Retrieved from http://www.dailykos.com/story/2012/03/06/1071600/-Separate-Unequal-and-Distracted

[ix] Thomas, P. L. (2012, July 15). Time as capital: The rise of the frantic class. *Daily Kos*. Retrieved from http://www.dailykos.com/story/2012/07/15/1110101/-Time-as-Capital-The-Rise-of-the-Frantic-Class

[x] Thomas, P. L. (2012, December 10). Clones, assembly-line capitalism, and wage-slaves. *Daily Kos*. Retrieved from http://www.dailykos.com/story/2012/12/10/1168718/-Clones-Assembly-line-Capitalism-and-Wage-Slaves

REFERENCES

Adams, C. J., Robelen, E. W., & Shah, N. (2012, March 6). Civil rights data show retention disparities. *Education Week, 31*(23). Retrieved from
http://www.edweek.org/ew/articles/2012/03/07/23data_ep.h31.html

Atwood, M. (2005). *Writing with intent: Essays, reviews, personal prose: 1983-2005*. New York: Carroll and Graf Publishers.

Atwood, M. (2011). *In other worlds: SF and the human imagination*. New York: Nan A. Talese/ Doubleday.

Bessie, A. (2010, December 29). To fix education: Fire teachers, hire holograms. *The Daily Censored*. Retrieved from
http://dailycensored.com/2010/12/29/to-fix-education-fire-human-teachers-hire-holograms/

Boser, U. (2011). *Teaching diversity matters: A state-by-state analysis of teachers of color*. Washington, DC: Center for American Progress. Retrieved from
http://www.americanprogress.org/issues/2011/11/increasing_teacher_diversity.html

Bracey, G. (2003). April foolishness: The 20th anniversary of A Nation at Risk. *Phi Delta Kappan, 84*(8), 616-621.

Chabon, M. (2000). *The amazing adventures of Kavalier & Clay*. New York: Picador.

Collins, S. (2008). *The hunger games*. New York: Scholastic Inc.

Collins, S. (2009). *Catching fire*. New York: Scholastic Press.

Collins, S. (2010). *Mocking jay*. New York: Scholastic Press.

Debs, E. V. (1918). Statement to the court upon being convicted of violating the Sedition Act. Eugene V. Debs Internet Archive. Retrieved from
http://www.marxists.org/archive/debs/works/1918/court.htm

Duncan, A. (2010, December 7). Secretary Arne Duncan's remarks at OECD's release of the Program for International Student Assessment (PISA) 2009 results. Washington DC: U.S. Department of Education. Retrieved from
http://www.ed.gov/news/speeches/secretary-arne-duncans-remarks-oecds-release-program-international-student-assessment-

Fielding, S. (2008, April 9). Inside the middle class: Bad times hit the good life. Washington, DC: Pew Research Center. Retrieved from http://www.pewsocialtrends.org/2008/04/09/inside-the-middle-class-bad-times-hit-the-good-life/

Freire, P. (1993). *Pedagogy of the oppressed*. New York: Continuum.

Freire, P. (2005). *Teachers as cultural workers: Letters to those who dare to teach* (D. Macedo, D., Koike, & A. Oliveira, Trans.). Boulder, CO: Westview Press.

Giroux, H. (2010, October 5). When generosity hurts: Bill Gates, public school teachers and the politics of humiliation. *truthout*. Retrieved from http://archive.truthout.org/when-generosity-hurts-bill-gates-public-school-teachers-and-politics-humiliation63868

Hicks, G. (1952). The engineers take over. *The New York Times*. Retrieved from
http://www.nytimes.com/books/97/09/28/lifetimes/vonnegut-player.html

How to fix our schools: A manifesto by Joel Klein, Michelle Rhee and other education leaders. (2010, October 10). *The Washington Post*. Retrieved from
http://www.washingtonpost.com/wp-dyn/content/article/2010/10/07/AR2010100705078.html

Holton, G. (2003, April 25). An insider's view of "A Nation at Risk" and why it still matters. *The Chronicle Review, 49*(33), B13.

Ishiguro, K. (2006). *Never let me go.* New York, NY: Vintage.

King, M. L., Jr. (1967). Final words of advice. *Wealth and Want.* Retrieved from http://www.wealthandwant.com/docs/King_Where.htm

Krashen, S. (2010, October 8). The Manifesto got it all wrong. *Schools Matter* [Web log]. Retrieved from http://www.schoolsmatter.info/2010/10/manifesto-got-it-all-wrong.html

Krashen, S. (2011, January 2). The freedom in education act. *Susan Ohanian.org* [Web log]. Retrieved from http://susanohanian.org/outrage_fetch.php?id=840

Krashen, S. (2012, February 26). Resolution opposing common core standards and national tests. *Schools Matter* [Web log]. Retrieved from http://www.schoolsmatter.info/2012/02/resolution-opposing-common-core.html

Le Guin, U. (1975). *The wind's twelve quarters.* New York, NY: Harper Perennial.

Lewin, T. (2012, March 6). Black students face more discipline, data suggests [sic]. *The New York Times.* Retrieved from http://www.nytimes.com/2012/03/06/education/black-students-face-more-harsh-discipline-data-shows.html

Maher, B. (2010). Episode 193. Guests John Legend, Markos Moulitsas, Dana Loesch, and Dan Neil. [Television series episode]. In *Real time with Bill Maher.* New York, NY: HBO. October 15, 2010.

Michie, G. (2011, January 9). How to be taken seriously as a reformer (don't be an educator). The Answer Sheet [Web log]. *The Washington Post.* Retrieved 10 January 2011 from http://voices.washingtonpost.com/answer-sheet/guest-bloggers/how-to-be-taken-seriously-as-a.html

Mitchell, D. (2004). *Cloud atlas.* New York, NY: Random House.

Niccol, A. (Director). (2011). *In time* [Motion picture]. United States: Regency Enterprises.

Noah, T. (2010, September 3). The United States of inequality. *Slate.* Retrieved from http://www.slate.com/id/2266025/entry/2266026

Orwell, G. (1983). *Nineteen eighty-four* (60th anniversary ed.). New York, NY: Plume.

Orwell, G. (2003). Politics and the English language. *The complete works of George Orwell.* Retrieved from http://www.george-orwell.org/Politics_and_the_English_Language/0.html

Parramore, L. (2012, July 12). Fifty shades of capitalism: Pain and bondage in the American workplace. *AlterNet.* Retrieved from http://www.alternet.org/story/156291/fifty_shades_of_capitalism%3A_pain_and_bondage_in_the_american_workplace

Perrotta, T. (2011). *The leftovers.* New York, NY: St. Martin's Press.

Professor Beth. (2012, December 10). The yes adjunct [Web log]. *Adjunct project.* Retrieved from http://www.adjunctproject.com/the-yes-adjunct/

Reed, P. (1995). "Player piano" overview. *The Vonnegut web.* Retrieved from http://www.vonnegutweb.com/playerpiano/pp_peterjreed.html

Rothstein, R. (2010, October 14). How to fix our schools. Issue Brief 286. Washington DC: Economic Policy Institute. Retrieved from http://www.epi.org/publications/entry/ib286

Statement by U.S. Secretary of Education Arne Duncan. (2012, February 23). Washington, DC: U.S. Department of Education. Retrieved form https://www.ed.gov/news/press-releases/statement-us-secretary-education-arne-duncan-1

Thomas, P. L. (2010, October 16). "Don't ask, don't tell": There's a reason Captain America wears a mask. *OpEdNews.com.* Retrieved from http://www.opednews.com/articles/Don-t-Ask-Don-t-Tell--T-by-Paul-Thomas-101014-950.html

Thomas, P. L. (2011). The educational hope ignored under Obama: The persistent failure of crisis discourse and utopian expectations. In P. R. Carr & B. J. Porfilio (Eds.), *The phenomenon of Obama and the agenda for education: Can hope audaciously trump neoliberalism?* (pp. 49-72). Charlotte, NC: Information Age Publishing.

Thomas, P. L. (2011, December 22). Poverty matters!: A Christmas miracle. *Truthout.* Retrieved from http://www.truth-out.org/poverty-matters-christmas-miracle/1325264564

Thomas, P. L. (2011, November 15). Diversity and the rise of majority-minority schools. *Daily Kos*. Retrieved from http://www.dailykos.com/story/2011/11/15/1036589/-Diversity-and-the-Rise-of-Majority-Minority-Schools

Thomas, P. L. (2011, October 30). Le Guin's "The ones who walk away from Omelas": Allegory of privilege. *Daily Kos*. Retrieved from http://www.dailykos.com/story/2011/10/30/1031651/-Le-Guin-s-The-Ones-Who-Walk-Away-from-Omelas-Allegory-of-Privilege

Thomas, P. L. (2011, October 23). Testing support for TFA and KIPP: Whose children matter? *Daily Kos*. Retrieved from http://www.dailykos.com/story/2011/10/23/1029321/-Testing-Support-for-TFA-and-KIPP:-Whose-Children-Matter

Thomas, P. L. (2011, October 20). Whence come *The Leftovers*?: Speculative fiction and the human condition. *Daily Kos*. Retrieved from http://www.dailykos.com/story/2011/10/20/1028381/-Whence-Come-The-Leftovers-Speculative-Fiction-and-the-Human-Condition

Thomas, P. L. (2011, October 11). Education in the Corporate States of America. *Daily Kos*. Retrieved from http://www.dailykos.com/story/2011/10/11/1025307/-Education-in-the-Corporate-States-of-America

Thomas, P. L. (2011, March 3). The Bill Gates problem in school reform. The Answer Sheet [Web log]. *The Washington Post*. Retrieved from http://voices.washingtonpost.com/answer-sheet/guest-bloggers/the-bill-gates-problem-in-scho.html

Thomas, P. L. (2011, January 3). Calculating the Corporate States of America: Revisiting Vonnegut's *Player Piano*. *OpEdNews*. Retrieved from http://www.opednews.com/articles/Calculating-the-Corporate-by-Paul-Thomas-110103-130.html

Thomas, P. L. (2012). *Ignoring poverty in the U.S.: The corporate takeover of public education*. Charlotte NC: Information Age Publishing, Inc.

Thomas, P. L. (2012, December 10). Clones, assembly-line capitalism, and wage-slaves. *Daily Kos*. Retrieved from
http://www.dailykos.com/story/2012/12/10/1168718/-Clones-Assembly-line-Capitalism-and-Wage-Slaves

Thomas, P. L. (2012, July 15). Time as capital: The rise of the frantic class. *Daily Kos*. Retrieved from http://www.dailykos.com/story/2012/07/15/1110101/-Time-as-Capital-The-Rise-of-the-Frantic-Class

Thomas, P. L. (2012, March 6). Separate, unequal ... and distracted. *Daily Kos*. Retrieved from http://www.dailykos.com/story/2012/03/06/1071600/-Separate-Unequal-and-Distracted

Thomas, P. L. (2012, February 27). The education games: Reform as double-speak. *Daily Kos*. http://www.dailykos.com/story/2012/02/27/1068659/-The-Education-Games-Reform-as-Double-Speak

Thomas, P. L. (2012, February 24). Education as "politically contested spaces." *Truthout*. Retrieved from http://www.truthout.org/education-politically-contested-spaces/1330105517

Thomas, P. L. (2012, February 13). Rotten to the (common) core. *Daily Kos*. Retrieved from http://www.dailykos.com/story/2012/02/13/1064342/-Rotten-to-the-Common-Core

Thomas, P. L. (2012, February 11). It's the end of equity as we know it (but we should all feel fine. *Daily Kos*. Retrieved from http://www.dailykos.com/story/2012/02/11/1063803/-It-s-the-End-of-Equity-as-We-Know-It-But-We-Should-All-Feel-Fine-

Vonnegut, K. (1952). *Player piano*. New York, NY: Delta.

Vonnegut, K. (1963). *Cat's cradle*. New York, NY: Delta.

Vonnegut, K. (1965). On science fiction. *The New York Times*. Retrieved from
http://www.vonnegutweb.com/archives/arc_scifi.html

Weinstein, A. (2011, October 11). Rick Scott to liberal arts majors: Drop dead. *Mother Jones*. Retrieved from http://motherjones.com/mojo/2011/10/rick-scott-liberal-arts-majors-drop-dead-anthropology

White, J. (2005, May 4). Army withheld details about Tillman's death. *The Washington Post*. Retrieved from http://www.washingtonpost.com/wp-dyn/content/article/2005/05/03/AR2005050301502.html

Wilder, T. (1938/2003). *Our town: A play in three acts*. New York, NY: Harper Perennial Modern Classics.

AUTHOR BIOGRAPHIES

Roymieco A. Carter, M.F.A., is Associate Professor and Director of the Visual Arts Program and University Galleries at North Carolina A&T State University. He teaches courses on graphic design, digital media, visual literacy, theory, and social criticism. He has written articles on graphic design education, art education, gaming, human computer interaction, and graphics computer animation.

Sean P. Connors is an Assistant Professor of English education in the College of Education and Health Professions at the University of Arkansas, Fayetteville. His scholarly and research interests include multimodality, graphic novels, and the application of diverse critical perspectives to young adult literature.

Erin Brownlee Dell is a doctoral student in Educational Leadership and Cultural Foundations at the University of North Carolina, Greensboro. Her research interests include pop culture as curriculum, critical pedagogy and critical whiteness studies. In her day job, Erin serves as an assistant academic dean at Guilford College.

Jennifer Lyn Dorsey is a doctoral student at the University of Oklahoma in the Instructional Leadership and Academic Curriculum department where she researches critical literacy, literacy practices, and critical thinking. Prior to entering OU, Jennifer taught English for thirteen years at the middle and high school levels.

John L. Hoben is a teaching consultant at Memorial University of Newfoundland. A former practicing lawyer, in 2007 he was awarded a Canada Graduate Scholarship (Doctoral) from the Social Sciences and Humanities Council of Canada to conduct a three year qualitative study of teachers' perceptions of free speech. He has authored publications and given academic presentations on an array of topics including: critical research and literacy; progressive assessment; education and the imagination; the law, cultural memory and loss; free speech and public schooling; and democratic approaches to education. At present, he continues to teach teaching skills to faculty and graduate students at Memorial, as well as graduate and undergraduate courses in the areas of education and law and society with an emphasis on civil rights, international humanitarian law and public law.

Aaron Passell is an assistant professor of sociology and urban studies at Furman University. His research focuses on the convergence of the social and material in urban and suburban development and neighborhood change. He is an eager teacher and ardent reader of SF and other stuff.

Michael Svec, Associate Professor of Education at Furman University, earned a Ph.D. in curriculum and instruction (secondary science) from Indiana University-Bloomington. His teaching and scholarship includes the culture of schools, and both elementary and secondary science teaching methods. He was a 2005 Fulbright scholar in the Czech Republic.

P. L. Thomas, Associate Professor of Education (Furman University), taught high school English in South Carolina before moving to teacher education. He is currently a column editor for *English Journal* (National Council of Teachers of English) and author of *Ignoring Poverty in the U.S.* (IAP). Follow his work at http://radicalscholarship.wordpress.com/ and @plthomasEdD.

Leila E. Villaverde, is Associate Professor of Cultural Foundations in the Department of Educational Leadership at the University of North Carolina, Greensboro and Director of PhD in Educational Studies. She teaches curriculum studies, visual literacy, feminist theory, and aesthetics. She has written books on white privilege and secondary education, and has written articles on identity, art education, and critical pedagogy.

Mike Winiski is the Associate Director for the Center for Teaching and Learning at Furman University. He consults with Furman faculty and teaches courses on geographic information systems, emerging learning technologies, and a first year seminar about Mars. Mike taught high school physics and chemistry for seven years.

CPSIA information can be obtained at www.ICGtesting.com
Printed in the USA
LVOW04s1937211015

459181LV00005B/51/P